HOW WALL STREET WORKS

HOW WALL STREET WORKS

STREET

WORKS

Second Edition

DAVID L. SCOTT
Professor of Accounting & Finance
Valdosta State University
Valdosta, Georgia

McGraw-Hill
New York   San Francisco   Washington, D.C.   Auckland   Bogotá
Caracas   Lisbon   London   Madrid   Mexico City   Milan
Montreal   New Delhi   San Juan   Singapore   Sydney
Tokyo   Toronto

Library of Congress Cataloging-in-Publication Data

Scott, David Logan, date.
  How Wall Street Works / by David L. Scott.   2nd ed.
      p.   cm.
  Includes index.
  ISBN 0-07-134112-9
  1. Wall Street.   2. New York Stock Exchange.   3. Investments — United States.
  4. Investment analysis.
HG4572.S37   1999
332.63—21   98055402
                                                                              CIP

McGraw-Hill

A Division of The McGraw·Hill Companies

1 2 3 4 5 6 7 8 9 0   DOC/DOC   9 0 9 8 7 6 5 4 3 2 1 0 9

ISBN 0-07-134112-9

The sponsoring editor for this book was Stephen Isaacs, the editing supervisor was Donna Muscatello, and the production supervisor was Suzanne W. B. Rapcavage. It was set in Times Roman by Carol Barnstable of Carol Graphics.

Printed and bound by R. R. Donnelley & Sons Company.

CONTENTS

PREFACE TO THE SECOND EDITION

One of the exciting and unnerving aspects of life is change. We experience changes in our interests, our abilities, our environment, and our physical selves. Nowhere is change more evident than the world of investing. Since the original edition of *How Wall Street Works* was published in 1992, new industries have emerged, existing industries have evolved, new investment products have come to market, taxes relevant to investors have been altered, and many individuals have developed a seemingly insatiable appetite for business news and commentary. Most aspects of investing and finance seem to be moving in fast-forward. A big part of this change stems from financial data and news being more readily available to individual investors, who now have the ability to gain access to current events almost as quickly as professionals. No longer does an individual investor have to call a broker or wait for the morning paper in order to determine what has happened to exchange rates, interest rates, and stock and bond values. Investors can sit in front of their personal computers, gain the information they need, and trade stocks and bonds just as readily as if they were living next door to a brokerage firm or in the middle of Wall Street.

This second edition of *How Wall Street Works* addresses many of the changes that have occurred during the decade of the nineties. You will find new terminology, additional material on new investment products, expanded coverage of the over-the-counter market, and updated tax information. Despite all of the changes and the emergence of new products, the basics of intelligent investing remain unchanged. Thus, the fundamentals discussed in the first edition are still valid, just as the ideas that Benjamin Graham popularized decades ago are as useful now as they were during his lifetime.

David L. Scott
Valdosta, GA

HOW WALL STREET WORKS

1

CHAPTER

What and Where Is Wall Street?

Chapter summary

Wall Street is as much a concept as it is a place. In a physical sense, Wall Street is a street in the financial district of New York City. At the same time, it represents a central market in which securities are issued and traded. Thus, in a broad sense Wall Street can be thought of as encompassing the financial district of New York City, but also all of the other financial districts around the globe. This chapter presents an introduction to Wall Street: who works there, what they do, how it is regulated, and how it assists economies to function more efficiently.

What is Wall Street?

Wall Street is a real street surrounded by buildings in which people conduct the country's and the world's financial business. Wall Street is where businesses sell shares of ownership; where the United States Treasury routinely borrows billions of dollars; where financial professionals trade a variety of financial claims, including stocks and bonds; and where financial services companies distribute mind-numbing amounts of financial information. Wall Street is a place where huge money-center banks make megasized loans; where frenzied traders wearing bright jackets with dangling name tags shout orders to buy and sell stock, bonds, and options; and where powerful computers process the daily record for hundreds of thousands of transactions. The activities on Wall Street are closely monitored by financial professionals around the world.

Is there a single street on which all these activities take place?

Wall Street certainly does exist. It is at the south end of Manhattan Island in downtown New York City. However, "Wall Street" is often spoken of in the sense that it is a marketplace encompassing all the activities that are related to the issuance and trading of financial assets. For example, the term *Wall Street* is frequently used as a frame of reference to identify the major financial institutions and markets that are scattered across the country. In a more narrow sense, *Wall Street* refers to the major financial institutions and markets that are located in and around New York City. The more restrictive definition still includes financial institutions that are near but not directly on Wall Street as well as institutions that enjoy a Wall Street address. In this sense, *Wall Street* is a reference to financial markets as opposed to a particular location.

How did Wall Street evolve from a street in New York City to being a major player in the world's financial system?

The financial system has experienced a major evolution, especially during the last several decades. At one time, nearly all major financial transactions either took place in New York City or else had some direct connection with the city. Not surprisingly, many firms engaged in financial activities had a presence on Wall Street even though they conducted most of their business elsewhere. As population and wealth gradually shifted away from the Northeast toward the West and the South, and as computing and communications technologies raced ahead, many of the functions that were once confined to the Wall Street area began to move outside New York City. However, Wall Street has historically been the place where most major financial transactions originate, and use of the term continues even though it often refers to similar activities that occur away from the historic financial district of New York City.

Have foreign financial markets stolen any of Wall Street's luster?

Wall Street is no longer the only game in town, and in some financial activities it is not even the main game. Financial markets in other areas of the world have captured an important place in the issuing and trading of securities. Financial professionals on Wall Street must now check each morning to see what has occurred overnight in markets around the world. Market conditions in Europe and Asia have an important effect on what takes place on Wall Street. Major financial markets are in London, Frankfurt, Tokyo, and other big cities around the world. As more investors have become interested in foreign stocks, financial media have begun providing increased security price information about each of these markets.

Exactly what is stock?

Stock represents partial ownership of a business. One share of stock indicates one unit of ownership in the business that issued the stock. For example, Procter & Gamble, a large consumer products company, has 1,337 million shares of stock outstanding. Each of these 1,337 million shares represents a single unit of ownership in the business. Some of Procter & Gamble's owners may hold only a few shares of stock, while institutional investors may each own hundreds of thousands of shares of the stock. The result is that Procter & Gamble has many more shares of ownership than it has owners. At the end of 1998, the firm had only 273,000 owners, including individuals and institutions such as mutual funds, bank trust departments, and pension funds.

What is a bond?

A bond represents a debt that is owed to the owner of the bond. The investor who holds a bond is a creditor, or lender, and the issuer of the bond is a borrower. Businesses, national governments, state governments, and municipalities borrow money by issuing bonds to individuals and institutions that have money to lend. Bonds generally require the borrower to make scheduled interest payments and to repay on a specific date the principal amount borrowed. As a lender, the bondholder is not involved in ownership of the company or organization that issued the bond.

Is trading stocks and bonds the main activity of Wall Street?

Issuing and trading stocks and bonds are two of Wall Street's major activities but certainly not the only activities. A whole host of new financial assets have been promoted, sold, and traded by Wall Street institutions during the last 10 to 15 years. In fact, developing new financial vehicles has itself become a major activity. Investment vehicles such as calls, puts, warrants, investment trusts, futures contracts, and partnerships are only a few of the multitude of investments in which Wall Street deals. Any asset of a financial nature is likely to have a connection with Wall Street. Still, Wall Street is best known for stocks and bonds.

Are financial assets issued and subsequently traded in the same markets?

Financial assets such as stocks and bonds are issued in what is called the *primary market,* a part of Wall Street in which investors' funds flow directly to businesses and governments that issue the financial claims, or securities. Once issued, most of these securities continue to be traded among investors on stock exchanges or in the over-the-counter market. Trading in securities following the initial issue occurs in the *secondary market.* In other words, an investor may purchase an original issue of stock in the primary market and later sell the same shares of stock in the secondary market. The process of issuing securities in the primary market is separate from the subsequent trading of these securities in the secondary market. The ability to resell stocks and bonds in the secondary market is important both for individuals and institutions who buy new issues of stocks and bonds in the primary market. Without an easily accessible method for reselling securities, most investors would be hesitant to commit funds to new issues of stocks and bonds. Ask yourself if you would buy shares of AT&T if you would have difficulty locating a buyer in the event you wanted to sell the stock.

How does an organization that has issued stock or bonds keep track of who owns its securities?

Organizations must stay current on ownership of their securities in order to know where to send reports, interest and dividend checks, and debt repayments. Businesses and other organizations that issue securities generally employ other firms to do this work for them. The issuers are informed each time their securities are traded so they can replace the name of the investor who sold a security with the name of the investor who bought the security. Although issuers of securities are not actively involved in the trading of their securities in the secondary market, these organizations must keep track of who owns the securities.

Is the New York Stock Exchange part of the primary market or the secondary market?

The New York Stock Exchange is a place for trading already-issued securities, not for issuing securities. In other words, the New York Stock Exchange is part of the secondary market, not the primary market. All of the activity on the floor of the exchange involves stocks and bonds being traded for investors. The investors include individuals, banks, mutual funds, pension funds, and insurance companies. The firms that originally issued the securities (i.e., the firms whose names are imprinted on the face of the certificates) are not involved in trading their own securities on the exchange, although these firms are obviously interested in what takes place on the exchange.

Is Wall Street part of or somehow associated with the federal government?

Activities on Wall Street are heavily regulated by the federal government, but most of the financial institutions that operate on Wall Street are privately owned and independently operated. These private concerns include commercial banks, securities dealers, stock exchanges, brokerage firms, and investment banking companies. Wall Street prides itself on being the heart and soul of the free enterprise system, even though financial institutions tend to be subject to substantial oversight by the federal government.

So no government organizations are represented on Wall Street?

The Federal Reserve is one government organization that *is* a major player on Wall Street. The New York branch of the Federal Reserve System regularly auctions U.S. Treasury securities and implements the government's monetary policy. The actions of the Federal Reserve have a major impact on interest rates, inflation, and security prices. Other Federal Reserve banks are situated in major cities around the United States, but none have the impact of the New York branch.

Are foreign firms represented on Wall Street?

Foreign firms are represented on Wall Street just as U.S. firms are represented in foreign markets. Investors and businesses, both foreign and domestic, increasingly have a global perspective. Thus, financial institutions need to have a foreign presence in order to satisfy the business needs of their customers. Individuals and businesses in foreign countries are major investors in the U.S. stock and bond markets.

When did the "real" Wall Street commence operations?

Commodities such as tobacco and grains were traded at the foot of Wall Street as early as the early to mid-1700s. In the late 1700s, a separate market developed for financial securities and Wall Street commenced trading Revolutionary War bonds and stock of the First Bank of the United States. The first formal agreement among brokers for what was later to become the New York Stock Exchange was drawn up about this same time, and the organization adopted the name *New York Stock and Exchange Board* in the early 1800s. By the mid-1800s, substantial trading was taking place in stocks and bonds of transportation companies, especially railroads and canals. Industrial expansion following the Civil War brought a broader spectrum of securities to Wall Street.

Where else are securities traded?

New York continues to be the financial hub of the United States and home for two of the country's major organized exchanges: the New York Stock Exchange and the American Stock Exchange. Similar but smaller financial markets are in Chicago, San Francisco, Los Angeles, and Philadelphia. A great variety and an increasing number of financial assets are traded via computer and telephone rather than in a central location. Continuing improvements in computers and communications are likely to produce additional changes in the methods by which financial assets are traded. Many financial experts believe that trading securities at a central location such as the New York Stock Exchange is an inefficient method of conducting business and that it will eventually be replaced by computerized trading.

Does this mean activities currently associated with Wall Street will increasingly take place outside New York City?

It seems likely that financial activities once relegated to the New York City area will increasingly move to other locations, if for no other reason than the high expense of conducting business in New York City. Many important financial activities already take place outside New York. For example, Chicago has always been a major center for futures contracts and serves as a location for much of the trading in stock options. Some professionals foresee the day when security trades will occur in the most remote locations, so long as individuals have access to a good communications system. A computer linked with current price quotations and other traders will permit an individual, regardless of location, to perform the same activities that now take place in New York City. Most of the required technology for such a system is already available.

If centralized markets are obsolete, why do these markets continue to be so important?

Many individuals and institutions associated with the organized exchanges have a vested interest in keeping things as they are, or at least slowing change. A great amount of money is invested in the existing financial marketplaces, and it is not always in the interest of the people who have made these investments to have competing markets gain status.

If I purchase stock through my local broker, will the order end up in New York?

Your broker's firm may route the order to New York, or it may decide to utilize another marketplace. The market where your order is executed depends on where the brokerage firm has its trading facilities and the location where your security is normally traded. For example, the order may be routed to San Francisco and executed on the floor of the Pacific Stock Exchange. If the stock is traded in several markets, your brokerage firm should attempt to have the transaction executed in the market where you will obtain the best price, which may or may not be in New York. Many stocks are not listed on an exchange, and your broker may have to locate a dealer who makes a market in the stock. Alternatively, if you have placed an order to purchase shares of stock in a foreign company, the brokerage firm may have to transact the order on a foreign exchange.

Is Wall Street an important part of the U.S. economy?

Wall Street plays a major role in both the domestic and the international economies. Wall Street facilitates the raising of capital by both businesses and governments. The capital raised by Wall Street firms allows businesses and governments to construct buildings, manufacture products, supply services, and provide jobs to the country's citizens. Large and active securities markets make it easier for businesses and governments to raise funds because individuals who invest in these organizations have confidence that the investments can subsequently be sold without great difficulty to other investors. Without Wall Street (or something akin to Wall Street), organizations would find it relatively cumbersome and more expensive to raise capital. Inefficient financial markets result in reduced economic growth, less competitiveness on the part of domestic businesses, fewer jobs for the country's citizens, and a lower standard of living.

Is a healthy economy important to Wall Street?

History has demonstrated that a sick economy—large amounts of inflation or deflation, high unemployment, and declining business activity—is generally accompanied by troubles on Wall Street. Businesses facing a bleak sales outlook are unlikely to be in the market to raise additional capital to pay for an expansion of facilities. Likewise, individual investors who become apprehensive about the economic outlook are likely to be more conservative in their investments so that Wall Street firms will find their own business deteriorating. A healthy economy is good medicine for Wall Street. Individuals who have good jobs and a lot of confidence are more likely to invest than people who are concerned they may get laid off from their jobs.

Do other countries have their own versions of Wall Street?

Developed countries with a capitalistic economy require some method for bringing together savers and users of capital. That is, an economy must have some means of connecting individuals and organizations having spare capital with other organizations that have a need for capital. A number of financial centers around the world provide this service, several of which are of a size to rival Wall Street. Keep in mind that foreign-based companies and governments often come to Wall Street to raise capital in the United States, and U.S. firms frequently use foreign markets for raising capital overseas. U.S. companies may choose to borrow in Europe or Asia if interest rates are lower there than in the United States. Financial markets in Hong Kong, London, Tokyo, Toronto, and Frankfurt are competitive with Wall Street. Other exchanges are in Korea, Taiwan, Amsterdam, Milan, and Zurich. Stock exchanges have recently been established in emerging countries, including China, Hungary, Poland, and Russia. As in the United States, many countries have more than one exchange. For example, Japan has eight stock exchanges, while Switzerland has three. Wall Street has gone global as financial centers around the world are linked and trading of securities moves to a 24-hour day.

What types of employment are available on Wall Street?

Wall Street is home to brokers, dealers, portfolio managers, bankers, lawyers, financial analysts, investment advisors, specialists, bond traders, stock traders, and a whole host of other professionals who make their living buying, selling, researching, and managing investments and offering investment advice. Most of these job specialties, some of which may be unfamiliar, will be discussed in a later chapter.

Do people employed on Wall Street make a lot of money?

As with most occupations, some individuals on Wall Street earn very high incomes, whereas other individuals have difficulty making ends meet. In addition, Wall Street tends to be a boom or bust environment. Some years tend to be very good, while other years are very bad. Income earned by brokers, traders, and investment managers is subject to substantial variation from year to year because all or a large portion of the income is directly dependent on the business they conduct rather than on salaries paid by their employers. Some brokers and investment managers have been on top of the world one year and out of a job several years later. Wall Street's riches to rags stories are just as real as the more frequently heard rags to riches stories.

How heavily regulated is Wall Street?

Wall Street activities are heavily regulated, primarily by the federal government. Regulation applies to new issues of securities as well as to trading previously issued securities on the exchanges and among securities dealers. Many of the people who work on Wall Street must be licensed, and brokerage firms and banks are subject to a great amount of government oversight. Brokers must generally obtain several licenses. Similar, although generally less strict regulations are imposed by state governments.

If Wall Street is so heavily regulated, why do investors frequently lose money?

Wall Street regulations are designed to ensure that financial activities are undertaken in an honest manner and that investors have access to relevant information prior to investing their money. Wall Street regulations are not designed to guarantee that investors avoid the purchase of overpriced stock and bonds. Regulations also don't guarantee that individuals won't choose inappropriate investments or put their money at great risk. Businesses and governments sometimes face hardships and therefore are unable to earn a profit or pay interest. Wall Street regulation doesn't protect investors from this type of risk.

Why is Wall Street so heavily regulated?

Much of Wall Street's regulation has been spurred by investor complaints about unethical behavior of the individuals and organizations that operate on Wall Street. A substantial amount of present-day regulation owes it existence to the major stock market decline and financial panic of the late 1920s and early 1930s. Extensive speculation, fraud, and excesses in the securities markets that preceded and accompanied the Great Crash brought forth a public clamor for government regulation of the financial markets. Additional changes followed the stock market crash of October 1987. Much of the current regulation originates with the U.S. Securities and Exchange Commission (SEC). Strict regulations cover a host of financial activities, including the information that must be provided prior to new securities issues and the methods by which brokers and dealers must operate.

Are any other regulations applicable to Wall Street firms?

Many institutions operating on Wall Street are subject to a combination of regulations by private organizations, government agencies, and professional groups. Many of these rules and regulations are over and above restrictions from the Securities and Exchange Commission. For example, the securities exchanges impose many rules by which employees and other individuals and institutions associated with the exchanges must abide. Likewise, the National Association of Securities Dealers (NASD) establishes standards for securities dealers in the United States. Commercial banks are regulated by the Federal Reserve Board and the Federal Deposit Insurance Corporation. Regulations by professional organizations often concern ethical standards as well as specific rules on how various activities are to be conducted and supervised.

Is Wall Street a safe place to invest my money?

Wall Street can be a safe place for investing your money. It can also be a very risky place to put your money. Many people have lost money investing in Wall Street, often because they were too greedy and chose investments that appeared to offer very high returns. Brokers sometimes make promises they can't keep, and investors sometimes put themselves in very risky situations they didn't foresee. Investing in Wall Street should be accompanied with some basic understanding of the potential consequences and a good dose of common sense. One rule of thumb is to never trust your money to an investment you don't understand. Another rule is to determine which types of investments are compatible with your own investment needs.

Do investors in close proximity to Wall Street have an advantage over those of us who live hundreds or thousands of miles away?

Opinion is divided as to whether it is to your advantage to be close to the action of Wall Street. Consider that one of America's premier investors, Warren Buffett, chooses to reside in Omaha, Nebraska, when he is wealthy enough to live anywhere he wants. Some investors feel that staying away from Wall Street allows them to gain better access to the "big picture" of investing. In other words, investors who are removed from the day-to-day activity don't get bogged down in the small bits of news that can cloud their thinking. This feeling is not universal, however, and other investors would rather be in the center of the activity. It is doubtful that most individual investors with a medium- or long-term investment horizon would benefit by being on Wall Street. With improved communications it isn't like you must wait days to receive the latest news from Wall Street.

2 CHAPTER

What Is Stock?

Chapter summary

The issuing and trading of stock are two of Wall Street's major activities. Investors who purchase shares of stock become part owners of the companies that issue the shares. Stockholders generally have the right to elect a firm's directors. An investment in stock offers the potential for substantial returns, mostly from gains in the value of the shares that are acquired. This chapter discusses what shares of stock represent, how stock ownership can produce substantial returns, and why stocks can be risky investments.

What is stock?

Stock represents ownership in a business. One share of stock represents one share of ownership in the business that issued the stock. Purchase shares of Microsoft Corporation stock and you become a partner with Bill Gates as part owner of the firm. The more shares of stock in a company you acquire, the greater your proportional ownership of that business. For example, owning 1000 shares of stock in a company that has 10,000 total shares outstanding means you hold a 10 percent ownership stake in the firm. Owning 1000 shares in Exxon Corporation, a mammoth firm that has nearly 2.5 billion shares of stock outstanding, means you own only .00004 percent of the company. In general, the more shares you own in a business, the more say you have in how the business is operated. The number of shares you own must, however, be compared to the total number of shares that are outstanding.

Where do shares of stock originate?

Shares of stock are issued by businesses to investors who supply the firm with something it needs, most likely money. Initially, stock is issued when a business is first organized. Some of the original owners may supply the business with money, while other individuals may contribute ideas, property, or labor. As the organization grows and requires additional money to purchase buildings, equipment, and items to sell, the owners of the firm may decide to bring in new owners by selling additional shares of stock. Companies sometimes issue new shares of stock in order to pay for the purchase of another business. Thus, many businesses periodically issue additional units of ownership in order to raise funds that allow the firms to grow. Over several decades a growing firm may issue tens of millions of new shares of stock.

Can companies raise money without selling new shares of stock?

Successful companies may be able to earn enough profits to provide most of their investment needs. Of course, relying on reinvested profits means these same profits cannot be distributed to the owners. Many growing companies choose to reinvest most or all of their earnings rather than distribute the profits to owners. Companies can also borrow money. They may borrow from financial institutions such as commercial banks or insurance companies, or they may issue bonds to investors. Bonds are discussed in the following chapter. Using profits or borrowed money means the company will issue fewer shares of stock, so the proportional ownership of existing owners remains the same. Growing a business without having to issue additional shares of stock means that existing owners will not be required to share profits or control with new investors.

Can I purchase stock directly from a company?

Raising funds directly from investors is most effective when a company does not require a very large amount of money. Smaller businesses will sometimes solicit funds directly from investors. In addition, some existing companies have chosen to sell shares directly to investors. Large businesses that choose to sell shares directly generally do so for public relations purposes rather than for efficiency. Still, it is possible for you to purchase shares directly from some companies. Exxon and Procter & Gamble are among several hundred large companies that sell shares directly to investors. In general, however, you will need to utilize a broker to buy and sell shares of stock of most companies.

What factors determine the value of a share of stock?

The value of a share of stock depends on the value of the business that issued the stock and the number of shares of stock the business has outstanding. The greater the value of a business, the greater the value of the shares of ownership of the business. Likewise, the fewer the number of shares outstanding, the greater the value of each share. The value of one share of ownership in a given business is less when 10,000 shares are outstanding than when only 1000 shares are outstanding. The more ways a company splits the pie, the less each piece of the pie is worth.

What determines the value of a business?

The value of a business is a subjective judgment; two individuals with the same basic information may place very different values on the same company. Although management quality, customer loyalty, sales, and the assets that are owned are all factors influencing the value of a business, the bottom line is the amount of cash the company is able to generate. Cash is king, not only the cash the company currently has available but also cash the business is expected to produce in future years. The cash flows that will become available in future years and the time when these cash flows are expected to be available give a company its value. The problem in valuation is accurately estimating the amounts, timing, and certainty of a company's cash flows. Even expert financial analysts have difficulty with this task.

Can you provide an example?

Suppose you talk with an insurance agent about buying a retirement annuity that would pay you an income for life. In deciding whether the income is worthwhile, you take into account the amount of annual cash you will receive, the timing of the payments, and the number of payments you can expect. In other words, the amount, timing, and certainty of the cash you can expect to receive over your lifetime determine the value of the annuity you are buying. Companies are valued in the same manner. The value of General Electric depends on the amount and timing of cash the firm is expected to generate. Cash is king because cash can be reinvested, used to pay suppliers, employees, or taxes, or distributed to stockholders. A company is not particularly valuable if it owns a large amount of assets that fail to generate much cash. On the other hand, a company with few assets that generate large amounts of cash is very valuable.

How can I be expected to estimate a company's future cash flows when I have difficulty balancing my own checkbook?

Even financial experts and company management often have difficulty forecasting a company's cash flows. As a result, most investors rely on someone else's judgment or on their own intuition when they select stocks to buy. Additional material on valuation of investments is provided in Chapter 4.

Why do stock prices jump around so much?

Stock prices change so much because stocks are difficult to value. Unexpected news regarding a company's products or earnings will cause investors to reevaluate their projections for the firm's future income and cash flows. This, in turn, will result in selling pressure (if the news is bad) or buying pressure (if the news is good) that may cause a major change in the firm's stock price. Stock prices reflect investors' expectations of the future, and the future is uncertain. For many companies, it is very uncertain. Even experts who are paid a lot of money to evaluate the value of stocks don't always produce accurate recommendations.

What do shares of stock look like?

Actually, a stock certificate looks a little like a fancy diploma with engraving on expensive paper. The corporate name, stockholder's name, and number of shares represented are printed on the face of the certificate. The face of the certificate is also likely to include some type of sketch relevant to the company or its products. The back of a stock certificate includes a form for transferring the shares to another investor. This part of the certificate must normally be completed and endorsed by the seller when the shares are sold. One certificate is issued no matter how many shares of stock are purchased at a given time. If you purchase 125 shares of IBM, you will receive one certificate for 125 shares. Buying another 100 shares a year later will result in receiving a second certificate.

Will I have to sell the entire 125 shares represented by the certificate if I later decide to sell the stock?

You may sell any number of shares up to 125 as represented by the certificate. You may sell more than 125 shares if you own additional shares of the same stock as a result of prior purchases. If you decide to sell 50 shares, you will deliver the certificate to your broker and later receive a new certificate for 75 shares (the difference between the shares represented by the certificate and the number of shares that you sold). If you have made two separate purchases of 100 shares each and later decide to sell 150 shares, you must deliver both certificates to the selling broker. Several weeks later you will receive a new certificate for the 50 shares of stock you owned but did not sell.

Is it difficult to resell stock I have purchased?

The ease or difficulty of selling stock depends on the particular stock you own. Stock in a small firm with few shareholders may be difficult to sell. For example, an attempt to sell shares in a local bank may find few interested buyers. On the other hand, shares in a large company with publicly traded stock are likely to be very easy to sell. Owning 300 shares of stock of a well-known company whose stock is listed for trading on one of the organized stock exchanges means the sale of your stock is only a telephone call away. A call to your broker will result in your shares being sold within a few minutes of your order. Most likely it will be sold at a price equal to or near the last price at which the stock traded. You may have difficulty getting a fair price when you are in a hurry to sell shares in a company whose stock rarely trades.

Am I able to purchase shares of stock in foreign companies?

Shares of ownership in foreign companies have become an important part of many investors' portfolios. Stocks of many foreign companies are traded on exchanges or in the over-the-counter market in the United States. Thus, you will find it just as easy to buy shares of Sony Corporation, a Japanese company, as General Motors. Not all foreign company shares can be purchased this easily, but many can. In truth, most investors choose to invest in the stocks of foreign companies by purchasing the shares of mutual funds that specialize in owning foreign securities. Investing through a mutual fund is probably the best method for acquiring a stake in foreign companies or bonds. Also, keep in mind that many U.S. companies have a major presence in foreign countries and earn much of their income outside the United States. For example, Coca-Cola typically earns much more profit overseas than in the United States.

I have read that some investors buy ADRs to acquire foreign securities. What are these?

ADR, an acronym for *American Depositary Receipt,* offers investors an indirect method for acquiring ownership of a specified number of shares of a foreign company. The foreign shares are held on deposit in a bank in the issuing company's home country (for example, Japan), while an affiliated U.S. bank issues the ADRs. The bank holding the foreign shares collects dividends, pays applicable taxes, converts the foreign currency into dollars, and forwards the dollars to holders of the ADRs. ADRs allow you to invest in foreign stocks without having to worry about converting currencies.

If I am a shareholder of a company that decides to issue additional stock, will I be offered the right to buy some of the new shares?

Your entitlement to shares of a new stock issue by a company in which you already own shares depends on the company charter. Their corporate charter requires some firms to first offer newly issued shares to existing owners. If this restriction applies to the company in which you are a stockholder, you will be offered an opportunity to buy new shares in proportion to the shares you already hold. For example, currently owning 5 percent of all the firm's outstanding stock means you will be offered the right to buy 5 percent of the shares in the new issue. Many firms' charters do not require that a new issue of stock be offered to existing shareholders. These firms may choose to offer a new issue of stock to outside investors. Thus, a stockholder of this firm may or may not be offered the right to buy newly issued shares.

Am I required to buy the new shares?

No, you don't have to buy shares that are part of a new stock issue. If you don't want to invest additional money in the same company, you should see about selling your right to buy the new shares to another investor. On the other hand, if you have been considering the purchase of additional shares of the firm, a new issue is a good time to invest because the issuing firm picks up brokerage fees. That is, you will not be charged a commission to purchase shares that are part of a new stock issue.

Is all stock basically the same?

Two major types of stock are issued by businesses, although one type is by far the most popular. If a company has only a single type of stock outstanding, it will almost certainly be common stock. Actually, companies sometimes issue more than one class of common stock. Preferred stock, the other major kind of stock, is much less popular. Nearly all companies have common stock outstanding, but a much smaller number have preferred stock outstanding.

The name implies preferred stock is better to own than common stock. Is this true?

In general, preferred stock is not better to own. This class of stock derives its name from its priority claim to any profits or assets distributed to the firm's owners. In other words, preferred stockholders have the right to be paid prior to common stockholders. Preferred stockholders also have priority over common stockholders with respect to a distribution of assets in the event a company is liquidated. The downside to ownership of preferred stock is the fixed amount of the dividend distributions. With fixed dividends the owners of preferred stock do not participate in future profit growth of a successful company. If you are to receive $80 in annual dividends the first year after buying shares of preferred stock, you will receive the same $80 of annual dividends years later no matter how successful the business may become.

How does this differ from common stock?

Unlike preferred stockholders, who are promised a specified cash distribution each year, profit distributions to common stockholders are less certain, but they are subject to being increased if and when the firm's income grows. Of course, profit distributions to owners of common stock can also be decreased or eliminated in the event a firm runs into financial difficulties. Distributions to preferred stockholders can also be cut, but this is much less likely to occur.

How can I profit from owning shares of stock?

The value of ownership in a business will vary with current and expected future profitability of the business. If the profitability of a business improves, the value of the business and the value of the firm's stock will generally increase. (See Figure 2-1 for an overall picture of how stocks performed between 1953 and 1998.) Thus, you may purchase a company's shares for $30 each that grow in worth to $40 several years later. The difference between the price paid and the current value represents the profit earned (called a *paper profit* because you have not yet sold the stock to realize the gain). The more shares you purchased, the greater the total profit earned. Of course, if the price of the shares falls back to its former level before you decide to sell, the paper profit will evaporate. Also, the price of the shares may initially decline rather than increase, in which case you would have a loss rather than a profit. The potential for gains in value is the primary reason most individuals invest in common stock.

If the stock of a successful company continues to increase in value, won't it eventually reach too high a price for investors to afford?

An extended increase in the value of its stock is likely to cause a company's directors to divide, or split, the shares. That is, the company will issue additional shares of stock to current shareholders. Because the company acquires no additional funds or other assets while the number of units of ownership is increased, the price of the stock will decrease. For example, if the directors decide to send one additional share for each share already owned (termed a *two-for-one split*), the market price of the firm's stock can be expected to decline to half the presplit price. If the directors send out three additional shares for each share owned (a *four-for-one split*), the price of the stock will decline to approximately a quarter of its presplit price. In the latter example, if you own 150 shares, you

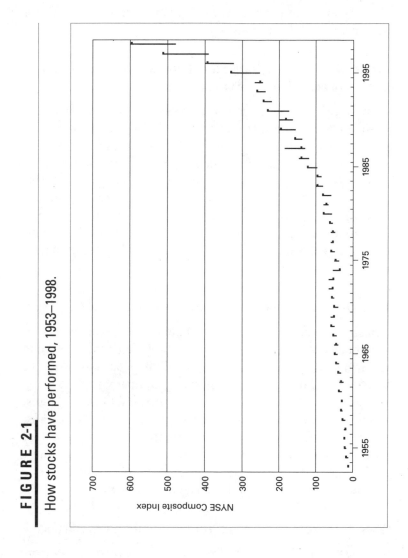

FIGURE 2-1

How stocks have performed, 1953–1998.

will receive an additional 450 shares for a total of 600 shares. The directors of most companies establish a "desired range" for the price of their stock and declare a split when the price moves above the upper end of the range.

As a stockholder, can I earn a profit from anything other than increases in the value of the stock I own?

Many companies distribute to the owners a portion of the firm's profits. These profit distributions, or *dividends,* are generally declared and paid by check every three months, although some companies choose to pay dividends annually or semiannually. Dividends are a source of stockholder income, just as an increase in the value of stock is a source of income. In fact, because dividends are generally paid in cash, investment income from dividends can be spent. On the other hand, profit from increases in the value of stock isn't available to buy things unless some shares of stock are sold.

Are companies required to pay dividends?

A business is not required to distribute profits to its owners. In fact, many companies retain most or all of their profits to use in acquiring additional assets, such as buildings or inventories, or for paying off debt. A rapidly growing company is most likely to need all of its profits for reinvestment in additional assets. Businesses that don't expect to need much additional capital for growth are most likely to distribute profits to the owners. A firm's directors are in charge of determining what portion of profits, if any, will be distributed to stockholders. The directors must also determine when the dividends will be paid.

When do I have to own a stock in order to qualify for the dividend?

You must own the stock on the stockholder of record date in order to receive the dividend that has been declared. The stockholder of record date is the date on which the company checks its ownership list to determine who will receive the dividend. If you are on the list as of that date, then you qualify for the dividend that will be paid. The stockholder of record date is often nearly a month prior to the date the dividend will actually be sent to stockholders. Directors announce the stockholder of record date and the payment date at the same time they announce the amount of the dividend to be paid.

So I will receive a dividend if I purchase stock by the stockholder of record date?

Actually, you must purchase stock at least one day prior to the ex-dividend date, which is three business days before the stockholder of record date. Stock transactions currently settle in three days, which means that you are required to pay for stock three days after the purchase date. Likewise, sell stock and you must deliver the certificate within three business days of the sale date. Buy stock on Monday and you must pay on Thursday. Thus, the system requires three days to transfer stock to a new owner. If you buy stock on the stockholder of record date, you will not receive the dividend because your name will not be transferred as an owner for three more business days. Buy stock one day prior to the ex-dividend date and ownership will be transferred just in time for you to receive the upcoming dividend payment. Important dividend dates for stockholders are described in Figure 2-2.

How is a stock's dividend yield calculated?

Dividend yield is equal to the annual dividend divided by the market price of the stock. For example, if a stock selling for $40 per share currently pays an annual dividend of $1.50, the dividend yield is $1.50/$40, or 3.75 percent. If you buy the stock at the current price, annual dividend payments will provide an annual return of 3.75 percent. A stock's dividend yield changes

FIGURE 2-2

Important dividend dates for stockholders.

A firm's directors normally meet at least four times per year to conduct the company's business. One of the important issues discussed at quarterly meetings is the dividend to be paid to stockholders. Directors must decide if a dividend is to be paid and, if so, what amount is to be paid. They must also determine when the payment will be made and establish the date that will be used to determine which stockholders are to receive the dividend. The four important dates relating to a dividend are:

Declaration date: The date directors convene and decide on the dividend. The firm's directors announce the amount of the dividend, the date that stockholders must be recorded as owners in order to be entitled to the dividend, and the date the dividend will be paid.

Ex-dividend date: The first day that new buyers of the firm's stock will not be entitled to the upcoming dividend that the firm's directors have declared. Investors who purchase shares of stock on or after the ex-dividend date will not receive the dividend that was declared at the last directors' meeting.

Record date (also called *stockholder of record date*): The date the firm closes its corporate register of security owners in determining who is to receive the announced dividend. The ex-dividend date precedes the record date by two business days. The two-day difference results from investors having three business days to pay for shares of stock that have been purchased.

Payment date: The date the firm or the firm's agent makes the dividend payment to individuals and institutions who have been identified as stockholders on the record date. Firms sometimes mail the dividend a day or so early so stockholders will receive their check by the payment date.

As an illustration of a typical dividend payment sequence, suppose a firm's directors convene on September 3 (the declaration

Continued

F I G U R E 2-2

Concluded

date) and determine that a dividend of $0.30 per share will be
paid to stockholders of record on September 20 (the record
date), with payment to be made September 30 (the payment
date). Examining the September calendar shown below, we see
that investors who have purchased the stock on or before the
close of business on September 17 will receive the dividend.
Thus, beginning September 18 (the ex-dividend date), new buyers of the stock will not receive the September 30 dividend. A
buyer of stock on September 18 will not receive the upcoming
dividend because payment on the stock is not due for three business days, or September 21, when the shares will be transferred.

Sun	Mon	Tues	Wed	Thur	Fri	Sat
1	2	**3**	4	5	6	7
8	9	10	11	12	13	14
15	16	17	**18**	19	**20**	21
22	23	24	25	26	27	28
29	**30**					

with the market price of the stock and with changes in the dividend. Dividend yield is a measure of the current yield you will
earn from owning a stock. It does not consider any change in the
value of the stock. Thus, dividend yield is relevant to evaluating
a stock, but it is certainly an incomplete measure of the yield
you can expect to earn.

What happens to the dividend if a company splits its stock?

A stock split will almost certainly result in a corresponding dividend reduction on a per-share basis. Suppose you own 200
shares of a stock that pays a $1 per share dividend and the direc-
tors declare a two-for-one split. You will end up with 400 shares

of stock (after receiving an additional 200 shares) that is likely
to pay a $ 0.50 per share dividend. In the aggregate, nothing has
changed because you own twice as many shares, each worth
half as much, and receive the same total dividends as before the
split. A firm's directors will sometimes declare an increase in its
dividend at the same time it announces a stock split. In the example just cited, the firm may declare a 55-cent dividend on the
split shares, which is the equivalent of $1.10 on the presplit
stock. You will receive a dividend check of $220 on the split
shares, as opposed to receiving a dividend of $200 on the
presplit shares.

If stockholders are the owners of a business, why don't the stockholders vote on whether the firm should pay dividends?

Stockholders influence a firm's dividend policy but in an indirect manner. Stockholders elect the firm's directors, who, in
turn, establish the dividend. The directors will be slow to anger
stockholders by paying too low or too high a dividend (as
judged by stockholders), because the stockholders theoretically
have the power to elect new directors who are more sympathetic
to the stockholders' desires.

Aren't investors penalized when a firm's directors choose to retain all of the firm's profits?

Not necessarily. A company's value should increase if its
managers are wise enough to reinvest the firm's income in
profitable assets. A decision by managers of an oil company
to forgo dividends in order to invest in a productive new oil
field is likely to benefit stockholders, who will see an increase in the value of their ownership. On the other hand, if
managers reinvest profits in unprofitable assets, the owners'
investment is likely to suffer a decrease in value. It is also
important to keep in mind that profit distributions are taxable

when received by shareholders, while increases in the value of ownership are not taxable until stock is sold. In other words, retaining profits for reinvestment has the effect of deferring any taxes to be paid by shareholders. The tax aspect of investing is discussed in a subsequent chapter.

What if I need current investment income for spending needs?

If you require current income to meet daily living expenses, you may want to choose preferred stock or the common stock of a company that pays a generous dividend. On the other hand, you may be better off investing in bonds which generally pay greater current income than stocks. An alternative is to invest in a growing company that pays a meager dividend and plan on selling some of your shares whenever you need money. This can be a risky strategy, especially if you rely heavily on current income to make ends meet, because there is no way to determine the price you will receive from the shares you must sell. This practice can also result in substantial brokerage fees.

Do dividends change from year to year?

Hopefully, dividends on the stock you own will increase over the years. Increased dividends are most likely when a company experiences an increase in revenues and profits. Without corresponding increases in profits, continually increasing dividends will eventually eat up all the profits and the firm won't have any funds available for reinvestment. Some companies have a proud history of raising dividends at frequent intervals. Other firms raise dividend payments sporadically as conditions warrant. A business with fluctuating revenues and profits (e.g., large profits one year and small profits or losses the following year) may pay a dividend that is a small part of profits one year and a dividend that is actually greater than profits earned the following year.

Do firms ever reduce or quit paying dividends?

Firms may reduce or even eliminate dividends during difficult economic periods, especially when these conditions persist for several years. A firm's directors are likely to view a reduction or, especially, an elimination of dividends as a fairly desperate measure because the news sends a negative signal to the investment community. However, a reduction in dividends may be in order when a firm needs to conserve cash in order to pay its bills. Remember, dividend payments on common stock are not guaranteed. Eastern Airlines paid dividends for many years before finally eliminating these payments in 1969. Although the airline operated for another 20 years, it failed to pay another dividend before it finally declared bankruptcy and was liquidated.

Do companies ever skip dividends to owners of preferred stock?

Companies are much more reluctant to omit a dividend to preferred stockholders. Most preferred stock is *cumulative,* which means any promised preferred dividends that have been omitted (omitted dividends are called *dividends in arrears*) must be made up in full before any dividends can be paid to common stockholders. This restriction on common stock dividends is a strong incentive for a company to maintain dividends to preferred stockholders. Dividends to preferred stockholders are seldom reduced or omitted unless a company is in serious financial difficulty.

Are dividends always paid by check?

Dividends are generally paid by check. However, companies sometimes distribute property or additional shares of stock in lieu of cash, or occasionally in addition to cash. Stock dividends are paid when a firm's directors wish to conserve cash but feel a need to distribute something to the owners. Likewise, a company's directors may distribute property the firm no longer needs. Cash dividends (paid via check) are by far the most popular form of distribution.

Can I have cash dividends automatically reinvested by the company?

Many companies offer dividend reinvestment plans (DRIPS) in which current shareholders can choose to have dividends automatically reinvested in additional shares of stock. These plans are typically administered by large banks that send a quarterly report to participants regarding the amount of the dividend paid, the number of shares purchased, and the number of shares being held in the account. These plans sometimes entail a nominal charge, both for annual maintenance and for stock purchases and sales. In some cases the company offering the plan picks up all the fees. These tend to be a good deal, although you will still be required to report dividend payments that are reinvested as income on your tax return.

How does a stock dividend work?

When a company in which you own stock declares a stock dividend, you will receive additional shares of stock in proportion to the stock you already own. For example, owning 100 shares of stock in a company that declares a 5 percent dividend means you will receive a new certificate for five shares of stock. Following the distribution, you will own 105 shares rather than 100 shares. If your existing stock is being held in a brokerage account, the new shares from the stock dividend will be credited to your account. New shares of stock do not come without a cost, since the market price of the shares you already own will decline in price. The extent of the decline will depend on the size of the stock dividend that is paid. A stock dividend decreases the price of the stock because it results in more shares of ownership without any corresponding increase in a company's assets or earning power.

What will happen to the value of my stock if the company goes out of business?

The reason a company goes out of business is important in determining how the owners of the business will fare. If the firm has suffered losses over an extended period, the value of ownership may be close to zero by the time the firm goes out of business. If the firm no longer has any value, the shares of ownership will also have no value and you will lose whatever you have paid for the stock. If the owners of a successful company decide to shut down the business, liquidate the assets, and distribute everything to the owners, stockholders may receive a substantial amount of money. Most corporate liquidations lie somewhere between these two extremes, but since most liquidations are among firms that are no longer competitive, the assets owned by the firm are not likely to have much value and the stock will sell at a low price.

What is the relationship between a firm's stockholders, directors, and managers?

Very simply, stockholders are the owners, who elect the directors, who, in turn, establish the firm's policies and hire its managers. Directors tend to be concerned about the big picture, while managers concentrate on day-to-day activities of the firm. Directors lay out broad policy guidelines under which the managers are expected to operate. A firm's board of directors is likely to include several of the firm's managers, some of its former managers, and individuals from outside the firm. Outside directors of a board can provide the business with independent and fresh perspectives. The power and effectiveness of directors varies from firm to firm. Some boards are very active, while other boards allow managers a free hand. Directors are sometimes selected for the prestige of their names or the organizations they represent rather than for the advice they can offer.

How do stockholders go about electing a firm's directors?

Stockholders generally vote annually for either a portion or all of a firm's directors. Most firms have staggered terms for directors, which means that at any one time, only a portion of the board will be up for election. For example, a firm with 16 directors, each with four-year terms, may specify that four positions are voted on each year. Voting generally takes place via ballots (called proxies) that the firm sends to stockholders prior to the annual meeting. Stockholders are asked to mark, sign, and return the proxies to the firm. By returning a signed proxy, you give someone else the right to vote your shares as you indicate. Shareholders are permitted to change their votes prior to the annual meeting.

Who decides on the nominees listed on the proxy?

The firm's existing directors generally appoint several of their members to a nominating committee. The committee members then nominate candidates for the board. Generally, one person is nominated for each position so that stockholders are only given the opportunity to vote for or not vote for a nominee. That is, you vote yes or withhold your vote. You are not permitted to write in someone else's name. Many investors consider the election of corporate directors to be no more than a rubber stamp for candidates friendly to current management and who have been selected by the board's nominating committee.

How many votes can a stockholder cast?

Most stock gives a shareholder one vote for each share owned
for each contested position. Thus, a stockholder with 200 shares
would have 200 votes to be applied to each position. Another investor with twice as many shares would have twice as many
votes. Some firms specify a special voting arrangement called
cumulative voting in which a stockholder can accumulate the
votes to be cast for all the positions and direct these votes for a
single position. Thus, if four positions are contested, a stockholder with 200 shares would control 800 votes that could be
cast for a single position. Regardless of which voting method is
utilized, the more shares a stockholder owns, the more votes and
the more power the stockholder possesses.

Do all types of stock provide owners with the right to elect directors?

Most, but not all common stock carries the right to vote for a
firm's directors. Some companies issue multiple classes of
common stock, with one of the classes having all or most of the
voting power. For example, a company with two classes of
stock may have one class with 10 votes per share and another
class with one vote per share. Preferred stock may or may not
provide shareholders with the right to participate in the election
of directors except under special circumstances. For example,
preferred stockholders may have the right to elect a specific
number of directors in the event the company's directors fail to
declare a preferred dividend for two years.

Should I care if a stock is traded on an exchange?

Quality stocks are traded on both the organized exchanges
and in the over-the-counter market. Stocks must meet certain
minimum standards in order to be traded on an exchange or

as part of the Nasdaq over-the-counter system. However, it is certainly possible to acquire a losing stock in either market. The over-the-counter market includes more stocks. It also includes a wider range of stocks with regard to quality. Subsequent chapters discuss both the organized exchanges and the over-the-counter market.

Do you have any last pointers on stock investments?

First, buy stock for the long term. Stocks tend to experience large fluctuations in price, so it is very risky to invest money you are likely to need within a year or less. Second, invest in stock issues that are consistent with your investment goals. It is one thing to invest in risky new issues or the stock of small untested companies when you have a substantial amount of excess funds. It is quite another thing to invest in these stocks when you need to preserve the principal of your investment. Third, don't invest in a stock without first undertaking some research on your own. Check a reputable investment publication such as the *Value Line Investment Survey* to obtain an independent appraisal of a stock. Fourth, continually reevaluate your investment needs with a view toward rearranging your portfolio. The stocks that fit your investment needs at age 25 are unlikely to be the same stocks that fit your needs at age 55. In general, you want to move toward a more conservative portfolio as you grow older.

C H A P T E R

What Are Bonds?

Chapter summary

A bond represents debt in which the bondholder is a lender and the issuer is the borrower. Most bondholders are entitled to periodic interest payments and repayment of the principal amount (face value) of the bond on a specified date. Bonds are issued by a variety of organizations, including businesses, cities, states, and the federal government. This chapter discusses the types of bonds that are available, how these securities are issued and traded, and how bonds are valued.

What are bonds?

A bond represents a debt that is owed to the bondholder by the issuer of the bond. Thus, a bond is an IOU given by one party (the borrower and issuer) to another (the lender and bond-holder). The bond obligates the borrower to repay the bond's face value (also called the *principal* or *principal amount*) on a specific date (the *maturity date*) and generally to make semiannual interest payments.

Do bonds represent a particular type of debt?

Different names are applied to different types of debt. The term *bond* generally refers to a long-term debt obligation with payments to the lender secured by a specific asset. For example, a book publisher needing to raise money to pay for a new editorial building may issue $20 million of bonds. The publisher pledges the building as security for the debt and promises to repay the amount borrowed 20 years from the date the loan is made. Because the building is pledged as collateral, bondholders can take possession of the building in the event the publisher is unable to pay interest on the debt or repay the principal of the loan at maturity. This is a description of a plain vanilla bond.

What other types of debt are available as investments?

Long-term debt without the pledge of a particular asset is called a *debenture.* Basically, a debenture is a promise to pay but without the added security of specific collateral. In the above example, the publisher might issue the debt but not use the building as collateral for the loan. In this instance, the securities issued would qualify as debentures because the loan is not backed by earmarked assets creditors can claim in the event the borrower fails to make the required payments.

Notes are another security that represent debt to be repaid within an intermediate time period, generally two to seven years from the date of issue. Notes are identical to bonds and debentures except that notes are scheduled for an earlier repayment. Several securities, including U.S. Treasury bills, represent debt with a maturity of one year or less. Although investors will encounter many variations on the basic debt described above, and the differences can be important, the basic characteristics of most debt securities are similar, and it is convenient to refer to all these securities as bonds.

What are some terms that will help me understand bonds?

The *face value,* or *principal amount,* is the amount of money that the borrower must pay the bondholder on the date the loan is due. A $1000 face amount bond entitles the bondholder to receive $1000 on a scheduled date. The *coupon,* or *coupon rate,* is the rate of interest paid by the borrower based on the bond's face value. For example, a 6-percent coupon, $1000 principal amount bond will pay annual interest equal to 6 percent of $1000, or $60. A bond's principal amount and coupon rate are established when the bond is issued, and both will remain unchanged until the bond's principal is repaid. The date on which the borrower is scheduled to repay the principal is known as the bond's *maturity.* Face value, coupon, and maturity are three very important characteristics of any bond. Some other helpful terms and information regarding bond rates is offered in Figure 3-1.

Where do bonds originate?

Businesses, the federal government, state governments, cities, counties, hospitals, churches, school districts, foreign governments, and a host of other organizations issue bonds. The U.S. Treasury, the state of Minnesota, New York City, Canada, and General Motors each issue bonds. Unlike stock, which is issued only by businesses, bonds are issued by a wide variety of organizations. A bond is nothing other than a piece of paper that represents a debt on the part of the organization that issued the bond.

How are bonds issued?

Bonds are issued in much the same manner as stocks. The organization planning to borrow will generally employ the services

FIGURE 3-1

Important short-term interest rates.

Bankers acceptance   Rate offered on negotiable bank-backed business credit instruments.

Broker call money   The rate commercial banks charge brokerage firms on loans collateralized by securities. This affects the rate investors pay on margin loans.

Certificates of deposit (CDs)   Rates paid on negotiable deposit certificates in amounts of $1 million and over.

Commercial paper   Rate paid by major corporations for unsecured short-term debt sold at a discount to face value; the corporate version of U.S. Treasury bills.

Discount rate   The rate charged on loans to depository institutions by the Federal Reserve. A change in the rate is an indication of the Federal Reserve's outlook for the economy.

Federal funds   The rate charged on overnight loans among commercial banks. Changes in the rate indicate whether the Federal Reserve is easing or tightening the money supply.

LIBOR (London Interbank Offered Rates)   Rate paid by British banks for dollar deposits.

Prime rate   The rate commercial banks charge on unsecured loans to their most creditworthy business borrowers; changed infrequently and generally in response to other interest rate changes.

Treasury bills   Rates paid by the U.S. government on short-term U.S. Treasury bills auctioned each Monday.

of an investment banker that helps plan and execute the borrowing. The investment banker, for a fee, will advise the borrower on the least expensive and best method of raising the needed funds. The firm will take care of all the details, including an intimidating amount of paperwork that must precede the actual issuing of the bonds. An investment banker often agrees to purchase the bonds directly from the borrower with the intention to resell the securities to investors at a slightly higher price. For example, an investment banker might purchase bonds from an issuer for $995 per $1000 bond and then immediately resell the same securities to the public for $1000 each. The difference between the price paid by the investment banker and the price at which the investment banker sells the bonds to investors is called the *underwriting spread.*

Why do businesses and governments issue bonds rather than borrow from a bank?

Organizations such as businesses do borrow from banks and other commercial lenders, of course. However, a business desiring a loan may determine that funds can be obtained at lower cost with a public bond issue than from a commercial lender. Also, a borrower is likely to find commercial lenders such as banks are often reluctant to provide funds for a very long period of time, say 25 or 30 years. Large organizations sometimes need to borrow huge amounts of money, more than a single commercial lender will be able or willing to provide. Another reason to prefer a public bond issue is that commercial lenders may require more collateral for a loan than a business wishes to commit. For example, a firm may want to borrow money currently but leave its assets unencumbered in order to support additional borrowing at a later date.

In what respects is a bond different from stock?

Other than the fact that both securities represent a financial claim on the issuer, bonds and stocks have very little in common. Stock represents ownership and provides the investor with a claim to a portion of a firm's profits. Stock also generally grants the shareholder the right to vote for a firm's directors. Bonds represent debt and provide the holder with a contractual claim to specific payments from the borrower. Bonds legally obligate the issuer to make stipulated payments and eventually to repay the principal amount of the loan. The two securities are also different with respect to tax implications for the issuer. Interest paid to bondholders is permitted as a deductible expense in calculating the borrower's income taxes. On the other hand, dividends paid to stockholders are not allowed as a deductible expense for tax purposes, which means that dividends must be paid with after-tax income.

If interest expense is deductible and dividends are not, why don't companies always borrow instead of issue stock?

Relying too heavily on debt will put a company in a very risky position regarding its ability to make the required interest and principal payments. At some point, investors and lenders may judge a company to be so risky that they refuse to advance additional funds. Companies generally try to achieve a balance of debt and equity in their capital structures. Too heavy a reliance on debt and the company runs the risk of insolvency.

In what amounts are bonds issued?

Corporate bonds are nearly always denominated in multiples of $1000. Thus, you can purchase a single $1000 corporate bond or 10 bonds of $1000 each. You cannot, however, normally buy $1500 principal amount of bonds. Purchasing one or multiple bonds in one transaction will result in a single certificate that indicates the principal amount of the debt. Bonds issued by state and local governments are nearly always issued in $5000 increments (e.g., you cannot purchase less than $5000 principal amount at a time), while U.S. government bonds are issued in amounts of $1000, $5000, and $10,000, depending on the particular type of bond. This discussion does not address U.S. savings bonds, which are issued at a discount from face value and are not comparable to other types of bonds discussed in this book.

Are bonds always issued at face value?

Bonds are generally issued at face value or a price near face value. In some instances an investment banker may issue a $1000 principal amount bond at a discount or premium to face value. For example, a bond may be issued at a price of $980. Likewise, bonds are sometimes issued at a price above face value. A limited number of bonds with very low or no interest payments are issued at large discounts from face value. Investors who hold bonds to maturity will receive face value even though the bonds were originally issued at a discount or a premium.

Some bonds don't pay any interest?

Zero-coupon bonds, bonds without semiannual interest payments, are popular with some investors who have no need for cash flow. Zero-coupon bonds are issued at a deep discount to face value. For example, an investor may be able to purchase a $1000 principal amount zero-coupon bond for $500. If the bond has a 10-year maturity, the $500 investment will turn into $1000 ten years after the date of purchase. This would provide the investor with an annual return of approximately 7 percent. Obviously, a zero-coupon bond is desirable only if you don't need current income.

Why are some bonds issued for less than face value?

The price at which a bond is issued depends on the bond's coupon rate compared to the interest rate that is available on similar securities at the time the bonds are issued. If a bond's coupon rate is competitive with current market interest rates, the bond will be issued at face value. If a bond's coupon rate is somewhat lower than the market rate of interest at the time of issue, the bonds must be issued at a slight discount from face value. For example, if bonds with a 5-percent coupon are issued at a time when similar bonds are yielding 6 percent, the new bonds must be issued at a discount to face value. Investors will not pay $1000 for a bond that pays $50 in annual interest when other bonds paying $60 annually can be purchased for $1000.

Will a bond issued below face value be repaid at face value?

Bonds are redeemed for face value at maturity regardless of whether the bonds are originally issued for less or more than face value. When bonds are issued at less than face value, investors can expect to earn a return higher than the coupon rate because the bond will gradually increase in price in addition to making specified interest payments. From the borrower's perspective, the coupon rate of the bond represents only a part of the cost of borrowing since the borrower will have to pay more dollars to redeem the bonds than were received when the bonds were issued.

Will I receive a certificate at the time I buy a bond?

You are likely to have to wait several weeks for delivery of a certificate following purchase of a bond. The delay will occur whether you purchase a bond that is part of a new issue or buy a previously issued bond that is traded in the secondary market. As discussed in a subsequent chapter, you will have a choice of receiving the certificate or having it kept by the brokerage firm that took care of the order.

Can I require the issuer to redeem a bond prior to maturity?

Very few bonds allow a bondholder to force the borrower to repay a loan prior to the scheduled maturity date. Bonds with long maturities are generally issued in order to pay for the purchase of long-term assets such as land, buildings, or equipment. Thus, it is impractical to expect a borrower to be able to repay a long-term loan on very short notice. Imagine the bank, savings and loan, or credit union that holds your home mortgage sending you a letter demanding that you immediately repay the outstanding balance on the loan. The few bonds that do allow the bondholder to force an early redemption are called *put bonds*. Being able to force a borrower to redeem a bond early is so desirable from an investor's perspective that bonds with this feature offer relatively low yields.

What can I do if I need money I have invested in a bond, but the bond is not scheduled to mature for many years?

Bonds can be transferred to another investor at any time. This means you can sell a bond prior to the scheduled maturity date. Of course, you must locate another investor willing to pay your asking price, or you must be willing to sell your bond at the price being offered by another investor. It is generally impractical to locate a potential investor on your own, so you will almost certainly employ the services of a brokerage firm to do the job for you. Bonds are transferred in an identical manner as stocks. You must endorse the back of the certificate and send or personally deliver the security to your brokerage firm. The brokerage firm, in turn, will forward the certificate to an assigned transfer agent, which will issue a new certificate imprinted with the new owner's name.

If I hold a certificate for $15,000 principal amount of a bond, will I have to sell the entire amount designated on the certificate?

As with stock, you can sell less than the amount represented by a certificate. In this example, you could sell from $1000 to $15,000 of the debt you hold. Regardless of whether you sell all or part of the debt represented by the certificate, you will be required to endorse and surrender the certificate. If you sell $5000 principal amount of the bond, you will give up your certificate in order to receive a new certificate for $10,000 principal amount of the bonds plus a check for the proceeds from the sale.

Is there a possibility I may encounter difficulty locating another investor interested in purchasing my bond?

First, your broker, not you, will attempt to locate a buyer for your security. This is the reason you pay the broker a commission. Having said that, anything, including a bond, can be sold if you are willing to accept a low enough price. Some bonds are actively traded, which means you should have a relatively easy time obtaining a fair price for the bond you intend to sell. Heavy trading of certain bonds, such as U.S. Treasuries, makes the securities very easy to resell. Other bonds trade irregularly and can prove difficult to sell unless you are willing to accept a price that is somewhat lower than you might expect. Municipal bonds issued by an obscure county or corporate bonds from a small business may prove difficult to resell. Likewise, attempting to sell bonds that are part of a small issue may mean you will have to accept a reduced price in order to locate a willing buyer.

Can a bond issuer choose to redeem its bonds prior to the scheduled maturity?

Subject to certain restrictions, borrowers are often permitted to redeem bonds prior to the scheduled maturity. Bonds that can be redeemed early are termed *callable bonds,* and the date on which they can be redeemed is termed the *call date.* The ability of a borrower to redeem a bond prior to maturity is spelled out in the original borrowing agreement. In other words, both you and the broker that executes your order to buy the bond should be aware of an early redemption feature. The possibility of early redemption can be very important because it may force you to surrender the bond long before you had planned.

How will I find out if my bond has been redeemed early?

The issuer will send a letter informing you of the redemption prior to the redemption date so that you will have sufficient time to deliver the certificate to the issuer. In return, you will receive a check for the amount stipulated by the call. In the event your bond is being held in a brokerage account, your broker will take care of all the paperwork. Of course, you will still be informed that your bond has been redeemed.

Are issuers required to pay bondholders a premium when bonds are redeemed early?

Early redemption frequently requires the borrower to pay bondholders more than the principal amount of the debt. For example, early redemption might require a borrower to pay bondholders $1040 for each $1000 principal amount bond that is redeemed. A premium is often required when the issuer redeems bonds prior to the scheduled maturity in order to refinance the loan at a lower interest rate. The original borrowing agreement will specify whether a premium is required when bonds are redeemed prior to maturity.

Is there any other reason a borrower will redeem its bonds prior to the scheduled maturity?

Many bond agreements have a sinking fund provision that requires the borrower to redeem a specified number of bonds annually. Basically, a sinking fund provision means that a borrower must repay a portion of its outstanding debt each year rather than all at once at maturity. Companies typically call bonds at par to meet a sinking fund requirement. You might want to check if a bond is subject to a sinking fund redemption, because a sinking fund makes it more likely the bond will be called prior to maturity.

What if I don't agree to an early redemption?

Too bad. The possibility of early redemption is part of the contract between the borrower and lenders, so you really have no choice in the matter. The issuer will make no further interest payments following the effective date of the call. Thus, failing to surrender your bond to the issuer means you will hold a bond that earns no interest. In addition, the principal amount of the bond will be withheld until you surrender the certificate. Your broker automatically surrenders certificates held in your brokerage account.

How much interest is the issuer required to pay on a bond?

The rate of interest on the loan represented by the bond is established at the time the money is borrowed and the bond is issued. The rate of interest is determined by the market rate of interest at the time the money is borrowed. The dollar amount of interest that will be paid on a bond is a function of two items mentioned earlier: the coupon rate and the principal amount, or face value, of the bond. A $1000 principal amount bond with a coupon rate of 7 percent will pay annual interest of $70 (7 percent of $1000). Purchase 10 of these bonds ($10,000 principal amount), and you will receive annual interest of $700 until the maturity date or until the issuer calls the bonds.

Is bond interest paid once a year?

Bond interest is paid twice a year, with half the annual interest paid every six months. The date on which interest is to be paid will be stipulated in the loan agreement. Many bonds pay interest on January 1 and July 1. An 8-percent coupon, $1000 principal amount bond will pay $40 in interest each six months until redeemed by the issuer. The annual payment dates will remain the same until the bond is redeemed.

Do a bond's interest payments ever change?

Nearly all bond agreements stipulate fixed interest payments. That is, once a bond is issued, the semiannual interest payments remain the same until the issuer redeems the bond. Purchase a bond and you will be guaranteed a stream of equal semiannual payments for as long as you own the bond. The fixed stream of income guaranteed to a bondholder has both advantages and disadvantages.

What if market interest rates change following my purchase of a bond?

The interest payments on a bond are established at the time of issue and will not be affected by changes in market interest rates. If you purchase a bond with a 6-percent coupon, the bond will continue to pay you $60 of annual interest regardless of what happens to market interest rates. You have committed your funds at what you consider a fair return, and the annual interest payments promised by the borrower will remain the same until the bond is redeemed.

Are fixed interest payments a good deal?

It depends. Fixed interest payments are not a good deal if the purchasing power of the fixed payments is eroded by inflation. Seventy dollars in annual interest paid by a 7-percent coupon bond is unlikely to buy much in 20 years if inflation averages 8 percent annually. The purchasing power of a dollar from 1970 to 1998 is shown in Figure 3-2. By definition, fixed interest pay-

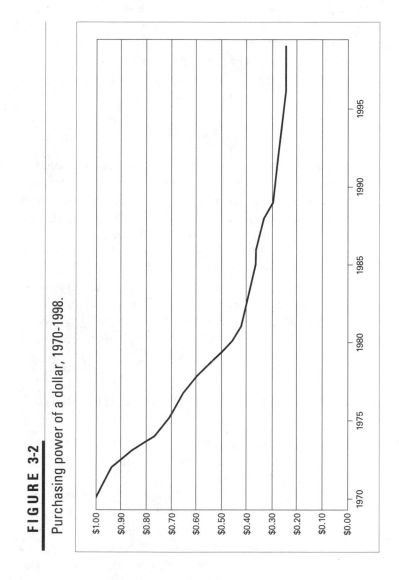

FIGURE 3-2

Purchasing power of a dollar, 1970-1998.

ments can't increase as can dividends, which depend on a firm's earnings. Fixed interest payments can be a good choice if you desire regular income. Of course, if consumer prices begin to decline, you will be happy to have a fixed stream of income because the purchasing power of your fixed interest payments will increase. Unfortunately for bond investors, declining consumer prices are probably unlikely, at least for any extended period.

Is interest the only income I will earn from owning a bond?

If you purchase a bond at face value and subsequently hold the security until its scheduled maturity, your income will consist of the interest payments you receive. On the other hand, if you buy a bond for less than face value and hold it until maturity, you will profit from a gain in value of the bond as well as from the interest payments. If you pay more than face value for a bond and hold it to maturity, you will suffer a loss in value that offsets a portion of the income from interest. There is another possibility: You may pay face value for a bond and then sell it prior to redemption at a price other than face value. Experiencing a gain or loss in value will affect the yield you earn from owning a bond.

How do I determine the return I will earn from investing in a bond?

Several measures of return apply to bond investors, but none is more widely used than yield to maturity, which takes into account both interest and changes in value, assuming you will hold the bond to the scheduled maturity. In other words, if you buy a 6-percent coupon, $1000 face amount bond for $850, the yield to maturity takes into account the stream of interest payments and the price appreciation of $150 ($1000 received at redemption minus the $850 price paid) from the time of your purchase until eventual redemption of the bond. A broker is most likely to quote the yield to maturity for a bond you are thinking about buying.

What other yields are applicable to bonds?

A bond's coupon rate has already been mentioned. This is the stated rate as applied to the principal amount of the bond. A bond's coupon rate remains the same from the issue date until redemption. The coupon rate is not the yield you will earn unless the bond is purchased at face value and sold at face value. Another measure of return is *current yield,* which is the annual interest payment divided by the current market price of the bond. For example a 6-percent coupon bond that is trading at a price of $850 will have a current yield of $60/$850, or 7.06 percent. Current yield takes into account the current price of the bond but not the fact that the bond will increase $150 in value by the time it is redeemed at maturity.

How will I fare if the issuer of my bond goes out of business?

If a business enters into bankruptcy and faces liquidation, you will have a legal claim that is superior to claims of the firm's stockholders. That is, you have a right to payment of principal and unpaid interest before stockholders have a claim to anything. Of course, few assets may remain to liquidate if the issuer has become a financial basket case. Claims of bondholders can be quite different depending on the type of bond you hold and the borrower's other outstanding loans. Owners of bonds secured by claims on specific assets generally fare much better in liquidation than do owners of debt securities backed only by the issuer's promise of payment. The more valuable the assets securing a bond issue, the more likely you will be paid what you are owed. How you will fare as a bondholder of a city, school district, or hospital that goes broke is less clear, since these organizations are unlikely to be liquidated.

Is there a possibility the bonds of a bankrupt organization will lose all their value?

It is possible that bondholders could lose their entire investment by failing to recover any of the principal amount that has been promised at maturity. It is also possible that bondholders will recover the full amount of their claims, although some delay is likely before any payment is received. Most likely, bondholders will recover some money but not their entire claim. The circumstances under which a firm goes out of business will play a major role in how bondholders fare in a bankruptcy. Firms that go out of business after experiencing years of financial losses are likely to have few assets available for unsecured bondholders to claim.

What factors determine the value of a bond?

A bond is desirable for the interest it pays and for the principal that will be returned at redemption. For bonds of a similar maturity, larger interest payments or a greater certainty the promised payments will occur as scheduled make the bonds more valuable. For example, a $1000 bond with a 7-percent coupon ($70 of annual interest) is more valuable than a bond of similar risk and maturity with a 6-percent coupon. Larger interest payments result in a more valuable bond. Likewise, a greater certainty regarding the promised payments results in a more valuable bond. A 20-year, 6-percent coupon bond issued by a financially strong company is worth more than a 20-year, 6-percent coupon bond issued by a financially weak company. Even large interest payments don't have great value if a borrower that is in weak financial condition promises the payments.

Is the length of time before a bond's scheduled redemption also an important consideration?

The redemption date is very important in valuing a bond. In general, the nearer a bond to its redemption date, the closer the value of the bond to the amount that is to be received at redemption. A bond that is to be redeemed in one month for $1000 cannot be worth much more or much less than the promised $1000. You are not going to sell a bond for much less than $1000 when you know you will receive $1000 from the issuer if you hold the security another month. Likewise, no one is going to pay you much more than $1000 when they know the bond will be redeemed for $1000 in another month. On the other hand, a bond that is many years from redemption can have a market value that is far more or far less than its redemption value.

Can the market value of a bond change after it is issued?

The value of any negotiable financial instrument can change, and bonds are no exception. Bond values change with variations in market rates of interest and with changes in the ability of the issuer to make the promised payments. Either an increase in market interest rates or a deterioration in the issuer's financial strength will cause the market value of a bond to decline. Conversely, the value of a bond should increase if market rates of interest fall or the financial strength of the issuer improves. A bond that sells for more or less than face value will move toward face value as the bond approaches maturity.

Are certain types of bonds subject to large price variations?

Changes in bond values are directly related to the bond's maturity length. During a period of rising interest rates, a bond scheduled for redemption in 20 years may drop in price by $150, while a bond with a two-year redemption drops in price by only $20. A period of declining interest rates would bring price changes in the opposite direction. That is, both bonds would increase in value when market rates of interest fall. Many investors prefer to own short-term bonds because of their relative price stability. These investors know they can sell the bonds for approximately the price they paid. On the downside, short-term bonds offer virtually no potential for appreciation in value.

Does this mean I should stay away from bonds with long maturities?

Not necessarily. Bonds with long maturities permit you to lock in a stream of fixed interest payments for many years. This may be desirable depending on your investment needs. Also, bonds with long maturities tend to offer higher interest payments compared to bonds with short maturities. In mid-1998, U.S. Treasury bonds with a 20-year maturity were yielding 6.0 percent at the same time Treasury bonds with two-year maturities were yielding 5.50 percent. You could earn an extra $50 per year in interest by investing $10,000 in the 20-year as opposed to the two-year bond. Keep in mind that this comparison of interest income does not consider any changes in either bond's value during the period of ownership.

Why are yields on long-term bonds generally higher than yields on short-term bonds?

Several theories attempt to explain the difference in interest rates paid on bonds of different maturity lengths. Some experts feel that long-term bonds present investors with more risk (greater variations in market values in addition to the simple fact that more things can go wrong to impair the credit quality of the issuer), and therefore bonds with long maturities must offer higher yields in order to attract buyers. Savers tend to prefer the return of their money sooner rather than later, which means they will generally accept a lower rate of interest for a short-term commitment.

Do bond prices vary as much as stock prices?

Bond values tend to be much more stable than stock values. Stocks sometimes double in value or fall in value by 30 percent or more within a year. This size price movement would be very unusual for a bond. In fact, price changes of 10 percent to 15 percent are considered fairly large for bonds, especially bonds with short maturities. Relative price stability is one reason many investors are attracted to bonds. The downside to price stability is the absence of the possibility for significant gains in value.

A friend told me her broker offered to sell her a bond with a very high yield. Is something wrong here?

Any investment that offers an unusually high yield should be suspect because ownership almost certainly entails high risk. Bonds that offer unusually high yields do so because investors are concerned the issuer will not be able to meet its promises regarding interest and repayment of principal. Ask yourself why investors are pricing a bond to yield 12 percent in a market where most borrowers are obtaining loans for 7 percent. The most likely reason is that investors who currently own the bonds and are offering to sell don't have great confidence that the borrower will be able to repay the loan. Investing in a bond with a very high yield will not prove to be a good investment if the issuer soon stops making interest payments.

How can I judge the ability of a borrower to make the required payments on a bond?

The best method for judging the credit quality of a bond is to check the credit rating. Several firms, including Moody's Investor Services and Standard & Poor's Corporation, regularly rate the credit quality of corporate and municipal bonds. The rating classifications used by the two firms are slightly different, but comparable. An AAA rating is awarded to bonds with the very highest credit quality. A BBB rating by Standard & Poor's or Baa rating by Moody's is the lowest grade for a bond to be considered investment-grade. In general, you should probably limit your bond investments to securities rated A or better. Some financial advisers suggest bonds rated AA or better. Bonds with a credit rating of BB or lower qualify as *junk bonds*. Junk bonds are also sometimes called *high-yield bonds*. Refer to Table 3-1 for more on corporate and municipal bond credit ratings.

Why would anyone consider buying a bond rated lower than AAA?

Bonds judged to have a high credit quality tend to offer low yields. At a time when BBB-rated bonds are yielding 6.5 percent, bonds rated AAA may be yielding only 5.7 percent. Thus, an investor may choose to purchase bonds rated A or BBB in order to earn a higher return. One axiom of finance is that higher yields generally expose an investor to higher risk. You may find it worthwhile to accept an increased likelihood of nonpayment to earn an extra half percent of interest. The choice is yours. Beware though. Investors sometimes chase high yields without thoroughly considering the risks inherent in owning bonds with a low credit rating.

Is any risk involved in owning a bond rated AAA?

Bond ratings are a measure of an issuer's ability to service the interest and principal requirements. Although the rating firms consider the past, present, and future when they judge the credit quality of a particular bond, even these experts are not 100 percent successful. Bonds that are initially judged high quality may later prove more risky. The financial stability of companies and municipalities changes over time, and these changes affect the riskiness of bonds issued by these borrowers. Keep in mind that bond ratings are not designed to measure fluctuations in value caused by interest rate changes. Even bonds rated AAA, especially those with long maturities, are subject to variations in

TABLE 3-1

Corporate and municipal bond credit ratings.

Moody's	Standard & Poor's	
Aaa	AAA	High-grade, with extremely strong capacity to pay principal and interest.
Aa	AA	High-grade by all standards, but with slightly lower margins of protection than AAA.
A	A	Medium-grade, with favorable investment attributes but some susceptibility to adverse economic changes.
Baa	BBB	Medium-grade, with adequate capacity to pay interest and principal but possibly lacking certain protection against adverse economic conditions.
Ba	BB	Speculative, with moderate protection of principal and interest in an unstable economy.
B	B	Speculative and lacking desirable characteristics of investment bonds; small assurance of principal and interest.
Caa	CCC	Issue in default or in danger of default.
Ca	CC	Highly speculative and in default, or with other market shortcomings.
C		Extremely poor investment quality.
	C	Income bonds paying no interest.
D		In default, with interest or principal in arrears.

value when market rates of interest change. In addition, even the most secure bonds make fixed interest payments, which can be eaten away by inflation.

What accounts for the popularity of bonds issued by state and local governments?

Most bonds issued by state and local governments (generally termed *municipal bonds*) offer one great advantage over other bonds: Interest earned from municipal bonds is exempt from federal taxation, and often from state and local taxation as well. The exemption of interest income from taxation causes municipal bonds to be very desirable investments for an investor who has substantial taxable income and pays a high tax rate. A limited number of municipal bonds pay taxable interest. An example of an offering statement for a new municipal bond issue can be seen in Figure 3-3.

What guarantees the interest payments on municipal bonds?

Municipalities issue both general obligation bonds (GOs) and revenue bonds. General obligation bonds are guaranteed by the full taxing power of the issuer. This is a powerful guarantee for most municipal issuers, especially states. Revenue bonds are generally backed by revenue generated from a particular project the bonds are used to finance. For example, cities and counties frequently use revenues from water and sewage systems to guarantee interest and principal payments on revenue bonds issued to finance these systems. General obligation bonds are usually, but not always, considered less risky to own.

Are municipal bonds purchased directly from the states and municipalities that issue them?

State and local bonds are purchased in the same manner as corporate and U.S. government bonds. That is, an investor must normally engage the services of a commercial brokerage firm to undertake the transaction. Commercial banks also deal in municipal securities. Municipal bonds can be purchased at the time of original issue or sometime later, when they trade in the secondary market. These bonds pay a fixed amount of interest semiannually, have a stated maturity date, and are usually issued in units of $5000. In other words, they are pretty much the same as corporate bonds except the interest payments don't have to be reported as income on your federal tax return. A com-

FIGURE 3-3

Offering statement for a new municipal bond issue.

CHEROKEE COUNTY WATER AND SEWERAGE AUTHORITY (GEORGIA)

MEMBERS

Douglas H. Flint, *Chairman*
Leon Bobo, *Vice Chairman*
Robert Campbell, *Secretary*
Hollis Q. Lathem
Dennis Lance

APPOINTED OFFICIALS

Thomas A. Heard, *General Manager*
Janice Henderson, *Director of Finance and Administration*

SPECIAL SERVICES

Authority's Counsel

Roach & Geiger
Canton, Georgia

Authority's Auditors

Donner, Weiser & Rosenberg, P.C.
Atlanta, Georgia

Bond Counsel

Alston & Bird LLP
Atlanta, Georgia

Consulting Engineers

Welker & Associates, Inc.
Marietta, Georgia

Continued

FIGURE 3-3

Concluded

NEW ISSUE

RATINGS
Moody's: Aaa
Standard & Poor's: AAA
See "MISCELLANEOUS — Ratings" herein.

In the opinion of Bond Counsel, subject to the limitations and conditions described herein, interest on the Series 1998 Bonds (including any original issue discount properly allocable to a holder thereof) is exempt from present State of Georgia income taxation, is excluded from gross income for federal income tax purposes, and is not an item of tax preference for purposes of the federal alternative minimum tax imposed on individuals and corporations; it should be noted, however, that for the purpose of computing the alternative minimum tax imposed on certain corporations (as defined for federal income tax purposes), such interest is taken into account in determining adjusted current earnings. The opinion contains greater detail, and is subject to exceptions, as noted in "LEGAL MATTERS — Opinion of Bond Counsel" herein.

$21,345,000

CHEROKEE COUNTY WATER AND SEWERAGE AUTHORITY (GEORGIA)
Water and Sewerage Revenue Bonds, Series 1998

Dated: December 1, 1998   **Due: August 1, as shown below**

The Water and Sewerage Revenue Bonds, Series 1998 (the "Series 1998 Bonds") are being issued by the Cherokee County Water and Sewerage Authority (the "Authority") for the purpose of financing the costs of making additions, extensions, and improvements to the Authority's water and sewer system. See "PLAN OF FINANCING" herein.

Interest on the Series 1998 Bonds is payable semiannually on February 1 and August 1 of each year, commencing on February 1, 1999 (representing two months' interest). All Series 1998 Bonds bear interest from December 1, 1998. See "INTRODUCTION — **Description of the Series 1998 Bonds**" herein.

The Series 1998 Bonds are subject to mandatory and optional redemption prior to maturity as described herein. See "**THE SERIES 1998 BONDS — Redemption**" herein.

The Series 1998 Bonds are **special limited obligations** of the Authority payable solely from and secured by a pledge of and lien on revenues derived by the Authority from the ownership and operation of its water and sewer system, remaining after the payment of expenses of operating, maintaining, and repairing the system. The Series 1998 Bonds will be issued and secured on a parity with the Prior Bonds (as defined herein) and any additional revenue bonds of the Authority hereafter issued on a parity with the Prior Bonds and the Series 1998 Bonds. See "SECURITY AND SOURCES OF PAYMENT FOR THE SERIES 1998 BONDS" herein.

Payment of the principal of and interest on the Series 1998 Bonds when due will be insured by a municipal bond new issue insurance policy to be issued simultaneously with the delivery of the Series 1998 Bonds by Financial Guaranty Insurance Company.

Financial Guaranty Insurance Company

The Series 1998 Bonds do not constitute a debt, liability, general or moral obligation, or pledge of the faith and credit or taxing power of Cherokee County. No governmental entity, including Cherokee County, is obligated to levy any tax for the payment of the Series 1998 Bonds. The Authority has no taxing power.

MATURITIES, PRINCIPAL AMOUNTS, INTEREST RATES, AND PRICES OR YIELDS

$6,045,000 Serial Bonds

Maturity	Principal Amount*	Interest Rate	Price or Yield	Maturity	Principal Amount*	Interest Rate	Price or Yield
2000	$255,000	3.40%	100%	2009	$360,000	4.20%	4.25%
2001	270,000	3.50	3.55	2010	375,000	4.30	4.35
2002	280,000	3.60	3.65	2011	390,000	4.40	4.45
2003	285,000	3.75	100	2012	405,000	4.50	4.55
2004	295,000	3.80	3.85	2013	425,000	4.60	4.65
2005	310,000	3.90	3.95	2014	445,000	4.70	4.75
2006	320,000	4.00	100	2015	470,000	4.70	4.83
2007	330,000	4.00	4.05	2016	485,000	4.80	4.88
2008	345,000	4.10	4.15				

$1,050,000 4.875% Term Bonds due August 1, 2018, Priced at 99.059% to Yield 4.95%

$3,110,000 4.875% Term Bonds due August 1, 2023, Priced at 98.374% to Yield 4.99%

$11,140,000 4.750% Term Bonds due August 1, 2028, Priced at 96.301% to Yield 4.99%

(Plus accrued interest from December 1, 1998)

This cover page contains certain information for quick reference only. It is *not* a summary of this issue. Investors must read the entire Official Statement to obtain information essential to making an informed investment decision.

The Series 1998 Bonds are offered when, as, and if issued by the Authority and accepted by the Underwriter, subject to prior sale and to withdrawal or modification of the offer without notice, and are subject to the approving opinion of Alston & Bird LLP, Atlanta, Georgia, Bond Counsel. Certain legal matters will be passed on for the Authority by its counsel, Roach & Geiger, Canton, Georgia, and for the Underwriter by its counsel, Kilpatrick Stockton LLP, Atlanta, Georgia, and William G. Hasty, Jr., Canton, Georgia. The Series 1998 Bonds in definitive form are expected to be delivered through The Depository Trust Company in New York, New York on or about December 15, 1998.

The Robinson-Humphrey Company

Dated: December 4, 1998

parison of yields on taxable and tax-exempt bonds for the period from 1955 to 1998 can be seen in Figure 3-4.

Are interest payments from U.S. Treasury bonds also exempt from income taxes?

Interest income from U.S. Treasury securities is not exempt from federal income taxes, but it is exempt from state and local income taxes. The state and local exemption can be valuable if you live in a state such as California or New York that levies a high state income tax. On the other hand, if you reside in Florida, Nevada, Texas, or Alaska, states without an income tax, you may as well invest in high quality corporate bonds that are likely to pay a higher rate of interest.

How does the safety of Treasury securities compare with the safety of corporate and municipal bonds?

U.S. Treasury securities are considered the standard by which all other bonds are measured in terms of credit quality. Securities of the U.S. government are considered risk-free from the standpoint of promised payments being made in full and on time. This high level of credit quality causes Treasury bonds to be in great demand, which, in turn, results in these securities having yields that are somewhat lower than you could earn on high-quality corporate bonds. Even though no credit risk is involved in owning U.S. Treasury securities, the bonds fluctuate in value when market rates of interest change. An increase in market interest will cause the price of outstanding U.S. Treasury securities to fall. Conversely, these bonds will increase in value when market rates of interest fall. The bottom line with U.S. Treasury bonds is that you know you will get paid, but you don't know how much you will receive if you need to sell the bonds prior to their scheduled redemption. As with corporate and municipal bonds, the longer the maturity length of a U.S.

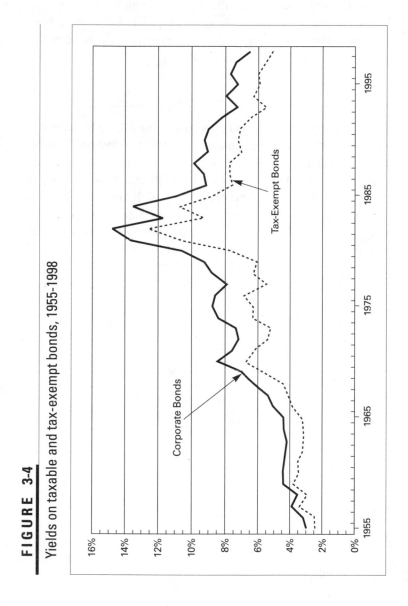

FIGURE 3-4

Yields on taxable and tax-exempt bonds, 1955-1998

Treasury bond, the greater the price fluctuations caused by
changes in market rates of interest. You also don't know how
much purchasing power the interest payments will have at the
time you are scheduled to receive them.

Do you have any general advice on buying bonds?

First, buy bonds on the basis that you will hold them to maturity.
Selling bonds in small amounts can be an expensive proposition
because most players in this market invest large amounts of
money. It is a good idea to stick with high quality, especially if
you don't have to give up too much in yield. If you plan to invest
a substantial sum of money in bonds, consider staggering the
maturity dates so that not all your securities will be redeemed at
the same time. Perhaps most important, locate a broker who is
knowledgeable about bonds. Many brokers spend little time
with bonds and as a result, are unlikely to provide good advice.

CHAPTER

How Are Securities Traded on Wall Street?

Chapter summary

Most individual investors would be hesitant to purchase securities that could not be transferred or resold to someone else. An important function of Wall Street is to provide a market mechanism that enables investors to sell securities they own to other investors. The New York Stock Exchange and the increasingly popular over-the-counter market are two of many marketplaces that facilitate investor buying and selling of securities.

Is the resale of securities a big business?

For the majority of Wall Street firms the resale of investor-owned securities is a much bigger business than issuing new securities. Most people who buy stocks don't intend to hold them for a lifetime, which means investors end up selling their shares to someone else who, in turn, sells them to yet another investor, and so forth. The same shares of stock may trade several times during the same day. The hundreds of millions of shares that are traded each day on the stock exchanges and in the over-the-counter market represent previously issued shares of stock that are being transferred from one investor to another investor. Even bonds that indicate a scheduled date on which investors will have their money returned often trade actively among investors.

Are securities easy to resell?

Most securities can be resold without great difficulty, although the ease of locating a buyer varies depending on the particular security. Thus, some securities are easier to sell than other securities. Factors such as the economy, availability of credit, and the outlook of investors also play a role in being able to quickly locate another investor who is interested in purchasing your securities. A security that is easily resold is said to have *liquidity*. A security that is difficult to resell and may require a major price concession to resell lacks liquidity and is said to be *illiquid*.

What types of securities enjoy the most liquidity?

Stocks of large, well-known businesses are generally very easy to resell. The common stocks of companies such as AT&T, Microsoft, Intel, General Electric, Southern Company, and Exxon are very actively traded. Reselling several hundred shares or several thousand shares will not create a ripple in either the market activity or price of the stock. U.S. Treasury securities trade in huge volume and set the standard for liquidity. Some corporate bonds are actively traded and are easy to resell.

Which securities may be difficult to resell?

Bonds and stocks that are part of a relatively small issue may prove difficult to resell. Small companies often have little name recognition and few shareholders, which means that a limited number of investors will be aware of or interested in the stock. Shares issued by these types of companies tend to have inactive secondary markets, so the stocks may be difficult to resell at a fair price. Many municipal and corporate bond issues and preferred stock issues do not have active resale markets. Regional firms, such as community banks, issue shares of stock that are traded locally or regionally but do not have an active secondary market.

What if I need to sell a security that does not have an active resale market?

An inactively traded security may have to be sold at a somewhat lower price than you feel is fair. Thus, a stock that last traded at $45 per share may have to be sold for $43.50, especially if you are in a hurry to achieve a sale. Likewise, a bond that recently traded at a price of $950 may fetch no more than $920 in a quick sale. When the security you wish to sell is not actively traded and you are determined to hold out for a price you feel is fair, days or weeks may elapse before a sale is completed.

What can I do to ensure I receive a fair price when I sell a security?

You can enter an order that specifies a particular price. For example, you can tell the broker to sell your stock only if you receive a price of $40 per share or more. Of course, your stock won't be sold immediately if the stock is currently trading for $35. This type of order ensures you receive the price you specify, but only if the stock trades at that high a price. If the stock fails to reach $40, you will continue to own the stock. This type order is not usually utilized when an investor is in a hurry to sell shares of stock. If you hold out for a specific price and the market price of the stock you own begins to decline, you will find yourself in an even deeper hole.

How can I determine if a security is inactive?

Any broker will be able to tell you if a particular security has little trading activity. Trading activity for many securities is published in major newspapers, in *The Wall Street Journal,* and on various websites. Keep in mind that if a security is very inactive, it may not trade every day. This means you may have difficulty locating price and volume information.

Should I avoid inactively traded securities?

The trading activity of a security is particularly important if you are likely to have a short holding period. If you are planning to buy stock this week and expect to sell this same stock during the next couple of months, then liquidity is important. On the other hand, if you normally invest for the long term, then the liquidity of a particular stock or bond is of less importance. Buying bonds you will hold to maturity means that trading activity isn't important at all, since you won't be selling the bonds. Likewise, if you plan to hold a stock for many years, then the liquidity of the stock isn't particularly important. In fact, some financial analysts feel that inactively traded securities offer greater profit possibilities because so many investors avoid them.

Is it easy to purchase securities that were issued months or even years ago?

Wall Street deals in thousands of different securities that were issued yesterday, last week, last year, and several decades ago. These securities are traded in the giant secondary market that includes stock exchanges and the over-the-counter market. Previously issued securities are often continuously available for purchase from former buyers who have decided, for whatever reason, to convert their investments to cash. These sellers may be individual investors such as you, institutional investors such as mutual funds, or professionals who purchase securities in order to make them available to other investors. Wall Street serves as a giant clearinghouse for both new and previously issued securities.

When might I be unable to purchase previously issued securities?

There are several reasons why you may be unable to purchase the securities of a particular issuer. Perhaps a firm issued shares of ownership years ago and subsequently went out of business. Many railroads issued shares of ownership that are no longer traded because the companies went bankrupt or were absorbed by other firms. A firm's shares may have been purchased by a small number of investors who have no interest in selling their shares. The publicly traded shares of some companies have been bought up by small groups of wealthy individuals who wanted to take control of the firms. No stock remains available for purchase by individual and institutional investors once other investors have acquired all the outstanding shares. Likewise, bonds of a particular issue are no longer available for trading once the issuer has redeemed the debt. Tens of thousands of corporate and government bond issues have been brought to market, subsequently traded by individuals and institutions, only to eventually disappear when the bonds were redeemed by their issuers. Just because a security is publicly traded does not mean it will always be publicly traded.

How does the resale market for securities differ from the market in which these securities are originally issued?

Perhaps the easiest way to understand differences between the secondary market and the primary market for securities is to relate the securities market to the market for baseball cards (or any other good for which ownership can be transferred). To build a baseball card collection, you can purchase packs or boxes of newly issued cards at a local drugstore or supermarket, or you can purchase previously issued cards from a friend, at a card show, or at a card shop. The cards at the card shop are being offered by the shop owner who has accumulated an inventory by buying cards when they were originally issued or by acquiring them from other collectors. In some instances, the card shop might also stock cards that other collectors have asked the shop owner to sell. The card shop and the card show each represent the secondary market for baseball cards. Prices in this market are negotiated between buyers who want to buy cards and sellers who previously purchased the cards and now offer them for sale. Cards in the supermarket and drugstore represent the primary market for baseball cards being offered for sale the first time.

Do the same financial firms that assist in the sale of new issues also participate in the market in which securities are resold?

Some firms are involved in both the original issue of securities and the trading of outstanding securities. In fact, many firms that help other companies sell securities to the public subsequently become market makers in these securities. Major broker-dealers such as Merrill Lynch are big players in marketing new issues of stocks and bonds, and they also participate in the secondary market in which securities are traded among investors. On the other hand, some firms are active in the resale market but do not become involved in the original issue market.

Why would the shop owner sell cards belonging to someone else?

The operator of the card shop may agree to take cards on consignment and retain a percentage of the sale price when and if the cards are sold. The owner of the shop does not buy the cards and, thus, has no money invested in an inventory of cards.

Selling cards on consignment reduces the risk to the shop owner, who doesn't stand to lose money if cards cannot be sold or if some cards decline in value during the period they are being held for resale. On the downside, the shop owner is likely to earn less profit on consignment sales than on sales of his own cards. Selling on consignment means a firm is being paid to bring together buyers and sellers.

How does a baseball card shop relate to the market for securities?

At the heart of the secondary market for securities are the many individuals and firms who buy and sell stocks, bonds, and other financial claims. Some firms act as dealers and purchase securities from investors. The firms then attempt to resell the securities to other investors at a price higher than they paid. This is similar to the card shop owner who purchases baseball cards from collectors and then offers for sale those same cards. In this instance, the card shop owner assumes ownership of the cards and is functioning as a dealer. At other times, a securities firm will act as a broker and bring two investors together. That is, the firm locates a buyer for an investor who wishes to sell a security or locates a seller for someone who wishes to buy a security. The card shop owner acts as a broker when cards are accepted on consignment. In this case, the shop owner seeks to locate a buyer for someone who wishes to sell.

Does the secondary market offer a greater variety of issues?

The secondary market offers a much greater variety of both stocks and bonds compared to the primary market. On any given day, a dozen to two dozen new stock and bond issues may come to market. If you want to buy stock or bonds in a particular company, you will almost certainly be out of luck if you limit your selection to new issues. On the other hand, the secondary

market offers thousands of different stock issues and bond issues that can be purchased by investors. Although some investors concentrate on buying new issues in the primary market,
most individuals buy stocks and bonds in the secondary market
where the selection is much greater.

Does a securities firm ever act both as a dealer and a broker?

Many Wall Street firms perform both jobs. These firms, termed
broker-dealers, act as dealers when they buy for themselves or
sell from their own inventory of securities. At other times these
firms act as brokers when they match buyers and sellers of securities. Nearly all of the large national securities firms, including
Merrill Lynch, Salomon Smith Barney, Charles Schwab, and
Morgan Stanley Dean Witter, are broker-dealers.

Do broker-dealers trade any and all securities?

Firms acting as dealers find it necessary to specialize in securities in which they make a market. For example, a firm may
choose to act as a dealer in 20 different securities. This firm
stands ready to purchase and to sell shares in each of the
stocks in which it has chosen to deal. A dealer must carefully
monitor the stocks and bonds in which it deals, which means
that no firm, no matter how large, finds it practical to buy and
sell every available security. On the other hand, a broker-
dealer is generally willing to act as a broker in any stock or
bond. Acting as a broker means the firm does not have to invest its own money and, thus, incurs no risk. Remember the
card shop owner who agreed to sell cards on consignment?
This person was acting as a broker and had no money invested in these particular cards.

Does a single firm serve as a market maker for each stock and bond issue?

Market makers for a particular security can range from one to several dozen. Stock exchanges have only a single market maker in each security that is listed for trading no matter how active that security may be. For example, one firm on the floor of the New York Stock Exchange acts as that exchange's market maker for a very active stock such as Compaq. Some of the other regional exchanges have their own market makers in this stock, so in a sense, some competition does exist. Depending on the level of trading activity, stocks traded in the over-the-counter market may have numerous market makers. Several dealers are able to earn a living as market makers when a security trades hundreds of thousands or millions of shares daily. On the other hand, only a single firm may be able to earn a profit by making a market in an inactive security that trades in the over-the-counter market. Compare this to the food world in which several restaurants are able to make a profit selling pizzas, even in a relatively small community. On the other hand, how many restaurants could specialize in Japanese food and still make money? Just as limited interest in Japanese food limits the number of restaurants selling Japanese cuisine, limited investor interest in a particular security results in a limited number of market makers for the security.

Should I be concerned about the number of dealers that make a market in a security I am thinking about buying?

Increased competition from multiple dealers of a security may result in a better price for your shares, especially if the shares are traded over the counter. A better price means paying less when you buy a security and obtaining more when you want to sell a security. A single dealer operates in an environment in which it easier to manipulate the price of a stock or bond. While multiple dealers must compete for your business, a single dealer has more flexibility to establish a price favorable to the dealer. Consider the case of a person who resides in a small town with a single supermarket as opposed to someone who lives in an area with several competing supermarkets. Which of the two individuals do you think enjoys the better prices?

Can I determine how many dealers make a market in a particular stock or bond?

Your broker should be able to determine the number of dealers who make a market in the security you are interested in purchasing. If a security is listed for trading on an exchange, you can count on a single dealer at that exchange plus the possibility of additional dealers at other exchanges that may also list the security. If the security is traded over the counter, the broker will be able to call up the security on his or her computer screen and read quotations from all the dealers who act as market makers.

Can you provide an example of a dealer's price quote?

The price a dealer will pay for a security is termed the *bid* and the price at which a dealer will sell a security is called the *ask*. The difference between the bid and the ask is the dealer's *spread*. A dealer quoting a bid of $27\frac{1}{2}$ and an ask of $27\frac{3}{4}$ is offering to buy the security for $27.50 per share and is offering to sell the security for $27.75 per share. The difference of $ 0.50 per share is the dealer's spread.

How does a dealer determine the bid and asked prices?

The dealer in a stock is continually attempting to establish a price that will equate shares being bought and shares being sold. Economists call this the *equilibrium price* because it is the price that equates the quantity supplied by sellers with the quantity demanded by buyers. When investors begin selling more shares than other investors are buying, the dealer must accumulate shares of stock. When investors buy more shares than they sell, the dealer must sell stock out of inventory. If investors begin selling large amounts of stock to a dealer who does not wish to accumulate additional shares, the dealer will lower both the bid price and the ask price for the stock. The lower price should attract fewer sellers at the same time it brings in additional buyers. Suppose investors are selling large amounts of a stock to a dealer who is bidding $35\frac{1}{4}$ and asking $35\frac{1}{2}$. To reduce the number and size of sell orders and at the same time stimulate the number and size of buy orders, the dealer might lower the bid to $35\frac{1}{8}$ and the ask to $35\frac{3}{8}$. The lower bid should attract fewer sellers and the lower asked should result in more buyers. If investors continue to sell more shares than they purchase, thus causing the dealer to accumulate even more stock, the bid and ask prices will be lowered another notch.

Conversely, the dealer will raise the bid and ask prices when investors begin buying more stock than they are selling. Thus, a dealer establishes price quotations in response to supply and demand for the security in which the dealer makes a market.

Do dealers in a security make a profit from the spread?

Buying at one price and selling at a higher price creates a profit for the dealer. The amount of profit earned depends on the size of the spread (a bigger spread results in more profit for each share traded) and the volume of trading. A dealer can also profit from price movements in the security. A dealer holding shares of Microsoft common stock for resale will profit from an increase in the price of the stock between the time shares are acquired and when shares are sold. The more shares of Microsoft the dealer is carrying in inventory, the more profit the dealer will earn if the price of the stock moves upward. A falling stock price will result in a loss for a dealer who is carrying an inventory of the stock.

Do Wall Street firms also make markets in bonds?

Dealers also act as market makers for bonds and a variety of other financial assets. Bid and ask quotations are established in the same manner as for stocks. That is, a dealer will quote both a bid price and an ask price for a particular bond. The bid is the price at which the dealer will buy the bonds, and the ask is the price at which the dealer will sell the bonds. When investors are selling more bonds than they are buying, the dealer will lower both the bid price and the ask price. The lower price quotations are intended to reduce investor selling and stimulate investor buying. Large investor demand for the bonds will cause the dealer to raise the quoted bid and ask prices. As with stock, a dealer attempts to establish a price that will cause investor supply and demand to be approximately equal.

How about debt securities issued by the U.S. government?

Treasury securities are initially sold to the public via regular auctions conducted by the Federal Reserve Bank of New York. The Federal Reserve deals directly only with a limited number of designated primary bond dealers who resell the securities to the public. Government bond dealers, including primary dealers who participate in the auctions for new issues, comprise the secondary market in U.S. Treasury securities. Like dealers in other securities, dealers in government bonds serve as market makers by providing bid and ask prices. The Federal Reserve will frequently enter the market to buy or sell Treasury securities, but this action is occasioned by a desire to affect the money supply and interest rates, not act as a market maker.

Are large commercial banks involved in the secondary market?

The big money center banks and large regional banks are active participants in the secondary market for securities. Commercial banks are major players in municipal bonds, for which they underwrite new issues and act as dealers in the secondary market. Investors can purchase and sell municipal bonds through commercial banks as well as through retail brokerage firms such as Merrill Lynch and Salomon Smith Barney. Commercial banks are also active in trading U.S. Treasury securities, and through their trust departments, these institutions trade in corporate bonds and in preferred and common stocks.

Is the opening price of a security always the same as the closing price from the prior day?

Although the opening price of a security is generally near the previous day's closing price, it is not always the same. Events following the close of business on one day can affect the price of a firm's stock prior to the opening of trading on the following day. Consider the case of a company announcement that the U.S. Justice Department commenced investigation of a charge that the firm has been engaged in anticompetitive practices. If the announcement comes after the close of trading in the firm's stock (as is likely), you can count on a reduced opening price the following morning as investors enter sell orders that flow in to the dealers. Companies often wait until after the close of trading to announce major news that may significantly affect their stock price. The delay is designed to provide investors with time to digest the news before they begin placing orders to buy or sell the stock.

Are security dealers interconnected?

Securities dealers have instant access to the quotations of competing dealers. This access means the prices quoted by any particular dealer are unlikely to be far out of line with prices quoted by other dealers who make a market in the same security. In fact, dealers trade with one another when they wish to adjust the inventory of a security they hold. A dealer desiring a smaller inventory of a particular security may sell bonds or shares of stock to another dealer who makes a market in the same security. Conversely, a dealer who wants to increase the inventory of a stock may purchase shares of the stock from a competing dealer.

Are most broker-dealers located in the Wall Street area?

While concentrated in the Wall Street area, broker-dealers in the U.S. are scattered throughout the country. In addition, many other countries have their own exchanges and system of broker-dealers. Domestic stock exchanges are in New York City, San Francisco, Los Angeles, Chicago, and several other cities in the United States. Broker-dealers in the over-the-counter market are spread all over the country. Stocks with primarily a regional interest are likely to attract dealers in that particular region of the country. The stock of a large bank headquartered in the Southeast may have dealers in Atlanta, Charlotte, Birmingham, and Nashville, in addition to one or more dealers elsewhere in the country. Likewise, broker-dealers who make markets in gold and silver stocks tend to be concentrated in the western United States where the issuers are located and the stocks have the greatest investor interest. Even though exchanges and the far-flung OTC market blanket the United States, the market makers are plugged in to what happens on Wall Street.

Am I required to locate the appropriate dealer in order to buy or sell a security?

The brokerage company you utilize to transact an order will locate the appropriate exchange or dealers that make a market in the stock you wish to buy or sell. It may turn out that your brokerage firm acts as a dealer in the security you wish to buy or sell. If so, the firm may execute the order internally as a dealer, and the confirmation slip sent to you several days following the transaction will identify the firm as a market maker in the security. If the brokerage company you use does not act as a market maker, your broker will contact the dealer offering the best price and execute the order through that dealer. The best price will be the lowest asked if you wish to buy and the highest bid if you wish to sell.

How do stock exchanges fit into this system?

A stock exchange is a physical location with a concentration of market makers for many different securities. For example, hundreds of market makers, each making markets in numerous individual securities, operate on the floor of the New York Stock Exchange. Other exchanges operate in other U.S. cities, and still more stock exchanges are located overseas. Brokerage firms from all over the world route investor orders to the floor of the various securities exchanges where market makers buy and sell assigned securities.

Is a stock exchange simply a gathering place for dealers?

Trading of securities on the floor of a stock exchange is different from trading in the widely dispersed over-the-counter market. Overall, however, the description of a stock exchange as a gathering place for dealers in many different securities is fairly accurate. Some of the members on the floor of an exchange are market makers in stocks and bonds. Other members perform different functions. Chapter 5 is devoted to describing the operation of stock exchanges, and Chapter 6 discusses the workings of the over-the-counter market.

Does it matter if I own stock that is not traded on a stock exchange?

A security traded on one of the stock exchanges is said to be *listed* on that exchange. For example, the common stock of AT&T is listed for trading on the New York Stock Exchange. AT&T stock is also listed for trading on other exchanges and is traded in the over-the-counter market. Some experts feel that securities gain liquidity, i.e., become easier to buy and sell without affecting the price, when they are listed on an exchange. On the other hand, many financial analysts make a case that securities traded on the exchanges are so closely monitored by professional financial analysts that it is easier to find undervalued stocks among those that have not been listed on an exchange. Overall, the average listed stock probably does have more liquidity than the average stock traded only by dealers in the over-the-counter market. However, many over-the-counter stocks trade in very large volume and are very easy to buy and sell.

Can I be assured of a fair price when I buy or sell a security?

The majority of security trades occur at prices that accurately reflect market conditions when the trades take place. Unfortunately, instances of investors being treated unfairly occasionally surface. In mid-1998, a government agency was investigating whether market makers on the floor of an exchange were trading for their own accounts in advance of executing customer orders, a practice that is prohibited. Paying an inflated price to buy a security or receiving an inadequate price when selling a security is most likely to occur when a security is relatively illiquid and has only a single market maker. With a lone market maker, the dealer becomes the market, a condition that makes manipulation of a security's price more likely. Investors are most likely to get bilked when they buy or sell very low-priced stocks of companies without a wide investor following.

How can investors be swindled in light of all the government regulation of Wall Street?

Unfortunately, state and federal regulators cannot monitor every broker, every dealer, and every security trade. History demonstrates that con artists are attracted to money, which happens to be the coin of the realm on Wall Street. Brokers have been known to convince individuals to invest in assets that enriched the brokers more than the investors. Likewise, occasional reports indicate individual investors don't always obtain the best price when an order is executed. Sadly, many investors get bilked because of their own greed when they plunge into investments that promise unrealistically high returns.

Can I count on being able to sell my securities if the market crashes?

During the crash of October 1987, some security issues could not be sold (or purchased, although few investors were trying to buy) because several market makers in the over-the-counter market failed to answer their telephones. Likewise, reporting by the exchanges was late, so investors were unable to determine current security prices. Such instances are rare, but under the worst of circumstances liquidity may prove to be a problem with some securities. It must be noted that changes in the securities markets since the 1987 crash may have improved liquidity. For one thing, the system is able to handle a much greater volume of trading. Also, consider that virtually anything can be sold if the price is sufficiently low. Thus, even during a crash you should be able to sell securities if you are willing to accept the price that buyers are offering. The problem is that you may receive a price that is substantially lower than you expect.

Are all of Wall Street's financial deals open to the public, or are some offerings kept private?

Investment bankers often engage in stock and bond offerings that exclude the general public. For example, an investment banker may assist an organization in raising funds from a single source such as an insurance company or pension fund. These *private placements* can often be accomplished more quickly and with less expense than a public offering, especially when a modest amount of money is being raised.

Will securities issued in a private placement be available in the secondary market?

Securities issued in a private placement may never reach the public because the institutions that purchase these issues may have no desire to sell the securities they purchase. No secondary market will exist for securities that are part of a private placement unless the original buyers decide to sell all or a portion of the securities. Even then, the sale may be made to another large institution rather than to individual investors. An active secondary market requires many buyers and sellers. The original buyers may never resell some stock and bond issues, so no secondary market can develop in these issues.

What other tasks are undertaken by Wall Street firms?

Wall Street firms perform a variety of tasks other than issuing and trading securities. Investment banking firms assist companies wanting to repurchase their own outstanding bonds or shares of stock. These securities may be purchased in the secondary market, or the company may make investors an offer to repurchase all or a portion of the securities at a specified price. The latter operation is called a *tender offer*. Wall Street firms also assist companies in paying dividends, transferring their securities from sellers to buyers, maintaining a record of stockholders and bondholders, and operating dividend reinvestment plans.

Why would an organization want to repurchase its own securities?

A firm's directors may feel investors are undervaluing the stock, that it sells at too low a price. Also, the company may not be able to identify enough investment projects for all the money it has available. Thus, it uses some of the excess funds to repurchase shares of its own stock. Fewer outstanding shares of ownership that result from the repurchase will mean fewer ways to split profits and less dividends to pay. If interest rates decline, a company may wish to retire some of its outstanding debt that was issued when rates were high. Many companies decided to repurchase their own stock during the 1990s. Likewise, an extended decline in interest rates caused many borrowers to retire their debt prior to the scheduled maturity.

Do companies repurchase securities directly from investors, or are the securities purchased in the market?

Companies use both methods to acquire their own shares or their own debt. In some instances, they will make an offer directly to the shareholders or bondholders. A direct offer from a company to investors is called a *tender offer*. For example, you might receive a letter from a company in which you own stock offering to buy your shares for $22 each. You can decide whether you wish to sell at this price and *tender* your shares. At other times, a company may buy its shares of stock or bonds in the open market. Thus, rather than make a direct offer to its own security holders, a firm may buy back its stock or bonds from whomever happens to be selling. You might sell your shares through a brokerage firm and never know that the issuing company is the buyer.

What are the takeovers I read so much about?

Takeovers are another financial activity engaged in by Wall Street firms. A takeover occurs when one investor or group of investors takes control of a company from the existing owners and managers. For example, a group of wealthy investors may make an offer to buy the outstanding stock of a company they wish to control. A group that is successful in purchasing enough shares of the target firm's stock is likely to install its own directors and managers. Investment groups that initiate takeovers nearly always employ the services of one or more Wall Street investment banking firms that attempt to purchase the stock and assist in providing financing for the takeover group.

What if shareholders of a firm do not wish to sell?

Existing owners of a company have every right to decide not to sell their shares. Owners may decide the price being offered is inadequate. In fact, managers and directors of a targeted firm may advise their shareholders not to sell. Sometimes the directors claim the price being offered is too low. In other instances, the directors may feel the firm's shareholders may be able to obtain a higher bid from another group. Perhaps the directors may simply not want the company to be taken over by any firm.

Are some takeovers unsuccessful?

A takeover may fail for a variety of reasons. Often, investors attempting the takeover may have difficulty arranging the financing required to pay for the stock they propose to buy. In other instances, the directors of the firm being taken over may be successful in convincing their stockholders not to offer their shares to the investment group attempting the takeover. Many companies have established financial and legal defenses that make it very difficult for another company to take them over unless the directors agree.

Are takeovers good for investors?

If the price offered for shareholders' stock is substantially higher than the price that existed prior to the takeover announcement, current shareholders will benefit, at least in the short run. Of course, the group initiating the offer must feel the company's shares are undervalued or they wouldn't be interested in purchasing the firm. Thus, investors who sell their shares may end up better off in the short run but worse off in the long run. While the stock price of the firm to be taken over will increase, the stock price of the company initiating the takeover often declines, at least in the short run. If everything works out as expected, the acquiring firm should eventually benefit from taking control of the new firm.

Will I be taxed on the shares I surrender in a takeover?

In general, no tax is due if you trade your shares of the company being taken over for shares of the takeover company. Any tax on a gain in value will be deferred to the date you sell the shares you received in the exchange. On the other hand, if you accept cash for your shares or trade the shares for debt of the takeover company (i.e., the takeover company swaps its own bonds for your shares of stock), you will pay tax on any gain you realize in the value of the shares you have surrendered. More extensive information about taxes on securities transactions is presented in a later chapter.

CHAPTER

How Do Stock Exchanges Function?

Chapter summary

A stock exchange is a central marketplace where buyers and sellers or agents of buyers and sellers meet to engage in securities transactions. Market makers on the exchange floor facilitate this trading by standing ready to buy and sell specific securities they have been assigned. The market makers execute trades for themselves and between other members of the exchange who represent individual and institutional investors. The majority of smaller transactions on the exchanges now take place electronically.

Are stocks the only securities traded on a stock exchange?

Although generally called *stock exchanges,* these facilities often serve as a marketplace for several types of securities, including bonds and options. In fact, option trading has become a very important part of the overall activity at several exchanges. Perhaps stock exchanges should more appropriately be called *securities exchanges*, because, often, a variety of securities are traded. Still, the country's largest securities exchange is the *New York Stock Exchange.*

Are securities exchanges the main mechanism for trading stocks and bonds?

Exchanges are an important cog in the country's mechanism for trading securities, but these organized markets are certainly not the only piece of the mechanism. In fact, a greater number and variety of securities are traded in the over-the-counter market than on the organized securities exchanges. In addition, many securities that trade on one or more of the exchanges also trade in the over-the-counter market. Although many academics and professionals contend that securities exchanges are relics of the past that should give way to computerized trading, stock exchanges continue to occupy an important position in the secondary market for security trading. Some professionals claim the exchanges provide a better trading environment than the over-the-counter market for relatively inactive securities.

Who owns the stock exchanges?

A stock exchange is a private company owned by its members, who are said to hold *seats* on the exchange. Memberships, or seats, are bought and sold by individuals and businesses. Basically, a stock exchange is organized like most other businesses, with owners, who vote for directors, who, in turn, hire employees and establish policy. Although the federal government has substantial regulatory powers over nearly all aspects of securities trading, the government is not part of the ownership of stock exchanges located in the United States.

Does each member of an exchange own only a single seat?

Some exchange members own a single seat, while other members who conduct a substantial amount of business may own several seats or memberships. For example, about 500 organizations hold the 1366 memberships available on the New York Stock Exchange, which means that some organizations have multiple memberships. Some members are partnerships, and other members are organized as corporations.

Do individuals become members of a stock exchange in order to trade for their personal accounts?

It is rare for an investor to purchase a membership for the sole purpose of trading for a personal account. An exceptional amount of personal trading would be required to justify the high cost of buying and maintaining a membership. The majority of investors would incur substantially lower expenses by paying commissions to a commercial brokerage firm to execute trades.

Do exchange members have help in conducting the business of the exchange?

Many individuals other than members are required to support the work of a securities exchange. For example, a specialist is likely to employ several individuals who assist in the market-making function. In addition, personnel are required to deal with the huge amount of recordkeeping involved in operating an active trading floor. A securities exchange must hire lawyers, accountants, receptionists, public relations personnel, guards, administrators, and so forth. Imagine the number of people it takes just to keep the electronics equipment up and working.

Is each stock exchange assigned a specific location in which to do business?

Stock exchanges tend to locate in financial centers, but no locations are assigned. New York City, which historically has been the center of financial activity in the United States, is the site for several exchanges, including the well-known New York Stock Exchange. Various regional stock exchanges are scattered throughout the United States, although recent years have seen a consolidation in the exchanges. Securities exchanges in foreign countries tend to be located in large cities. Table 5-1 is a list of websites of U.S. and major foreign securities exchanges.

TABLE 5-1

Websites of U.S. and major foreign securities exchanges.

U.S. Securities Exchanges	Major Foreign Securities Exchanges
American Stock Exchange www.amex.com	Bourse de Paris www.bourse-de-paris.fr
Chicago Board Options Exchange www.cboe.com	Frankfurt (Germany) Stock Exchange www.exchange.de/fwb/fwb.html
Chicago Stock Exchange www.chicagostockex.com	Hong Kong Stock Exchange www.sehk.com.hk
Nasdaq www.nasdaq.com/	London Stock Exchange www.stockex.co.uk/aim/
New York Stock Exchange www.nyse.com/	Tokyo Stock Exchange www.tse.or.jp/eindex.html
Pacific Exchange www.pacificex.com/	Toronto Stock Exchange www.tse.com/

Are exchanges assigned specific securities to trade?

Companies that issue securities have a major role in deciding where these securities will be traded in the secondary market. Some companies with outstanding securities desire a listing on one or more of the exchanges, while other firms prefer that their securities trade in the over-the-counter market. Each exchange has its own established standards for a security to be listed and traded, which plays a part in whether a firm's securities are listed on an exchange. In general, an exchange is interested in listing a security that has a large investor following and as a result, will produce a substantial trading. Large trading volume means more business for the exchange and extra profits for the exchange members.

Do some securities trade on more than one exchange?

Many securities are listed for trading on the New York Stock Exchange at the same time they trade on one or more of the regional exchanges, and in some instances, in the over-the-counter market. In fact, most trading volume on regional exchanges is in securities that are also listed for trading on the New York Stock Exchange. As an example, the common stock of General Motors is listed for trading on the NYSE, its major market, but it is also traded on several regional exchanges, including San Francisco and Chicago. Regional exchanges in the United States include the Chicago Stock Exchange, the Pacific Stock Exchange (San Francisco and Los Angeles), the PBW (Philadelphia-Baltimore-Washington) Exchange, the Boston Stock Exchange, the Spokane Stock Exchange, the Honolulu Stock Exchange, and the Intermountain Stock Exchange in Salt Lake City. Like the New York Stock Exchange, these regional exchanges have specialists who serve as market makers. Likewise, dealers throughout the United States also serve as market makers in the over-the-counter market.

Do regional exchanges serve as the only market for some stocks?

Some stocks are traded only on a regional exchange, although the stocks are also likely to be traded by dealers who serve as market makers in the OTC. A relatively small regional company may not meet the standards for listing on the NYSE but at the same time be actively traded on one of the regional exchanges. Stocks listed on a regional exchange but not the NYSE are likely to be regional companies with a regional investment following.

Are securities of any foreign companies traded on U.S. securities exchanges?

Shares, or at least claims to the shares, of many foreign companies are traded on domestic securities exchanges, just as stocks of U.S. companies are traded on foreign exchanges. Instead of actual foreign shares, U.S. investors generally purchase claims called *American Depositary Receipts* (ADRs). One American Depositary Receipt may represent a claim to one or more shares of a particular foreign stock, with the actual number of shares represented being specified by the ADR. Trading claims on foreign stock rather than the actual shares avoids some of the difficulties that would be encountered in dealing with a foreign currency.

Where do these American depositary receipts originate?

American depositary receipts are issued by American banks that hold in their foreign branches the actual shares represented by the ADRs. Investors who purchase ADRs incur slightly higher expenses than are involved in purchasing shares of U.S. companies. An ADR can be exchanged for the underlying shares, although shareholders generally have no interest in undertaking such an exchange.

Are bonds an important part of trading activity on the exchanges?

A large number of bond issues are listed for trading on the New York Stock Exchange and the American Stock Exchange, although many of these issues are relatively inactive. Most bonds listed for trading are corporate issues. Some foreign government bonds are also traded. The huge amount of trading in U.S. Treasury securities takes place among dealers in the over-the-counter market. Likewise, large trades in corporate bonds typically occur in the over-the-counter market.

Are listed securities ever dropped from trading?

The stock of a company that is liquidated or purchased by another firm will no longer be available for trading in any market because no shares will be outstanding for anyone to buy and sell. For example, Nationsbank purchased Barnett Banks in 1997 and absorbed all of Barnett's outstanding common stock. The New York Stock Exchange had served as the major marketplace for Barnett stock, but none of the shares of Barnett remained to be traded following the takeover. Thus, the stock was dropped from trading simply because no shares were publicly owned to trade.

Can companies still in existence be dropped from trading?

Companies that no longer meet an exchange's established standards for listing could have their shares dropped or delisted from trading. Just as an exchange has standards for listing of a security, it also has standards that must be met in order for a security to continue to be listed. A stock may be delisted when a company repurchases a large amount of its own stock so that the remaining shares are inactively traded. Likewise, a firm's stock may be delisted from an exchange if the company fails to promptly disclose required financial information.

Will I be able to sell a security that has been delisted by an exchange?

A security that is delisted by one stock exchange, say the New York Stock Exchange, is likely to be listed on some other exchange or to be traded in the over-the-counter market. Thus, you should be able to sell stock that has been delisted from trading on a particular exchange.

How are securities traded on the exchanges?

Most stock exchanges are operated as auction markets, in which securities are sold to the highest bidder and bought at the lowest offering. The heart of an exchange is the group of market makers who conduct business on the floor of an exchange. These market makers, formally called *specialists,* buy and sell securities for themselves and for others. In most trades they match orders from buyers with offsetting orders from sellers. In other instances, the specialists will actually buy stock from sellers or sell stock to buyers. Specialists function as dealers when they purchase stock for their own account, or sell stock from their own accounts. They serve as brokers when they bring together a sell order from one customer and a purchase order from another customer. Suppose a specialist receives a customer order to purchase 200 shares of a particular stock. If no offsetting order to buy shares of the same stock has been placed, the specialist will fill the order by selling 200 shares from inventory, i.e., the specialist's personal account. If a customer order to sell stock comes to the exchange and can't be matched with an offsetting customer buy order, the specialist will purchase the stock for his or her personal account. In each of these latter two trades, the specialist is acting as a dealer rather than as a broker.

Where do specialists' orders originate?

Orders to buy or sell stock originate with institutional investors and individual customers of retail brokerage firms. Orders are sent to the brokerage firm's trading desk, where they are rerouted to dealers in the over-the-counter market or to exchanges where exchange members make markets in the securities. If the order is routed to an exchange, the brokerage firm's representative at the exchange (called a *commission broker*) will convey the order to the specialist firm that has been assigned as market maker for the stock. The bottom line is that specialists' orders originate with investors, either small investors such as you and me or large investors like mutual funds that have decided to buy or sell stock.

With a huge volume of shares being traded every day, don't all the people on the floor of an exchange get in one another's way?

Orders of modest size are conveyed to an automated execution system, so no personal contact is required to complete many customer orders that flow to the floor of the exchange. Different exchanges have different names for the computerized systems designed to speed transactions and reduce the need for brokerage firm representatives to personally deal with specialists. Without automatic executions of small- and intermediate-size orders, activity on the floors of the exchanges would come to a standstill.

Do specialists roam around an exchange trading floor looking for business?

Specialists are stationed at trading desks called *posts,* where they conduct business on the floor of the exchange. A specialist who has been assigned particular stocks in which to be a market maker remains at the same location on the floor of the exchange each day. Thus, commission brokers who need to execute customer orders know where to go on the trading floor to buy or sell a particular security. Essentially, a specialist is in charge of a trading desk for a designated group of stocks.

Does a commission broker become my representative on the floor of the exchange?

The commission broker does indeed represent you when your order is conveyed to the exchange and, eventually, to the specialist's post. If you have entered an order to purchase a security, the commission broker's job is to obtain the lowest possible price. If you place an order to sell a security, the commission broker will attempt to obtain the highest possible price for the investment you wish to sell. In reality, a market order of modest size will be executed at whatever price is being quoted when the order reaches the post.

Do the commission broker and specialist meet at the specialist's post and negotiate a trade?

If specialists and commission brokers negotiated every order sent to the floor, the market would come to a standstill. The specialist quotes a bid price and an asked price, for example, 25 bid and $25\frac{1}{8}$ asked. In this case the specialist offers to buy stock for $25 per share (the bid) and sell stock for $25\frac{1}{8}$ per share (the asked). This quote leaves little room for negotiation unless the specialist is willing to split the difference and execute an order for $25\frac{1}{16}$. If the difference between the bid and asked prices is an eighth or larger, the commission broker might ask the specialist to raise the bid by a sixteenth (if the commission broker is holding a customer order to sell) or to lower the asked by a sixteenth (with a customer order to buy). In fact, negotiations are unlikely for relatively small orders from individual investors.

Can a specialist refuse to buy or sell shares of an assigned stock?

Specialists are required to provide a continuous market by furnishing bid and asked quotations for the stocks they have been assigned. Specialists must fill orders from commission brokers at the quoted price, either by matching other customer orders they are holding or by buying or selling for their own accounts. The specialist can limit the number of shares he or she is willing to buy or sell at the quoted prices. In fact, the quoted bid and asked prices will be accompanied by the number of shares the specialist agrees to buy at the bid and to sell at the asked. The specialist is not required to buy or sell stock when the commission broker stipulates a price that is away from the specialist's quote. For example, a specialist quoting a bid of 21 and asked of $21\frac{1}{4}$ will not be required to purchase shares of the stock for $21\frac{1}{2}$, which is 50 cents per share more than the quoted bid.

Do I have any control over the price at which I buy or sell a security?

Although an order you enter with a broker is unlikely to influence the market price of the stock or bond you buy or sell, an acceptable price can be included with the order. For example, you can specify the minimum price you will accept when an order to sell stock is entered. Likewise, you can specify the maximum price you will pay to buy bonds or shares of stock. Entering an order that includes an acceptable price is called a *limit order*. If AT&T common stock last traded at $65 per share and you would like to buy 100 shares at $63 per share or better, you can instruct your broker to enter a limit order to buy the stock at a price of $63 or less.

Can the specialist who makes a market in AT&T stock refuse to sell 100 shares at $63 per share?

If the asked price quoted by the specialist (the price at which the specialist will sell) is $63 at the time your order to buy at $63 is entered, the order will be executed at the limit price you have specified. If the $63 price you set is less than the asked quote at which the specialist will sell, the order will be left at the specialist's post for execution in the event the price eventually falls to the level you specified. If the market price subsequently increases rather than falls following the time your order reaches the exchange floor, the order will not be executed and you will not become an owner of the stock.

How long will the specialist retain my order?

You may enter a *day order,* in which case the order remains effective only for the day it is entered. A day order that is not executed is withdrawn at the end of the day but can be reentered the following morning. An alternative is a *good-till-canceled order* (also called an *open order*), which remains active until the order is executed or until you call your broker and request that the previous order be canceled. In practice, some brokerage firms will automatically cancel the order after a period of time unless the order is renewed. If you plan to enter limit orders, you should ask your broker about the brokerage firm's policy for dealing with these specialized orders.

How do specialists keep track of all these limit orders that have been left with them?

In the old days, specialists maintained a record of limit orders on note cards or in a notebook called the *specialist's book* or *limit order book.* The book contained all of the limit orders that had been left by commission brokers for their customers but had not yet been executed or canceled. Electronic recordkeeping has now replaced the old paper recordkeeping system, although the store of information continues to be referred to by the same name.

Does access to this information provide the specialist with an advantage over other investors?

One criticism leveled at specialists concerns their access to information unavailable to other investors. Critics contend this monopoly on purchase and sell orders allows specialists to earn unusually large profits. A specialist has information regarding the demand for and supply of a particular stock that may be useful in determining whether to own a large number of shares in the stock. For example, large orders to buy a stock at a price slightly under the current market price (information available to the specialist in that stock) allow the specialist to acquire a large position in the stock without being concerned about a big price decline.

Can you provide an example of how a limit order works?

Suppose you enter an order to buy 100 shares of Cincinnati Bell common stock and specify a maximum price (the limit price) of $30 per share. At the time your order arrives on the floor of the exchange, the specialist is quoting Cincinnati Bell at $31\frac{1}{2}$ bid and $31\frac{5}{8}$ asked. This quote indicates the specialist will purchase shares of Cincinnati Bell for $31.50 per share and will sell shares at a price of $31.62 per share. Your order will not be executed because the specialist is offering to sell at $31\frac{5}{8}$, over a point and a half more than your order specifies that you are willing to pay. In fact, the specialist is offering to buy the same stock for more than you are willing to pay. Your order will be kept by the specialist and eventually executed if the price drops to your specified limit price of $30 per share. Of course, if

Cincinnati Bell does not decline to the specified level and, instead, begins rising, you will be on the sidelines watching as your order stagnates at the specialist's post.

Is my order certain to be executed if the market price drops to $30 per share?

Your order may or may not be filled if the stock price drops to the limit you have specified. Orders are filled in chronological order and limit orders at the same price may have been entered earlier than your order. For example, the specialist may be holding many orders to buy Cincinnati Bell at $30 at a time when only 500 shares trade at that price. If the price subsequently increases after that trade, you will miss buying the stock, at least for the moment.

What happens if I don't specify a price?

An order to buy or to sell stock or bonds without a price specified is termed a *market order*. A market order is executed at the best possible price at the time the order arrives on the floor of the exchange. In practice, the best possible price means that you are likely to pay the price quoted by the specialist. A market order for an actively traded stock will probably result in buying or selling the stock at the same price as the last trade. However, one danger of using a market order is that you may end up paying a little more than you expect when stock is purchased, and you may receive a little less than you expect when stock is sold. No price guarantee is provided when you choose to place a market order.

Is it better to enter a market order or a limit order?

If you are buying or selling a fairly active stock and tend to hold securities for relatively long periods of at least several years, it is probably best to enter market orders that are certain to be executed. Attempting to save an eighth or a quarter of a point, i.e., 12.5 cents or 25 cents per share, when a security is to be held for many years or has been held for several years is probably shortsighted. If you enter an order for an inactive security or plan a short holding period, a limit order may be the preferred type of order.

Why do I hear so much about the New York Stock Exchange?

The New York Stock Exchange (NYSE) is the oldest, largest, and most active organized securities exchange in the United States. Sometimes called the *Big Board,* daily trading on the exchange regularly exceeds 500 million shares. The common stocks of most large publicly owned corporations are traded on the NYSE, and both the print and television media often illustrate stories related to economics, the stock market, and other financial topics with pictures of activity on the floor of the New York Stock Exchange. Although the stocks of only a small portion of America's businesses are traded on the floor of the New York Stock Exchange, these businesses include most of the country's largest and best-known firms.

Who owns the New York Stock Exchange?

Like other exchanges in the U.S., the New York Stock Exchange is a corporation owned by individuals who hold seats on the exchange. The NYSE has 1366 members, or owners, a number that is fixed. With a fixed number of seats, anyone wishing to acquire membership must purchase a seat from an existing member at a mutually agreeable price. The value of a seat varies with the profitability of membership. When trading is active and profits of existing members are high, memberships are valuable and seats change hands at high prices. When trading

TABLE 5-2

Prices of Membership on the New York Stock Exchange.

Year	Low Price	High Price
1950	$ 46,000	$ 54,000
1955	80,000	90,000
1960	135,000	162,000
1965	190,000	250,000
1970	130,000	320,000
1975	55,000	138,000
1980	175,000	275,000
1981	220,000	285,000
1982	190,000	340,000
1983	310,000	310,000
1984	290,000	400,000
1985	310,000	480,000
1986	455,000	600,000
1987	605,000	1,150,000
1988	580,000	820,000
1989	420,000	675,000
1990	250,000	430,000
1991	345,000	440,000
1992	410,000	600,000
1993	500,000	775,000
1994	760,000	830,000
1995	785,000	1,050,000
1996	1,225,000	1,450,000
1997	1,175,000	1,750,000

activity declines and member profits fall, seats on the exchange sell at low prices. Buying a seat on the NYSE is similar to investing in the stock of a business: The more profitable the business, the more valuable the stock. See Table 5-2.

Can anyone purchase a seat on the New York Stock Exchange?

Applicants for membership must be sponsored by at least two current members and must obtain the approval of the organization's board of directors. Of course, the applicant must also locate an existing member who desires to sell a membership and must have sufficient financial resources to pay the asking price. New members of the exchange are required to pay an initiation fee, and all members are assessed annual dues.

Once a seat on the exchange is purchased, can the new member walk onto the floor and begin trading securities?

The buyer of a seat assumes the duties and responsibilities of the seat that has been acquired. In other words, a new member cannot simply walk onto the floor and decide to become a specialist in a particular stock or a particular group of stocks. Members perform different functions on the exchange. The largest number of members are registered as commission brokers, who handle security orders that originate outside the exchange. A commission broker receives orders from a trading desk or from a member of the public by way of a brokerage firm. This exchange member then takes care of executing the order at the best available price or according to the customer's instructions that accompany the order. For example, a customer may enter an order to purchase stock at a particular price. The order will be left at the specialist's post if it cannot be immediately executed at the specified price.

What jobs do other members perform?

Many exchange members perform as specialists, who make markets in securities that are traded on the floor of the exchange. Each specialist is assigned securities (a typical specialist makes a market in about 15 different securities) for which the specialist is required to provide bid and asked prices. Specialists also act as brokers when they match a customer's order with an order that has been left by a commission broker representing another customer. The third largest group consists of floor brokers (formerly called *two-dollar brokers*), who assist other members in transacting orders. Commission brokers may need assistance during periods of especially heavy trading.

How many specialist firms operate on the floor of the New York Stock Exchange?

Consolidation has reduced the number of specialist firms that operate on the floor of the New York Stock Exchange. As of the end of 1997, only 35 specialist units were operating on the floor. The largest of these firms served as the market maker for 442 stocks and did nearly 22 percent of the exchange's dollar volume. A volatile stock market resulted in specialist firms requiring large capitalization that was unavailable to small firms.

Is the New York Stock Exchange always open?

The NYSE is open Monday through Friday (except legal holidays) from 9:30 a.m. to 4:00 p.m. eastern standard time. Many people expect the exchange to implement an expanded trading schedule in response to competition from other markets that are open during the hours the NYSE is closed.

How does the New York Stock Exchange decide which securities to trade?

To qualify for having its securities traded, a public company must apply and meet standards that have been established by the exchange. Standards include minimum requirements relative to earnings, assets, number of shareholders, shares outstanding, and the market value of publicly held shares. Standards set by the exchange tend to exclude the stock issued by recently formed companies and small firms with a limited number of shareholders. The exchange is particularly interested in listing securities that offer the potential for active trading.

Is it advantageous for a company to have its shares listed for trading on the New York Stock Exchange?

The exchange contends that listing benefits both the company and its shareholders. The listing company benefits from increased exposure in the financial press and more prestige among investors. Stockholders benefit because their securities become more marketable. That is, the exchange claims that securities are easier to buy and sell after being listed for trading. The improved liquidity stems from the continuous market provided by exchange specialists who serve as market makers, publicity and prestige that results from a listing, and a pool of investors who prefer to invest in securities listed on the exchange. Improved liquidity is good both for investors who find it easier to buy and sell the security and for the company whose stock is being traded because better liquidity may result in a reduced cost of capital for the company.

Are the securities of all large companies traded on the NYSE?

Not all large companies have securities listed for trading on the New York Stock Exchange. Some large firms, such as State Farm Insurance, are mutual companies owned by their customers. These firms don't have publicly traded shares of stock that can be listed on an exchange. A relatively small number of individuals own some firms, so although stock may be outstanding, none of the shares are publicly traded. Still other firms have many shares that are available for trading and meet exchange standards for being listed, but for one reason or another decide not to apply for listing on an exchange. The directors of these firms apparently feel their shareholders are just as well served by having the firms' securities traded in the over-the-counter market. A decision not to list has been especially prevalent among technology companies that appeared on the scene during the last decade. Another potential disadvantage for some companies (but not investors) is the New York Stock Exchange requirement that listed firms provide a minimum level of financial disclosure. Some firms are hesitant to produce this information.

What are some examples of large, well-known companies with stock not listed on the New York Stock Exchange?

The common stocks of many technology firms are traded in the over-the-counter market. For example, Microsoft Corporation, one of the world's best-known and most valuable firms, is traded in the OTC. Likewise, the common stocks of Intel, Yahoo, Dell Computer, and Cisco Systems are traded in the OTC rather than on the New York Stock Exchange. While the over-the-counter market was once considered the home of new issues and risky securities primarily purchased by speculative investors, this thriving market now includes the stock issues of many well-known corporations.

Does the over-the-counter market function in much the same way as the organized exchanges?

Organized exchanges and the OTC market operate in two very different fashions. While a listed stock has one market maker on the floor of an exchange, a stock traded in the over-the-counter market may have many market makers scattered around the country. The OTC market is discussed in more detail in the following chapter.

CHAPTER

How Does the Over-the-Counter Market Work?

Chapter summary

The over-the-counter (OTC) market is comprised of interconnected dealers who serve as market makers for thousands of different stocks and bonds. The OTC market is the primary market for debt securities and for thousands of equity securities. While the over-the-counter market once served as a market for common stocks that did not qualify for listing on an organized exchange, it has become the primary market for the common stocks of many large and well-known corporations.

How did the over-the-counter market acquire its name?

Many years ago, an investor who wished to purchase a stock that was not traded on an exchange would go directly to the firm issuing the security. The investor passed the appropriate amount of money over a counter through a window and received the certificate in return. Thus, the security was purchased over the counter. At least, this is one theory about how the term *over the counter* originated.

What types of securities are traded over the counter?

The over-the-counter market is the primary market for all debt securities, including corporate, government, and municipal bonds, and for money market instruments such as U.S. Treasury bills. Although a large number of corporate bond issues are listed for trading on one of the exchanges discussed in the last chapter, most large bond trades take place over the counter. The OTC is also the main market for thousands of different common stock issues. Basically, all securities not listed for trading on an exchange are traded over the counter.

Is the OTC market primarily a market for trading the stocks of small companies?

The stocks of most small companies are traded in the over-the-counter market. The securities of small companies do not generally meet the standards that have been established for trading on the New York Stock Exchange, and many do not meet the standards for trading on one of the regional exchanges. For example, a relatively small firm is likely to have too few shares outstanding or too few shareholders to meet the standards for listing on an exchange. The stock of these firms, if publicly traded, will trade over the counter. The directors and managers of many large companies that qualify for having stock listed on an exchange have chosen instead to stick with the over-the-counter market. Thus, although the OTC market is the home for stocks of nearly every small public company, it also serves as the primary market for many large companies.

Why do many investors consider stocks trading in the over-the-counter market as speculative?

To some degree, this characterization stems from the history of this market. For many years the OTC market consisted of traders linked via telephone. These traders conducted business among themselves and with brokerage firms that sought to execute investor orders. Most stocks in this market had a relatively small number of shares outstanding so that even moderate-size trades could cause large price movements that caused many stock prices to be extremely volatile. The markets for individual stocks tended to lack liquidity, and accurate price quotations were often difficult to obtain. Under this system, a broker with a customer order would be required to call several different firms that served as dealers in a stock. Even a conscientious broker found it difficult to determine if the best price had been obtained for the customer. Because public information on OTC stock prices was so sparse, individual investors could never determine if they had obtained a favorable price.

How has this changed?

The Nasdaq system of computerized trading introduced in the early 1970s allowed market makers in the OTC to electronically transmit their quotations to brokers and other dealers. In other words, dealer price quotations were made public so that brokers could instantly provide customers with firm bid and asked prices. It was no longer necessary for brokers to gather quotations by phone from a limited number of dealers, at least for the more active OTC stocks. Better price information also carried over to newspapers and financial publications that devoted increased space to OTC stocks.

Why do some companies that meet the guidelines for having their stocks traded on a stock exchange choose to have the securities continue trading in the OTC market?

The reputation of the OTC market and the quality and name recognition of some of the stocks traded in this market have undergone substantial improvement since the introduction of the Nasdaq system. The new technology, improved price information, and increased investor interest in this market resulted in increased trading volume and improved liquidity, so managements of some companies fail to see an advantage in acquiring a listing on one of the exchanges. Table 6-1 compares the major national markets in the United States.

What are some of the large firms with stocks traded over the counter?

The stocks of some large and successful companies—Dell Computer, Microsoft, Infoseek, Intel, MCI WorldCom, Novell, Oracle, Cisco Systems, and Sun Microsystems, among others—are traded in the over-the-counter market. Notice that these firms are all engaged in high technology

TABLE 6-1

Comparing the major national markets of the United States.

	NYSE	AMEX	NASDAQ
Monthly share volume (000)	14,188,256	582,404	17,915,219
Monthly dollar volume (000)	$641,105,200	$16,641,382	$561,429,081
Number of issues	3,752	916	5,983
Average price/share	$45.19	$28.57	$31.34

Data as of mid-1998.

products and services. Any of the organized exchanges would very much like to list and trade these stocks, which typically have very large volume.

Do substantial differences exist between the over-the-counter market and the organized exchanges?

One of the main differences between the OTC market and exchanges is the number of market makers in each security. An exchange has one designated market maker for each listed stock. For example, a single New York Stock Exchange specialist firm acts as market maker for General Electric common stock. All orders to the NYSE for shares of General Electric common stock are directed to the single specialist firm. Likewise, only one specialist firm on the floor of the exchange makes a market in General Motors common stock. Each specialist firm at an exchange generally acts as the exchange's exclusive market maker for several different securities.

How does this differ from the over-the-counter market?

Multiple dealers often act as market makers for securities in the over-the-counter market. The number of market makers for a particular stock depends on the amount of trading activity in the stock. Very active OTC stocks may have dozens of competing market makers, while relatively inactive stocks may have only one or two dealers that serve as market makers. The OTC market has no institutional restriction on the number of firms that may serve as market makers in a single stock. A new firm may enter the fray as a market maker for a particular stock for which several dealers already make a market. If the trading volume of a stock declines, one or more firms may withdraw as a market maker. Market makers require volume in order to earn an adequate profit.

Is the over-the-counter market bigger than the New York Stock Exchange?

The OTC market is larger than the NYSE in terms of the number of issues traded, but not in terms of the dollar value of securities that are traded. Both the NYSE and the OTC market are significantly larger than the American Stock Exchange, the other national equity market.

Are OTC stocks traded in overseas markets?

Both exchange-listed and OTC stocks are traded in overseas markets, just as the stocks of foreign companies are traded in the United States. Improvements in communications have resulted in a 24-hour trading day, so OTC and exchange-listed stocks can find buyers in overseas markets when U.S. markets are closed.

Do brokerage firms also serve as market makers in Nasdaq stocks?

Some brokerage firms act as both brokers and dealers. Thus, the possibility exists that the shares of stock you purchase over the counter will come from the portfolio held by your brokerage firm. If so, your order must be executed at a price equal to or better than the best price quoted by competing market makers. The same is true of orders to sell. That is, if your brokerage firm is a market maker in the stock you are selling, the broker must pay the highest price quoted by all other market makers in that stock.

Does it matter if I purchase a stock in the OTC market and the stock is subsequently listed for trading on an organized exchange?

The same shares you purchase over the counter can be sold on an exchange if the stock is eventually listed. At one time, it was a natural progression for a successful company to have trading in its stock move from the OTC market to an exchange. Improvements in the over-the-counter market have made an exchange listing less important in the view of many corporate managers and investors. In any case, don't worry if trading in a stock you own moves from the OTC market to an exchange. On the other hand, you may have reason for concern if a stock you own is moved off the Nasdaq National Market System to become a non-NMS stock.

What is Nasdaq?

Nasdaq (pronounced "Nazdak") is an acronym for National Association of Securities Dealers Automated Quotations. Nasdaq was established in 1971 and is a centralized quotation system for market makers to post firm bid and asked quotations for the best-known and most actively traded OTC securities. Minimum standards must be met for a stock to be included in the Nasdaq listings. Market makers are bound to honor the price quotations they enter on the system. In other words, a market maker that quotes a bid of $25 for a particular stock must stand ready to buy shares of the stock for $25 per share. The price quotations posted on Nasdaq are available to all other market participants.

How does a stock being included on Nasdaq affect my order to buy or sell an OTC stock?

Your broker will be able to enter a four-letter symbol on a computer terminal and obtain the current bid and asked prices if the stock you wish to trade is included in the Nasdaq system. The listing will include the bid price, asked price, and quotation size for each market maker. Thus, your broker will be able to determine which market maker is offering the highest bid (if you wish to sell) and the lowest asked (if you wish to buy). Competition among market makers should reduce the spread between the bid and asked, which means you should receive a fair price regardless of whether you are buying or selling.

Is the over-the-counter market divided into Nasdaq and non-Nasdaq stocks?

Actually, the Nasdaq system consists of two components, the National Market System (NMS) and regular issues. Stricter requirements regarding assets, income, number of shares available for trading, and number of shareholders apply to companies that wish to have their stocks included in the National Market System. NMS stocks are generally better known and more actively traded than regular Nasdaq stocks. Trading data available for NMS traded issues is much like the information available for securities listed on exchanges.

Are minimum standards required in order for a firm's stock to be included in the National Market System?

In order to acquire a listing on the NMS, a firm must have at least 1.1 million publicly traded shares, 400 shareholders who own at least 100 shares each, and a minimum bid price for its stock of $5. In addition, a firm must meet established standards relative to pretax income, tangible assets or market capitalization, or total assets and revenues. Separate standards have been established for a stock to retain a listing in this elite group of OTC stocks.

What about OTC stocks that are not included as part of Nasdaq?

Tens of thousands of stocks are not listed on any of the organized exchanges or included in the Nasdaq system. These stocks are typically of newer, smaller companies that have a limited investment following. Sometimes they are stocks of companies that have gone bankrupt. Regardless of the reason, these stocks generally offer less trading data and liquidity compared to stocks that are included as part of Nasdaq. The financial pages of many newspapers include closing prices for select exchange-listed and Nasdaq stocks only. Thus, you may find it necessary to call your broker to obtain a quotation for an OTC stock not included in Nasdaq.

Does this mean that OTC stocks not included in the Nasdaq system are more risky to own?

In general, OTC stocks outside the Nasdaq system are more risky to own. Securities issued by small companies and new companies without a track record tend to be risky assets to own. These stocks are difficult to value, therefore you may pay an inflated price to purchase the shares. Non-Nasdaq OTC stocks generally have few market makers, which means less competition to maintain low spreads and keep prices from being manipulated. Not surprisingly, relatively unknown stocks have substantial potential for both gains and losses. You must determine if the risk is worth the potential reward.

Are OTC stocks outside the Nasdaq system also traded electronically?

Stocks outside Nasdaq's regular system are based on quotations that are published daily either in the "Pink Sheets" or on Nasdaq's OTC Bulletin Board. The Bulletin Board is an electronic quotation system that permits brokers and dealers to locate current price quotations, trading data, and market makers in several thousand securities that don't meet the minimum standards for Nasdaq's regular system. The Pink Sheets, which do not include trading data, are published daily by an organization not affiliated with Nasdaq. Trading in Bulletin Board and Pink Sheet stocks generally takes place over the telephone.

Does the over-the-counter market have an automatic execution system similar to those used on the exchanges?

Nasdaq introduced the Small Order Execution System (SOES) in 1985 to automatically execute small orders in OTC stocks (generally fewer than 1000 shares). SOES is used both for market orders when no price is specified and for limit orders that stipulate a price. As with the NYSE's SuperDot system, SOES is designed to take care of the flood of relatively small orders that would clog the system.

Is it a good idea to determine where a stock is traded before buying shares of the stock?

There is no question that you should determine whether a stock is traded on an exchange or in the over-the-counter market. If it is an OTC stock, find out if it is included in the Nasdaq system. Where a stock is traded will affect how readily you will be able to obtain price and other relevant information about the stock. It will also influence how easily the stock can be resold. It is not unusual to receive calls from brokerage firms touting stocks and subsequently discovering the same firm that sold you the stock is the only market maker. As a result, you will be at the mercy of that firm when you decide to sell the security. Many naïve investors get taken to the cleaners in such situations.

Will a broker be able to determine in which market a stock is traded?

Any broker should be able to determine whether a stock is listed on an exchange or traded over the counter. If it is an over-the-counter stock, the broker should be able to tell you whether it is part of the National Market System. You may want to double-check information provided by the broker before you make a commitment to purchase shares of the stock, especially if the stock is being touted in an unsolicited telephone call.

Who oversees and administers the over-the-counter market?

The U.S. Congress established the National Association of Securities Dealers (NASD) in the 1930s to serve as a self-regulatory body for the over-the-counter market. The NASD includes more than 5000 firms involved in mutual funds, OTC trading, and investment banking. In other words, NASD is an industry-run organization with the responsibility to oversee the industry.

Does the federal government have regulatory powers in the OTC market?

The U.S. Securities and Exchange Commission has substantial regulatory powers over virtually every aspect of issuing and trading securities, including activities in the over-the-counter market. Basically, the same federal regulations apply to OTC securities as to exchange-listed securities. The individual exchanges enforce their own regulations, which are separate from rules imposed by the federal government. It is important to keep in mind that federal regulations are designed to keep you from being cheated, not to protect you from making dumb investment decisions or from losing money.

Does NASD establish commission schedules and regulate security prices?

The National Association of Securities Dealers establishes rules by which its members must conduct their business. The organization does not specify rates and prices that members can charge, but it does require that charges to customers must be reasonable. The most important stipulation is that only NASD members can trade securities with one another at wholesale prices. In other words, nonmembers are required to buy securities without receiving a price concession from member firms. This means that nonmembers must pay the same price paid by retail customers such as yourself. This regulation makes it impractical for most firms to participate in the securities business without being NASD members.

Will the brokerage commission to buy a stock traded over the counter be higher than the fee for the same size trade on an exchange?

The brokerage commission to purchase stocks traded over the counter is likely to be the same as the commission you would pay to purchase stock traded on an exchange. Any difference depends on the brokerage firm you choose to enter the order because some firms have a somewhat different commission schedule for OTC stocks than for listed stocks. Commissions on trades involving OTC stocks are sometimes a little less than commissions for trades in listed stocks. Purchasing the stock through a broker who is not also a dealer means you will pay the dealer's asked price plus the commission charged by your broker. If the OTC stock is relatively inactive, the spread between the bid price and the asked price may be relatively large. If the stock is active, however, the spread will be small. The key to price and commission is the trading volume of the stock and the fee schedule of the brokerage firm you use, not whether the stock is traded over the counter or on an exchange.

Are all securities firms members of NASD?

Small firms that concentrate on specialized products such as penny stocks and tax shelters are sometimes able to conduct business without membership, but nearly all firms that offer a range of products will almost certainly be members of the association. Although NASD is generally associated with the over-the-counter market, nearly all members of stock exchanges are also NASD members.

Should I make certain a broker is a member of NASD before placing an order to purchase stock?

It is a good idea to do business with a member of NASD. This helps protect you from some of the worst abuses in the industry. NASD has the authority to discipline members that engage in unethical practices, which means there is a strong incentive for an NASD member to treat you fairly.

Does doing business with a member of NASD protect me from unscrupulous sales practices?

NASD imposes rules of conduct on its members and has the ability to discipline individuals and member firms that fail to live by these rules. For example, NASD regulations prohibit manipulative and fraudulent practices by its members. Members found guilty of such practices can be fined, suspended, or expelled. Having said that, consider that members *have* been fined, suspended, and expelled, which means that they have been found guilty of these offenses. History demonstrates that some employees of NASD member firms and exchange member firms do occasionally engage in unsavory practices.

Does the OTC market represent the future or the past?

Many professionals believe that vast improvements in communications have made obsolete the single trading floor of an organized exchange. While at one time it was necessary to physically gather people together in order to create a working marketplace, changes in the business now allow participants to efficiently operate from many different locations. With new stock issues now being sold on the Internet and individuals trading stocks from their homes, the need for bringing people together in a physical sense has been replaced by bringing people and data together electronically.

7
CHAPTER

What Financial Investments Other Than Stocks and Bonds Are Available on Wall Street?

Chapter summary

Although stocks and bonds are the staples of Wall Street, brokerage firms offer a wide variety of products including options, convertible securities, and futures contracts. In fact, virtually all financial products, insurance and certificates of deposit to name two, can be purchased from your local broker. A large number of innovative financial products have been brought to market or made more accessible during the last several decades. This chapter discusses some of Wall Street's alternatives to stocks and bonds.

Why does Wall Street need to offer products other than stocks and bonds?

Wall Street companies have a desire to generate revenues and earn as much income as possible. These firms figure that becoming a place for one-stop shopping will allow them to corral all your assets. As part of this effort, Wall Street offers a product for every need and more than a few products that sometimes seem to meet no apparent need. Wall Street peddles products that will allow you to profit from gold, investments that can produce income from oil and gas exploration, and products that will allow investors to cash in on business ventures in foreign countries. Wall Street firms want to suck up and take care of your money, all of it. Brokerage firms compete with insurance companies, banks, and every other financial institution for your investment dollars. As such, brokerage firms feel they must offer a wide range of products that will allow them to capture business that might flow to competing institutions.

Are all these different investment vehicles actually necessary?

Issuing and trading stocks and bonds is an integral part of an efficient capitalistic economy. Securities that can be easily transferred from one investor to another help assure savers that these investments can be quickly turned into cash. Liquidity in the secondary market facilitates the process of raising capital in the primary market. Some of the other investments offered by Wall Street appear to have little to do with the economy and mainly serve the public's need for speculation and Wall Street's desire to make money. Of course, the firms that develop new investment products and the individuals who make a substantial portion of their income from selling the investments will argue that their products are integral and necessary parts of the capitalistic system.

Are these other investments primarily targeted at individual investors, or are they mainly aimed at institutions such as banks and pension funds?

Both individuals and institutions put money into some of these investments. Other investment vehicles are so complicated or involve such large amounts of money that institutions are the major buyers.

What are some examples of these other investments?

Derivatives are alternative investments that have become very popular among both individuals and institutional investors. They have also received a great deal of media attention. A big part of the news coverage has resulted from major financial losses suffered by some businesses that invested in derivatives. Basically, a derivative is an investment that derives its value from some other investment. For example, options to buy or sell shares of stock are considered derivatives because the options derive their investment value from the underlying stocks. Options to buy or sell futures contracts derive their investment value from the underlying futures contracts, which, in turn, derive their value from underlying agricultural commodities or financial assets. Convertible bonds derive at least part of their value from shares of stock for which the bonds can be exchanged.

Do Wall Street firms sell other investments?

Wall Street firms sell certificates of deposit, annuities, life insurance, partnerships, warrants, real estate trusts, mutual funds, and on and on. If you want to invest in something and have the money to pay for it, count on these firms being able to sell it. Firms operating on Wall Street have truly become financial supermarkets.

Many of these investments sound more complicated than stocks and bonds. Are they?

Some Wall Street products are so complicated that even the people who sell them sometimes don't have a thorough understanding of the fine points. It is often difficult to value a derivative investment product that is dependent on the value of some other product. Some investment products are so complicated, their value depends on the value of another investment, which, in turn, depends on the value of still another investment. For example, the market value for an option contract on coffee futures depends on the value of the underlying contract for coffee futures, which depends on the market price of coffee. The option is two levels removed from the investment that gives the option its value.

If I don't fully understand an investment, can I trust the advice of the person who is selling it?

A good rule of thumb is to avoid putting money into any investment vehicle you don't understand. Only when you understand an investment can you determine whether it meets your financial needs and fits with other investments you may already own. Always keep in mind that the person talking to you about the investment probably earns income from selling the product. Also remember that complicated investments often involve an above-average sales commission.

What are the options that were mentioned earlier?

An option represents a choice. The person or business that holds the option can choose whether or not to undertake a certain course of action. In finance, an option provides the owner of the option with the choice of whether or not to buy something or whether or not to sell something. An option specifically states whether it conveys the right to buy or the right to sell. For example, an option on a specific piece of property might allow the owner of the option the right to buy (or not to buy) the specified property, usually at a predetermined price.

Do some options apply specifically to stocks?

A stock option permits the owner of the option either to buy shares of a specified stock at a stated price (termed the *strike price*) until a predetermined date (termed the *expiration date*), or to sell shares of a stock at a fixed price until a predetermined date. Nearly all stock options specify 100 shares of stock. Depending on the type of option held, the option holder has the right either to buy shares of stock or to sell shares of stock, but not both. The right to buy stock is termed a *call* and the right to sell stock is termed a *put*. An investor who purchases a call option is forecasting an increase in the price of the underlying stock, while someone who buys a put option is expecting a decline in the price of the underlying stock.

Do stock options pay dividends or interest?

Investors who own stock options receive no income payments of any kind. Stock options have value only because they permit the option owner to purchase or to sell 100 shares of stock. Option holders are not owners or creditors, and they have no voting power and no rights in the event a company is liquidated. They get no annual reports or correspondence from the company, on whose stock the option can be used. The investor who owns an option to buy the stock will not receive any cash payments even when the underlying stock pays a dividend.

Can you provide an example of a call option?

Suppose in April 199X, a call option to buy 100 shares of Philip Morris stock for $45 per share until September of the same year traded for $200. At the time, Philip Morris common stock traded for $40.50 per share. Thus, the owner of the option had five months to decide whether to buy 100 shares of Philip Morris stock for $45 per share. If the stock price increased from $40.50 to $50 sometime during the five months, the option owner would be able to buy stock worth $5000 (100 shares @ $50) for $4500 (100 shares at the strike price of $45). The option that traded at a price of $200 in April should have been worth at least $500 when the underlying stock sold for $50 per share because the option conveyed the right to buy 100 shares of stock for $5 less per share than the stock's market value.

Who would sell 100 shares of stock for less than market value?

The investor who originated, or wrote, the call option will be called upon to supply stock that may be purchased by the owner of the call. The writer of the call agreed to give up any potential appreciation above $45 per share in return for a nonrefundable cash payment (termed the *premium*) from the investor who purchased the call. A call is a contract between two investors. The buyer of the call has the right (but not the obligation) to use the call to purchase stock at a predetermined price, while the writer of the call has the obligation to deliver the stock in the event the call is utilized.

What happens if the price of the stock remains below the strike price?

In the event the stock price stays below $45 for the life of the call, the owner of the option will choose not to buy the stock (why pay $45 per share for stock that is worth less than $45 per share) and the call will expire without value. The writer of the option will retain the stock and keep the premium that was received when the call option was written. The option writer may decide to write a new call option in order to earn another premium. There is also a possibility the call option will not be used if the stock price temporarily rises above the strike price and subsequently declines. Option owners tend to exercise options just prior to their expiration date.

How does a put option work?

A put option allows the holder of the option (the person who purchases the option) the right to sell 100 shares of a particular stock at a fixed price until a specified date. While a call option allows the option owner to buy stock, the owner of a put option has the right to sell stock. Investors generally purchase put options when they think the price of a stock may fall and they want to be able to lock in a price at which to sell it. The writer who originated the put option is obligated to buy the stock if the owner of the option decides to exercise the option and sell the stock. The writer keeps the premium and has no further obligation if the put expires without being used.

When would a put option not be used?

The holder of a put will not exercise the option to sell stock when the market price of the stock is higher than the price specified by the put option. Suppose you own a put option that gives you the right to sell shares of a stock at $25. Why would you use the put option to sell shares at $25 to the option writer if the market price of the stock was higher than $25? The answer is that you wouldn't. A put option that was issued some months ago and is near its expiration date has little or no value when the market price of the stock is higher than the strike price specified by the option.

How would I use a put option?

Suppose you purchased 300 shares of Coca-Cola common stock several years ago for $45 per share and the stock currently trades at a price of $65 per share. You would like to continue to hold the stock, but the sharp increase in value has caused you to worry about the possibility of a price decline over the next several months. One potential course of action is to purchase three put options (like calls, each put is generally for 100 shares of stock) with a strike price of $65. Holding these options would allow you to sell your 300 shares for $65 per share during the period the option is valid no matter how much the stock price declined. For example, if Coca-Cola stock suddenly fell to $58, you could force the writer of the put to buy your shares for $65 each. The length of time you have available to sell your stock at this price depends on the expiration date of the put option you purchase. An option with a longer life (i.e., a later expiration date) is more valuable to own and will cost more to buy. In the instance just described, you have acquired a put option in order to protect against a decline in the price of stock you own.

Can options be utilized in other ways?

Options are utilized in many ways. For example, you could purchase a put in order to speculate on a price decline in the underlying stock. If the stock price declines, the value of the put will increase in market value and you will make money on your investment. The lower the price of the stock, the more valuable the put option because the strike price remains unchanged. Alternatively, you can speculate on a price increase in a stock by purchasing a call option on the stock.

How about writing instead of buying options?

If you are considering the purchase of a particular stock, you might decide to write a put option on the stock. Writing a put option means you agree to buy the stock at a specific price, something you were thinking about doing anyway. Writing the option means you will receive a premium from the buyer of the option, who may or may not force you to purchase the stock. Of course, if the stock price increases, the put will not be used (the owner of the put will not force you to buy stock at a price below the current market price), and you will not own the stock during the period it is increasing in value. Put options, call options, and various combinations of the two are often used in complicated investment strategies that are beyond the scope of this book.

Can I purchase an option and then sell it to someone else?

Like stocks and bonds, options are traded in the secondary market. Thus, you can buy an existing option from another investor and then resell that same option to yet another investor. Suppose you expect IBM stock to increase in price and decide to buy a call option with a three-month expiration. If IBM stock does indeed increase in price, the call option you purchased should also increase in value. With a secondary market in options, you should be able to earn a profit by selling your call option to another investor. In other words, you don't actually have to use the option and buy the underlying stock in order to profit from owning the option.

Can I purchase these options through my regular broker?

Virtually all brokerage firms accept orders for put and call options. In fact, these are an important source of commission revenue for many brokers and their firms. Investors who buy and sell option contracts tend to undertake lots of trades and generate quite a bit of commission income for many brokers. Consider that investors often hold stocks and bonds for many years, whereas most put and call options expire within one year. This means that investors who choose to trade in options are constantly buying, selling, and reinvesting.

Are put and call options traded on exchanges or in the over-the-counter market?

Most stock options are traded on separate trading floors of the national and regional exchanges. The American Stock Exchange, the Pacific Stock Exchange, and the Philadelphia Stock Exchange all have their own trading floors specifically designed for options. The method of trading options is somewhat different than for stocks, but market makers are utilized in option trading as well as in stock trading.

Should I consider investing in options?

Options can be included as part of your investment portfolio, but first make certain that you fully understand these investments and the risks involved in their ownership. Options can be utilized to speculate on stock prices, either upward or downward. Likewise, put and call options can be used to hedge price changes for the stocks that you already own. However, be aware that options are subject to very rapid and large price movements. Modest changes in the price of the underlying stock can cause relatively large variations in the valuation of options to buy or sell the stock. Option prices are very volatile, and the investments are frequently worth nothing by the time they are ready to expire. Also keep in mind that buying and selling options can involve substantial brokerage commissions. Many investors who choose to invest in options make more money for their brokers than they do for themselves. The bottom line is that most individual investors would probably do themselves a favor by avoiding options.

What other kinds of investments should I consider?

Although not nearly as popular as puts and calls, stock warrants can be interesting investments. Warrants are similar to a call option in that they allow an investor to purchase a specific number of shares of stock at a fixed price until a certain date. Warrants are another example of a derivative because warrants derive their value from the underlying shares of stock they can be used to buy.

This sounds just like a call option. Is there a difference?

Warrants are issued by corporations that agree to sell shares of their stock to the warrant holders. Basically, corporations issue warrants in order to raise investment capital, both at the time the warrants are issued and at the time the warrants are exercised. Call options originate from individual and institutional investors who write options to earn premium income from other investors who purchase the calls. Exercise of a warrant causes shares of stock to be issued by the company that originally issued the warrants. When a call option is exercised, the stock comes from another investor who issued the call option. Another difference relates to the number of shares that can be purchased. Nearly all call options allow the option holder to buy 100 shares of stock, while warrants stipulate a whole range of shares. Some warrants give the holder the right to purchase two shares of stock; other warrants are for five shares. Each warrant is unique.

Are there any other differences?

While call options generally expire within a year from the date they are written, warrants may have a life of several years or more. In fact, a few warrants have been issued without an expiration date. Thus, a warrant owner generally has a much longer period of time to decide whether to purchase stock than does the owner of a call option. Like call options, warrants do not pay dividends or interest and do not give the holder a voice in the firm's business affairs, even though the warrant is issued by the company that is obligated to supply the stock.

Why would I want to buy a call option or a warrant rather than the common stock of the firm?

Options allow investors to obtain what finance people call *leverage*. Options and warrants permit you to control stock that has substantial market value with a relatively small amount of money. The earlier example of the Philip Morris option allowed an investment of $200 in the call option to control $4050 worth of Philip Morris stock (100 shares at a market value of $40.50 per share). This type of leverage allows you the possibility of doubling, tripling, or quadrupling your investment in a relatively short period of time. On the flip side, option ownership carries with it the real possibility that you may lose all the money you invest in an equally short period of time. Warrants also provide leverage, because a relatively modest investment gains control over a substantial amount of stock. Of course, the control lasts only until the option or warrant expires.

Is there any reason to buy a call option or warrant that allows me to buy stock at a price higher than the current market price?

An option that permits the purchase of stock at a price higher than the stock's current market price means betting (and *betting* is the appropriate term) on two things: (1) the market value of the stock will appreciate to a level above the price at which the option or warrant allows you to purchase the stock, and (2) the rise in price will occur before the call option or warrant expires. The option will expire without value if the stock price remains below the price at which you can exercise the call or warrant.

Are warrants as risky as options?

Warrants are risky investments but perhaps not quite so risky as options. In both cases, your entire investment may be lost if the underlying stock doesn't perform as you hope. Warrants give you somewhat more of a chance of success because they generally have longer lives than options. A longer time before an option expires makes it more likely you will be able to buy the underlying stock at a bargain price. On the downside, a longer life causes the premium to be higher, so a two- or three-year warrant will cost more to buy than a three-month call option with the same stock purchase price. Details aside, call options, put options, and warrants are all risky investments.

Will I be able to resell a warrant I purchase?

Warrants are traded like stocks and bonds. That is, most warrants have a secondary market of sellers and buyers. Although you will almost surely be able to resell a warrant, there is no way to determine ahead of time whether the price you receive will be higher or lower than the price you paid when you bought it. As long as the underlying stock increases in value, you will probably make a profit on the warrant. If the underlying stock declines in price or remains at the same level as when the warrant was purchased, you will probably have to sell the warrant for a lower price than you paid. In the meantime, no dividend or interest checks will have been coming in.

You mentioned earlier that bonds can be exchanged for shares of stock. How do these work?

Bonds that can be exchanged for shares of stock are called *convertible bonds*. Like ordinary bonds, these securities offer investors a steady stream of fixed semiannual interest payments in addition to the scheduled return of the principal amount of the bond. Interest and return of principal are the only payments that are promised by an ordinary bond. Convertible bonds have the added benefit of allowing bondholders to choose whether to swap their bonds for a specified number of shares of the issuer's common stock. The exchange is at the discretion of the investor, not the issuer.

Does ownership of convertible bonds have a downside?

The conversion privilege is a feature added to certain bond issues in order to allow the issuer to borrow funds at a reduced rate of interest. Thus, an investor who chooses to invest in a convertible bond will not receive as much interest income as when a similar bond without a conversion feature is purchased. At a time when a company's regular 20-year bonds pay 7-percent interest, a convertible bond with a similar maturity from the same firm might pay 4 percent or 5 percent in annual interest. The difference in yield between a regular bond and a convertible bond will depend on the likelihood that the convertible bonds will be converted. The bottom line for an investor is that the buyer of convertible bonds surrenders some interest income in exchange for the opportunity to participate in the firm's growth. The opportunity to participate in growth will prove profitable only if the firm's growth in revenues and profits is translated into a higher stock price.

If the stock price fails to increase and I choose not to convert the bond, will I eventually receive the principal amount of the bond?

Convertible bonds that remain outstanding until maturity will be redeemed just like other bonds that don't include a convertible feature. In fact, convertible bonds may be redeemed prior to the scheduled maturity if a call feature is included in the borrowing agreement. Payment of principal at redemption will be to whoever owns the bond on the date the bond is redeemed. The maturity date and call dates are determined at the time the bond is issued, and these dates will remain the same regardless of how many times a bond is resold.

Can you provide an example of a convertible bond?

Suppose a $1000 principal amount bond has a coupon rate of 5 percent and a maturity date of 2020. The borrowing agreement stipulates that each bond is convertible into 40 shares of the issuer's common stock at any time prior to maturity. The bond will pay an investor $50 annual interest (5 percent of $1000) until 2020, when the issuer is required to redeem the security and repay the $1000 face value. If the firm's common stock trades for $20 per share, a bondholder will have no interest in trading the bond for stock because the 40 shares to be received in the swap have a value of just $800 (40 shares worth $20 per share). However, if the company is successful and the price of the stock increases to $50, the bond could be traded for $2000 in stock (40 shares worth $50 per share). The bonds can be exchanged for shares of stock so the bonds rise and fall in value in response to increases and decreases in the price of the stock.

What about interest payments on the bond?

As long as the bond isn't converted into stock, the issuer must continue to pay interest to the bondholder. However, interest payments will cease once the bond is exchanged for stock. In addition, the issuer will not have to repay the principal amount borrowed when bonds have been converted into stock. For practical purposes, the bonds have disappeared once they have been exchanged for shares of common stock. The surrendered bonds are no longer in investor hands or on the issuer's financial statements. The debt is no longer owed to anyone. While interest payments on a bond cease when the bond is converted, the firm must pay dividends on new shares of stock that are issued in trade for the converted bonds. This assumes the company is indeed paying a dividend on its stock.

If I exchange a convertible bond for shares of stock, can I later reverse the exchange?

Exchange a convertible bond for shares of stock and you are stuck with the stock. Of course, you can subsequently sell the stock to another investor, but you cannot reverse the conversion. At the time a bond is converted, you give up all future rights to interest payments and to the principal amount of the bond at maturity. The bottom line is that a conversion causes you to shift from being one of the firm's creditors to being one of the firm's owners. Keep in mind that convertible bonds tend to increase in value along with the stock, so no advantage generally exists to converting a bond for the underlying stock until the bond nears maturity or is redeemed by the issuer. You are generally better off keeping the bond and continuing to receive interest payments that are likely to be higher than dividend payments on the stock you would receive in exchange.

Is a convertible bond risky to own?

Convertible bonds tend to be more risky than regular bonds from the same issuer but less risky than if you are a stockholder in the company. Interest rates, maturity length, and the credit quality of the issuer all influence the price of a regular bond. The price of a convertible bond is influenced by these factors and also by the price of the issuer's common stock, a variable that is often quite volatile. A convertible bond becomes particularly risky to own when the underlying stock has exhibited a substantial price increase, thereby causing the bond to sell at a big premium to face value. At this point the bond value will become more volatile as the bond price begins to closely track the stock value. A 10-percent decline in the stock price is likely to cause nearly a 10-percent decline in the value of the convertible bond trading at a big premium to face value. The promise of receiving a $1000 payment of principal at maturity is likely to provide little comfort if you are holding a bond that trades in the market at a price of $1700. In addition, convertible securities often have substantial credit risk (e.g., the risk that the promised interest and principal may not be paid on schedule) and a correspondingly low credit rating. Some convertible bonds are of such low credit quality that the issuers would have difficulty borrowing money unless investors were also given an ownership stake in the company.

Can I lose money if I purchase a convertible bond?

Several things could cause you to lose money. If the issuer encounters financial difficulty, you may not receive the principal at maturity. You may also find that interest payments cease. If the company does poorly but stays afloat, you are likely to find that the firm's stock never gains much value, which means you are stuck with a bond that pays below-market interest. You will get your money back, but only if you stick it out to maturity. Another possibility is that market rates of interest will rise, thereby putting downward pressure on the value of your bond. The price you receive may be less than you paid if you are required to sell the bond prior to maturity.

What are futures?

Futures are contracts for delivery of a specified asset. Historically, the contracts designated the delivery of agricultural commodities such as wheat, oats, corn, and cotton and livestock such as cattle and hogs. The contracts were useful as a method for farmers and their customers to guarantee the prices of goods with very volatile values. For example, a farmer could use a futures contract to guarantee the price to be received for a crop that would be harvested several months in the future. Likewise, a buyer of the commodity could use a contract to guarantee the price that would be paid for a crop that was not scheduled for delivery for several months.

So a futures contract is nothing other than a contract for future delivery?

Exactly. A person who sells a futures contract guarantees to deliver the specified item, and the person who buys the contract guarantees to accept delivery of the specified item. Someone who sells a contract for coffee agrees to deliver a certain quantity of coffee beans to a specified location on a certain date. The person who buys the contract agrees to take delivery of the same coffee on that date. Both the quantity and quality of the coffee are specified.

What if I don't have coffee to deliver or I don't want to buy coffee?

You don't have to actually make or take delivery to trade a futures contract. You can buy a contract (guarantee to take delivery) and subsequently sell the contract prior to the specified delivery date (called the *settlement date*). Selling a contract you already own means you no longer have an obligation to take delivery. Likewise, you could sell a futures contract (guarantee to make delivery) and subsequently purchase an identical contract. Purchasing a contract you have sold means you no longer have an obligation to make delivery. In each case noted above, you have eliminated your obligation by undertaking a second transaction that was the opposite of your initial transaction. In the first instance, you sold something you had purchased. In the second instance, you bought back something you had sold.

Do these contracts involve large amounts of money?

Futures contracts generally involve substantial amounts of whatever is to be delivered. For example, one contract for coffee stipulates the delivery of 37,500 pounds. A contract for orange juice concentrate requires delivery of 15,000 pounds. In currencies, a futures contract for Canadian dollars stipulates the delivery of $100,000. The dollar value of a contract depends on the value of whatever is to be delivered. If orange juice is selling for approximately $1.10 per pound, then one contract for 15,000 pounds will have a market value of $16,500. Keep in mind that to purchase a contract, you generally need to put up only a fraction of its value.

Is a futures contract an example of a derivative?

Like an option, a futures contract derives its value from something else. For example, the value of a futures contract on cotton is based on the value of the cotton required to satisfy the contract. Likewise, the value of a contract on a stock average is determined primarily by the current level of the average. If the stock average increases, the value of the contract will increase. Thus, making money on a futures contract requires that you correctly project changes in the value of the underlying asset.

Can I purchase a futures contract through a regular brokerage firm?

Orders to purchase or sell a futures contract are given to a broker, who transmits the order to the floor of the exchange where the contract is traded. Futures contracts are traded on exchanges where market makers specialize in these types of contracts. In other words, futures contracts are not traded on the floor of a stock exchange. Many brokerage firm offices employ one or more brokers who specialize in futures contracts. Brokers who deal mostly in stocks and bonds often have little knowledge of futures contracts.

Why would I want to trade futures contracts if I'm not interested in the underlying commodity?

You might want to buy or sell a futures contract in order to make money on the changing value of the contract. You would profit either by purchasing a contract that subsequently goes up in value or selling a contract that subsequently goes down in value. Trading futures contracts in this manner means you are speculating on the future price changes of the underlying commodity. If you believe wheat prices are going to increase, then you would consider buying a futures contract on wheat. If wheat does indeed increase in price, you should make a profit from the contract, which will increase in value. On the other hand, if you believe that wheat prices will decline, you would sell a contract on wheat. If wheat prices fall, you should be able to repurchase an identical futures contract at a price lower than you received.

Are futures contracts available for anything other than agricultural commodities?

In addition to agricultural commodities, futures contracts are traded for several metals, petroleum, interest rates, foreign currencies, and stock indexes. You can utilize futures contracts to speculate on the price movements of such things as copper, gasoline, gold, U.S Treasury bonds, or natural gas; changes in the value of currencies like Swiss francs or French francs; or changes in indexes like the Dow Jones Industrial Average. Wall Street has traveled a long way from the farm economy.

Should I become involved with futures contracts?

Probably not. Futures contracts tend to be risky investments, and you are likely to be playing in this game at a disadvantage. Many of the buyers and sellers of futures contracts are professionals who maintain close touch with the markets for the underlying assets. In other words, most people who trade futures on coffee have a strong interest in and knowledge of the coffee market. Likewise, traders of futures contracts for gold tend to be very knowledgeable about the gold market. These are the people you must compete with when you become involved with futures contracts. Futures contracts can be very alluring investment vehicles because they offer the potential to earn such high returns very quickly. The downside of these investments is that they also offer the potential to lose so much so quickly.

You mentioned earlier that my broker may offer certificates of deposit. Why should I prefer to invest in these through my broker instead of using a bank, credit union, or savings and loan?

Many brokerage firms offer certificates of deposit through an agreement with several banks or savings and loans that actually issue the certificates. These CDs are generally sold in units of $1000 and are insured up to $100,000 by the Federal Deposit Insurance Corporation. Investments in CDs through a brokerage firm generally entail no commissions because fees are absorbed by the issuing financial institution. The key factor as to whether to buy a certificate of deposit through your broker is whether you can obtain a higher yield compared to CDs offered directly by issuing financial institutions. You may also find it convenient to maintain CDs in the same account in which you hold stocks and bonds. Most brokerage firms maintain a secondary market in the certificates of deposit they broker so that you have the ability to sell a CD prior to maturity. Of course, the price you receive in a sale will depend on what has happened to market interest rates subsequent to the date the certificate was purchased.

CHAPTER

How Do I Locate a Good Broker and Open an Account?

Chapter summary

A broker serves as your connection with Wall Street. Brokers can provide advice, transmit orders, locate information, and resolve the snafus that will almost certainly occur from time to time. The quality of brokers and the firms that employ them varies widely. Some brokers provide reduced services at a substantial savings in commissions. Other brokers are employed by firms that offer every imaginable investment product and service. Trading via the Internet bypasses brokers and has become increasingly popular as a low-cost method for buying and selling securities. This chapter discusses the services that brokers provide and the fees they charge. It also addresses some of the decisions you will face when an account is opened.

Do I have to go through a brokerage firm to buy or sell securities?

In most cases you will need to employ the services of a retail brokerage firm to buy or sell securities. Brokerage firms have access to the over-the-counter dealer network and to trading floors of the various exchanges. In addition, many brokerage firms package and sell their own financial products. Some securities can be purchased without using a brokerage firm. A limited number of corporations sell stock directly to individual investors, but most do not (see Table 8-1). Also, many mutual funds sell shares of their stock to individual investors, who are thereby able to save a sales fee. Mutual funds are discussed in a later chapter.

How do I locate a brokerage firm?

Brokerage firms are often listed in the local telephone directory yellow pages, generally under *stock and bond brokers*. If you reside in a small town without a local brokerage firm, check the financial section of your local newspaper or the paper of a larger nearby town. You might also visit a library and check the telephone books of nearby towns. Many brokerage firms have toll-free telephone numbers for out-of-town customers, and nearly all the firms will accept collect calls. Most metropolitan newspapers and financial publications, such as *The Wall Street Journal* and *Investor's Daily*, contain numerous brokerage firm advertisements. Of course, you can always ask friends for their recommendations.

Does the brokerage firm I use really matter?

Your choice of a brokerage firm can be important, especially with regard to the commissions you will be required to pay. Each brokerage firm has its own schedule of commissions,

TABLE 8-1

Partial list of firms with direct stock purchase programs.

Ameritech	800-774-4117	Merck	800-774-4117
British Airways	800-711-6475	Mobil	800-648-9291
Chevron	800-774-4117	Nippon Telegraph	800-711-6475
Disney	818-560-1000	Owens Corning	800-472-2210
Enron	800-662-7662	Penney (J.C.)	800-565-2576
Equitable Cos.	800-774-4117	Procter & Gamble	800-764-7483
Exxon	800-252-1800	Reader's Digest	800-242-4653
Food Lion	800-232-9530	Sears, Roebuck	888-732-7788
Gillette	800-730-4001	Sony	800-711-6475
Hillenbrand Ind.	800-774-4117	Southern Co	800-774-4117
Home Depot	800-774-4117	Tenneco	800-446-2617
Lucent Technologies	888-582-3686	Texaco	800-822-7096
Mattel	888-909-9922	Unilever	800-774-4117
McDonald's	800-774-4117	Wal-Mart	800-438-6278

which means that depending on the firm chosen, it is possible to pay widely varying fees for the same type of transaction. Buying or selling 100 shares of a $40 stock may involve a commission of $100 or more at some firms and $20 or $25 at other firms. Larger transactions involving more money can produce even wider commission differences, depending on the firm you choose. The more money you expect to invest and the more trades you are likely to undertake, the more commission rates should be considered when you select a brokerage firm.

How can I find out about a firm's commission schedule?

Ask a broker about the fees the firm charges for the particular types of trades you are most likely to undertake. For example, if you plan to occasionally buy and sell a couple of hundred shares of stock, ask about the commission for 200 shares of stock priced at different levels. If you plan to invest mostly in mutual funds, ask about the sales or redemption fees that will be charged. Brokerage firms also employ different fee schedules for bonds, so ask about this if you plan to invest in debt securities. Ask about fees for trading options if you are likely to become involved in these investments. Keep in mind that commission rates are negotiable, especially if you expect to be making substantial investments or you plan to actively trade stocks or options.

Is there anything else I should consider?

Brokerage firms differ with respect to the types and quality of the services they provide. Firms that charge relatively low commissions may provide a reduced level of personal service or a limited array of financial products compared to brokerage firms with higher fees. Even brokerage firms that charge relatively high commissions differ in the services and products they provide. Your choices may be limited if you are determined to use a local broker whom you can occasionally drop in and visit. On the other hand, if a personal relationship with a broker is unimportant, your choice of firms is wide open.

How do I locate a brokerage firm that offers low commissions?

Brokerage firms that offer reduced fees are generally called *discount brokers*. It is not difficult to locate a discount brokerage firm. If you live in a metropolitan area, several of these firms are likely to be listed in the telephone yellow pages or the business

section of your local newspaper. Discount brokers also advertise on television and in national financial publications such as
Money, Kiplinger's Personal Finance, The Wall Street Journal,
and *Barron's.* Call several of these firms and request a kit for
opening an account. The kit will detail each firm's services and
fee schedule. In fact, you might want to obtain one of these
schedules just so you can compare it with the fees you are
quoted at a full-service firm.

Should I consider using a discount brokerage firm?

Discount brokers can be a good choice if you feel you can get by
without relying on the advice of a broker to help you decide
which securities to buy and sell. Perhaps you regularly read an
investment advisory service such as the *Value Line Investment
Survey* or an investment newsletter to help with your investment
choices. Discount brokers are set up to transact orders, but most
of these firms do not maintain a research department and do not
offer advice on which securities to buy and sell. In other words,
you generally obtain a reduced commission (compared to full-
service firms) by accepting a reduced level of service.

Are all discount brokers pretty much the same?

Actually, this segment of the industry includes firms with a
wide range of fees, products, and services. Some discount firms
are much like full-service firms in that they offer a wide variety
of products and have branch offices in many of the major cities.
Firms such as Charles Schwab and Quick & Reilly fall into this
category. Many discount firms operate from a single office and
conduct nearly all their business via a toll-free telephone number. These firms, often called *deep discounters,* generally offer
commissions that are half or less of those charged by the bigger
discount firms. Avoiding the considerable expense of branch
offices and a research department produces a low overhead and

permits these firms to offer low commissions and still make a profit. Yet another category includes firms with offices in several cities but with commission rates between the large national discount firms and the deep discounters. Table 8-2 represents a partial listing of discount brokerage firms.

What about brokerage firms that offer trades via the Internet?

Trading securities on the Internet is a relatively new activity, but it is growing very rapidly. Brokerage firms on the Internet offer some of the very lowest commissions you will find anywhere. Thus, doing business with a firm that offers Internet trading is both convenient and cheap. Like other discount brokers, these firms execute orders but generally don't provide advice. See Table 8-3 for some of the largest on-line brokerage firms.

What if I'm a novice investor?

With limited knowledge of Wall Street products and practices, you are probably best served by utilizing a full-service broker-

TABLE 8-2

Selected list of discount brokerage firms.

Brown & Company	800-822-2829
Charles Schwab	800-648-5300
Fidelity Brokerage Services	800-343-3548
Muriel Siebert & Company	800-786-2511
Scottrade	800-619-7283
Seaport Securities	800-732-7678
StockCross	800-225-6196
Waterhouse Securities, Inc.	800-841-2424

TABLE 8-3

List of large on-line brokerage firms.

Firm	Website
Ameritrade	www.ameritrade.com
Charles Schwab	www.schwab.com
Datek Online	www.datek.com
Discover Brokerage Direct	www.dbdirect.com
DLJdirect	www.dljdirect.com
Dreyfus Brokerage Services	www.edreyfus.com
E*Trade	www.etrade.com
Fidelity Investments	www.fidelity.com
National Discount Brokers	www.ndb.com
Quick & Reilly	www.quick-reilly.com
SiebertNet	www.msiebert.com
Suretrade	www.suretrade.com
Waterhouse Investor Services	www.waterhouse.com

age firm, especially if you will be occasionally investing relatively small amounts of money. Although the fees at full-service firms are higher than at discount brokers, the counseling provided by most full-service firms is likely to be worth the extra expense you will incur. Some investors choose to open one account at a discount broker and a second account at a full-service firm. Whether or not you want to do this will depend in part on the amount of money you expect to be investing.

How will I come into contact with a broker when I visit a local firm?

The receptionist is the first person you are likely to encounter when you walk into a brokerage firm. You should inform the receptionist you would like to talk with a broker about open-ing an account. Depending on your preferences, you may want to add any preferences regarding whether the broker is female or male, young or older, new or experienced, well-versed in bonds or stocks, and so forth. It is to your benefit and the benefit of the brokerage firm that you be matched with a broker who is compatible. Being unhappy with your broker means it is more likely you will eventually move the account somewhere else. In general, younger brokers are more likely to advocate a relatively aggressive investment policy, especially if the broker hasn't experienced a serious bear market since beginning in the business.

What should I say to the broker?

A broker will want to know what type of investor you are. This will include some idea of your income, assets, and investment goals. If you plan to rely on your broker's advice, be prepared to supply more information. For example, you should provide in-formation on your family status and why you are investing. A broker cannot provide useful investment advice without the es-sentials of your financial status. You will also be asked to com-plete and sign some papers in order to open an account.

Will I be able to buy or sell a security the same day I open the account?

You will be able to enter an order immediately after opening an account. Some firms require that new customers make a deposit of cash or securities into their account prior to the first trade. Brokerage firms are sometimes concerned that new customers may enter an order but fail to settle up when the money is due, or in the case of an order to sell, when the securities are due to be delivered. Requirement of a deposit of funds will depend in part on whether the broker knows you and the quality of the references you list on your account application.

What are the rules on payment?

You will be required to pay for stocks and bonds within three business days of a transaction. The date that payment is due is called the *settlement date*. Purchase stock on Monday and your broker must receive payment by Thursday. Sell stock on Friday and you must deliver the certificate by the following Wednesday. A legal holiday extends the payment date or the security delivery date by one day. Weekends are not considered in the three-day calculation. Payment for options is required on the business day following the transaction. Remember, the settlement date is when your payment is due at the brokerage firm, not the date on which you put your check in the mail. Payment by a brokerage firm to you is made on these same terms. That is, proceeds from the sale of a security are due to you three business days following the date of the transaction. Sell bonds on Wednesday and the proceeds are credited to your account on Monday.

If I am interested in investing but don't know what to buy, will the broker have some ideas to get me started?

One thing you don't have to worry about is the possibility a broker won't have any ideas on how to invest your money. Brokers earn their keep by coming up with both proven and innovative ways to put your money to work. The broker is likely to initially suggest that you invest in a mutual fund, especially if you have only a modest amount of money to commit. An initial investment in one or more mutual funds is often a good idea that provides some diversification along with professional management of your funds. The downside to buying shares of a mutual fund involves the fees you are likely to have to pay. Be certain to ask about the fees of the

particular funds your broker recommends, and then compare these
fees to those charged by other mutual funds.

Any hints on how I should react to the broker's recommendations?

You can learn a lot about a broker at this first meeting, so keep
your eyes and ears open. You will probably be best served by
taking home the broker's recommendations to give yourself
time to digest what happened during the encounter. You certainly have no obligation to give your broker an order at the time
your account is opened.

Should I visit more than one broker?

There is certainly nothing wrong with soliciting several opin-
ions on where your money should be invested, especially if you
have a substantial amount of money to invest. You should feel
free to solicit the advice of two or three brokers before deciding
with whom to entrust your money. Choosing a broker is one of
the most important decisions you will make, so you may as well
take time to make the correct choice the first time.

Are all brokerage accounts similar?

All brokerage accounts are not the same, although most brokerage
firms offer a similar array of accounts. One decision you will be
required to make is whether to open a cash account or a margin account. A margin account allows you to purchase securities with a
greater value than the money you put up. The remainder of the
purchase amount is borrowed through a loan arranged by the broker. A cash account requires that you pay in full for securities you
purchase. If you decide to open a margin account, you will be required to sign an agreement that spells out (in very small print) the

details of the account, including the method by which interest is calculated on money that is borrowed.

How does a margin account work?

Suppose you have $6000 of your own money and are interested in purchasing shares of the common stock of a particular company. The stock currently sells at a price of $30 per share, which means you can afford to buy $6000/$30, or 200 shares. A margin account permits you to borrow up to 50 percent of the amount invested (the percentage is established by the Federal Reserve, the U.S. government agency that controls domestic credit and monetary policy), which means you can use borrowed money to purchase additional shares of stock. Taking maximum advantage of margin would allow you to purchase $12,000 worth of stock, half with borrowed money and half with your own money.

Do I have to pay interest on the borrowed money?

Interest will be charged on the money you borrow. The clock begins on the date the money is borrowed and stops on the date the loan is repaid, typically through the sale of stock purchased with the proceeds of the loan. The lowest rate will generally go to customers with the greatest amount of money borrowed. The rate of interest on a loan can fluctuate, since it is tied to a short-term interest rate such as the broker call rate or the prime rate charged by commercial banks on loans to their best customers. The fact that the interest rate can change during the period of the loan presents one of the dangers of a margin account. Of course, the rate can go down as well as up. If you plan to open a margin account and use securities as collateral for loans, you should inquire about the brokerage firm's policy regarding interest charges because not all firms charge the same rate.

Does having a margin account mean I have to borrow?

Just because you choose a margin account rather than a cash account does not mean you are required to borrow when you purchase stocks and bonds. In fact, your broker will be happy to accept full payment in cash for each and every transaction, even though you have a margin account. A margin account only gives you the option of borrowing.

Is it risky to buy securities with borrowed money?

It is very risky to buy securities with borrowed money. Using borrowed funds to double the amount of stock you purchase also doubles the gains and losses compared to paying in full and buying half as much stock. In the above example, assume the price of the stock rose from $30 to $40. Paying in cash and buying 200 shares means you would have made a $2000 profit (200 shares times the $10 gain in price). Borrowing so that you could buy twice as much stock means you would have made a profit of $4000 (400 shares times the $10 gain in price). Had the price of the stock declined from $30 to $20, your losses on the same purchases would have been $2000 and $4000, respectively. In other words, you would lose $2000 with 200 shares and $4000 with 400 shares. None of these profit and loss calculations take into account interest you would have to pay on the money borrowed or any dividends you may have received on the stock you bought.

So what's the bottom line?

The bottom line is that buying on margin leverages your investment and multiplies gains and losses. In good times you benefit and in bad times you suffer. You will look like a genius if the stock goes up and like a fool if the stock goes down. Novice investors and conservative investors should stay away from buying stock on margin.

Will I be allowed to borrow against securities in my brokerage account and use the proceeds for something other than investing?

Most stocks and bonds serve as excellent collateral for a loan, since they are easy to value and easy to liquidate. Securities held in a margin account can be used as collateral for a loan as long as you are not already borrowed up to the maximum allowed. The proceeds of this type of loan can be used for any purpose, including buying a new Corvette, taking a vacation, or paying blackmail. Borrowing is as easy as asking your broker to send a check for a specific sum of money. Keep in mind that the securities to serve as collateral must be held in your brokerage account before you can arrange a loan from your broker. Securities being held at home or in a lockbox must be delivered to your broker before you can borrow against them. Of course, you don't have to borrow from a brokerage firm. You could take certificates for shares of stock to a commercial bank and arrange for a loan from the bank.

Are cash accounts and margin accounts the only account options offered?

These are the two main types of brokerage accounts. Some brokerage firms also offer *wrap accounts*. These are specialized accounts in which the broker matches you with an independent money manager who will decide how to invest your money. The account wraps all expenses, including commissions, periodic reports, and management expense, into one comprehensive fee that tends to run about 3 percent of the value of the assets being managed. These accounts nearly always require a minimum amount of assets, generally about $100,000. The percentage fee is often reduced for very large accounts.

Is any other type of account available?

Some investors sign a power of attorney that permits their brokers to buy and sell securities without consulting the investors. This type of account, called a *discretionary account,* is fraught with possibilities for abuse because the broker has free reign over assets held in the account. Most people would find it in their best interest to avoid opening a discretionary account.

If I choose to open a cash account, can I later change it to a margin account?

There is no problem in changing from a cash account to a margin account, although you will be required to sign a margin agreement. Likewise, nothing keeps you from converting from a margin account to a cash account as long as no margin loan is outstanding. Simply call your broker and request the change. There is no charge for such a conversion, and the entire process will be handled internally by the firm.

Can I open more than one brokerage account?

Many investors maintain more than one brokerage account. For example, you may want to have one account at a discount brokerage firm and a second account at a full-service broker. Likewise, having accounts at more than one full-service broker would allow you to have access to additional sources of investment research. Having more than a single account is especially valuable when you invest in bonds because each firm will have a different inventory of bonds available for sale. Some individuals choose to open more than one account with the same broker. Perhaps you want an account in your own name and a separate account in joint name with your spouse or your children. Keep in mind that multiple accounts will generally entail more account maintenance fees than having only one account.

How often will I receive information about my account?

Brokerage firms typically send customers a statement in any month in which investment activity has occurred in the account. Buy or sell stock or bonds in March and you will receive a March statement. Customers with inactive accounts generally receive statements each quarter. A statement will provide information on assets being held in the account along with account activity for the period.

Will most brokerage firms be able to transact an order on any exchange or in the over-the-counter market?

Any full-service or discount brokerage firm will be able to enter orders on any of the national or regional exchanges or in the over-the-counter market. From the standpoint of carrying out orders for most securities, including stocks, bonds, options, and warrants, nearly all brokerage firms will offer virtually identical service.

Will I receive certificates for the securities that I purchase?

One of the questions you will be asked when opening a brokerage account is whether you want securities delivered to you, i.e., sent to your home via mail, or kept in your account. Stocks and bonds purchased on margin must be retained in your account because the securities serve as collateral for the margin loan. You can always ask for delivery of securities that are not being utilized as collateral.

Should I choose to have securities delivered or kept in my account?

It is certainly more convenient to have securities kept in your account. Leaving securities with your broker means that your brokerage company, not you, is responsible for safekeeping of the certificates and for collecting dividends and interest payments. You won't have to worry about losing a certificate or delivering a certificate to your broker when the stock or bond is sold. Having securities held in your account is less trouble for you, especially when you use an out-of-town broker and would be required to send certificates via registered mail.

Are there any advantages to taking delivery of securities?

Having certificates in your possession allows you to utilize a different brokerage firm to sell a security than was used to buy the security. You may be able to save on commissions by selling your stock through a discount broker, for example. Holding certificates also means dividends and interest will be mailed directly to you rather than to your brokerage company. This is a particular advantage if your brokerage company doesn't immediately sweep cash balances into a money market fund. Perhaps the biggest advantage of holding shares of stock is that it allows you to enroll in the firm's dividend reinvestment plan. Shares held in brokerage accounts are generally ineligible for dividend reinvestment plans.

What happens if I lose a stock or bond certificate?

Lost certificates must be replaced. Replacing a lost certificate requires that you post a bond costing about 2 percent of the security's market value. Lose a certificate for 500 shares of a $40 stock and you will have to purchase a $20,000 bond at a cost to you of approximately $400. This is a one-time expense on your part. The company that issued the lost certificate or the company's transfer agent will be able to provide instructions on how to obtain a replacement certificate. Keep in mind that choosing to have securities held in your account relieves you of worrying about certificates being lost.

Do brokerage firms charge a fee for maintaining an account?

Each brokerage company has its own unique policies regarding account maintenance fees. Some firms levy an annual fee of $25 to $50 on nearly all their accounts. Other firms levy an annual maintenance fee only for inactive accounts. For example, a firm may require one or two trades per year in an account in order to avoid the annual fee. Still other firms don't levy an account maintenance fee of any type. You should discuss the firm's policy regarding fees before opening an account.

How about a charge for having securities delivered?

Some brokerage firms charge a fee to deliver a certificate. This charge will be in addition to any monthly or annual maintenance fee that is charged. Other firms will deliver a certificate without charge. If you intend to have certificates delivered rather than kept in your account, this fee may be an important consideration in choosing a firm. As an aside, some bond issuers do not issue certificates, but rather credit bonds in what is called *book-entry form*. No delivery is possible if you purchase book-entry bonds.

What happens to dividend and interest payments on securities held in my account?

Interest and dividends from securities held in your brokerage account will be paid into the account. The same is true of proceeds from the sale of securities. Some brokerage firms provide for an automatic sweep of cash into a money market fund so that the funds will earn a nominal amount of interest. The sweep may occur daily, weekly, monthly, or quarterly, depending on the firm. A minimum cash balance is sometimes required for an automatic sweep. You can leave standing instructions to have cash balances forwarded to you, in which case most firms will send checks on the first day of the month following receipt of dividends and interest. Again, these are important details you should ask about before an account is opened. It is to your advantage to have an account with automatic sweeps of any and all cash balances. The sooner cash is converted into an interest-earning asset, the more income you will earn.

What about voting shares of stock held in my account?

The brokerage firm will forward all financial reports and proxies when securities are being held in your account. In fact, the company in which you own stock or bonds is unlikely to know you are one of its owners or creditors. Forwarding means you should receive all of the financial reports that are normally sent directly by the company, although these may arrive a little late. Proxies are returned to the brokerage firm, which forwards the voting instructions to the company that sent the proxy. Having the brokerage firm hold your securities effectively places a shield between you and the company in which you are an owner or creditor.

A friend told me about a special brokerage account that includes a credit card and a checking account. How can I obtain one of these?

Some of the larger brokerage firms offer accounts in which all cash balances are automatically swept into a money market fund. For example, Merrill Lynch has its Cash Management Account and Salomon Smith Barney its Financial Management Account. Most other large brokerage firms offer similar accounts with different trademarked names. These accounts fall under the generic title of *asset management accounts* (see Figure 8-1). Balances in an asset management account can be accessed either by check or by a credit card, both of which are supplied when an account is opened. Some firms include a debit card with the account and offer a credit card as an extra-cost option. The accounts generally allow unlimited check-writing, with checks supplied free of charge. Asset management accounts are margin accounts that permit you to use the credit card or checks to borrow against securities held in the account. These special accounts often entail an annual fee of from $50 to $100, although the fee is sometimes waived for customers with large account balances. As an account holder, you will generally receive a more elaborate monthly statement and end-of-the-year report than if you had a regular account.

Are asset management accounts aimed at big investors?

Asset management accounts are useful for big and small investors because they combine so many activities and assets into a single account. Consolidating all this information simplifies recordkeeping and may result in lower fees, especially if you currently pay an annual fee for a credit card and a monthly charge for your checking account. Most asset management accounts require a minimum initial deposit of securities and cash (generally $20,000), although the value can fall below this level after an account is activated. The annual charge to maintain an asset management account ranges from $50 to $100, depending on the firm. Investors with substantial assets can sometimes have the annual maintenance charge waived.

FIGURE 8-1

Comprehensive asset management accounts.

Merrill Lynch introduced the first comprehensive brokerage account, termed the Cash Management Account (CMA), in the late 1970s. The CMA was soon imitated by a number of other brokerage firms as asset management accounts gained popularity during the 1980s. The limited number of brokerage firms that offer this type of account do so under various trademarked names, but the accounts have similar features that generally include:

1. Automatic daily or weekly sweeps of any cash in the account into an interest-bearing money market fund sponsored by the brokerage firm. Some firms provide daily sweeps (an advantage), while other firms sweep weekly unless an especially large amount of cash is involved. Most firms provide investors with a choice of several money market funds, including a regular fund, a tax-exempt fund, and a fund that invests only in U.S. government securities.

2. Unlimited check-writing privileges against money market fund balances. Funds in the account earn interest until checks are presented for payment, at which time shares in the fund are sold.

3. Automatic investment of dividends and interest from securities maintained in the account and proceeds from any securities sales into the money market fund.

4. A comprehensive monthly account statement and an end-of-year statement of itemized income items for tax reporting.

5. A debit or credit card, with purchase amounts from card use deducted from the account's money market fund. Shares in the money market fund are sold to produce a cash balance that is used to pay the charge. Most firms provide a debit card (money market fund shares are sold when the purchase

Continued

FIGURE 8-1

Concluded

---

amount is presented for payment) as part of the account and offer a credit card at an additional annual fee of $25 or $35. With a credit card, shares of the money market fund are sold at the end of the month to pay for card purchases.

6. Account insurance from private insurers is provided beyond the $500,000 coverage of the Securities Investor Protection Corporation.

7. Margin loans use as collateral the securities being held in the account. Checks and the debit or credit card can be used to access credit.

Is my brokerage account insured in the same manner as my bank account?

Insurance coverage applies to financial losses you may suffer as a result of a collapse of your brokerage firm but not to losses you may incur from declines in the value of your securities. In other words, the insurance doesn't protect you against poor investment decisions, but it does protect you against a financially unstable brokerage firm. In 1970, Congress established the Securities Investor Protection Corporation (SIPC) as part of the Securities Investor Protection Act. The insurance fund covers each account against losses of up to $500,000, including a maximum of $100,000 in cash. The SIPC is similar to the Federal Deposit Insurance Corporation that insures accounts at your local bank. Some brokerage firms carry additional insurance from private companies so that individual accounts may be insured for several millions of dollars.

Will securities in my brokerage account continue to have value even if the brokerage firm fails?

The SIPC is designed to take care of losses up to the specified limits in the event your brokerage firm fails and regulatory authorities are unable to locate your securities or cash. Make certain the value of securities held in your account doesn't exceed SIPC limits unless the brokerage firm has additional insurance. You should not be charged for additional insurance protection that a brokerage firm provides.

Should I open an account in my name only or in joint name with someone else?

This is a tough call and varies depending on individual circumstances. Having an account in joint name is more flexible because either person normally has access to the account and can make investment decisions. A joint account is also likely to reduce administrative fees compared to having two individual accounts. A joint account generally ensures a relatively smooth transition of assets to the survivor in the event that you or your spouse should meet an untimely death. On the other hand, a joint account sometimes results in a less-than-optimal distribution of assets at the death of one of the account holders, especially if children are involved and the account is substantial. Also keep in mind that several types of joint accounts exist.

What types of joint accounts are available?

The most common type of joint account, especially among married couples, is *joint tenancy with rights of survivorship,* often abbreviated as JTWROS. With this type of account, all property passes directly to the surviving account holder in the event of the death of the other. This account designation may produce some difficulties in the event of a divorce. Another type of joint account is known as *tenancy in common*. With this account each party's interest is independent of the other. Thus, in the event of the death of one party, only the assets of that tenant pass to his or her estate. The surviving tenant then has sole ownership of the remaining portion of the account.

What if I become unhappy with my broker?

You should encounter no problem if you wish to transfer your account from one broker to another within the same firm. Merely inform the office manager that you would like to have your account assigned to someone else. You will probably also want to discuss why you are dissatisfied and what you expect from a new broker. You may discover that you prefer to work with a broker who is more experienced, more conservative, or will spend more time with you than your current broker. You may also decide that you would prefer a broker who has greater knowledge of a particular type of investment in which you are interested.

Will I be able to move my account to another firm?

It is certainly possible to have your account moved to another firm, although the process can sometimes take longer than you might hope. If all your securities are already in your possession, i.e., you have taken delivery of the securities you have purchased, then you merely need to withdraw any cash, close your existing account, and open an account somewhere else. If securities are being held in your existing account, the process is somewhat more complicated, although the new firm should be able to take care of the paperwork and transferring the assets. One course of action is for you to ask your broker for delivery of all the securities in the existing account. Upon receipt, the certificates can be deposited in your new account. Another choice is to request that all the assets being held in your current account be transferred to your account at the new firm. This type of transfer should be completed within a week or two if you are dealing with mainline brokerage firms. Moving an account from a small firm can sometimes prove more troublesome.

Can all of the assets in my account be transferred to another account?

You may experience difficulty if you own a proprietary investment product such as shares of a mutual fund sold only by the firm you are leaving. However, it is now possible to transfer many of these investments from one firm to another.

CHAPTER

How Do I Interpret Financial Information?

Chapter summary

Most financial information is not difficult to interpret if you are able to wade through the slang, acronyms, and abbreviations. A little study can go a long way toward understanding the complexities of security price listings and market activity. This chapter is devoted to locating and interpreting some of the most frequently sought financial data that regularly appear in the business sections of most large newspapers.

Where can I locate price quotations for stocks that I own?

Widely held securities of large corporations are generally included in listings for the New York Stock Exchange. The

NYSE listing is always a good place to begin a search unless you are looking for the stock price of a small regional firm. Similar quotations are provided for stocks listed on the American Stock Exchange and actively.traded stocks in the over-the-counter market. All of these listings are carried by national dailies such as *The Wall Street Journal* and *Investor's Business Daily* and in the financial sections of most metropolitan newspapers. If you are unable to locate *The Wall Street Journal* or *Investor's Business Daily* at a newsstand, try your local library. *Barron's* publishes more comprehensive listings each Monday on a weekly basis.

How will I determine whether a stock is traded on the New York Stock Exchange, the American Stock Exchange, or in the over-the-counter market?

One obvious way to determine where a stock is traded is to look in each of the three listings noted above. Large, widely held stocks generally trade on the NYSE. In fact, the NYSE listing is probably a good place to begin searching for a stock price. If you are unable to locate the stock on the New York Stock Exchange, try the over-the-counter Nasdaq listing. The American Stock Exchange should be your next choice. If the stock has been issued by a very small company, you may be unable to locate the price in any of these three listings.

Can I use my computer to locate stock prices on the Internet?

With access to the Internet, you can obtain stock prices without having to know whether the stocks are traded on an exchange or in the over-the-counter market. It helps to know a stock's ticker symbol, but the symbols can be obtained from most of the same services that offer price quotes. Just enter the ticker symbol and you can obtain the latest stock price (usually 15 minutes old). Figure 9-1 shows selected websites with comprehensive invest-

F I G U R E 9-1

Select list of websites with comprehensive investment information.

CBS MarketWatch

cbs.marketwatch.com/news/newsroom.htx
Business news, price quotations, market commentary, public offerings, world markets, mutual fund profiles, and annual reports.

CNNFN

www.cnnfn.com/
Business news, market updates, currency exchange rates, world
markets, price quotations, reference information.

FinancialWeb

www.financialweb.com
Links to a multitude of other sites providing business news,
stock quotes, options quotes, stock recommendations, interest
rates, market analysis, and so forth.

Individual Investor Online

www.iionline.com/
Analyst recommendations, mutual fund screening, business
news, price quotations, investment information.

The Motley Fool

www.fool.com/
Business news, price quotations, money management ideas,
market overview, stock selection ideas.

PCQUOTE

www.pcquote.com
Financial news, price quotations, currency exchange rates, stock
charts, broker recommendations, earnings estimates, initial public offerings, stock screening.

Continued

FIGURE 9-1

Concluded

Smartmoney

www.smartmoney.com/
This site includes business news, price quotations, mutual fund descriptions, information on retirement, credit management, and home ownership.

Streetnet

www.streetnet.com/
Company research reports, online investing, and price quotations.

USA Today Money

www.usatoday.com/money/mfront.htm
Business news, interest rates, mutual fund information, price quotations, initial public offerings of securities, and recommended business books.

---

ment information. Best of all, most popular Internet sites provide stock prices without charge. What a deal!

What if I am unable to locate a stock listing in any of the three markets?

First, keep in mind that most daily newspapers publish only partial listings for these three markets, so your stock may be listed but simply not included in the listings by that particular newspaper on that particular day. Some newspapers publish much more comprehensive listings than other newspapers. For example, *The New York Times* stock listings are much more complete than listings of regional newspapers such as the *Indianapolis Star* or the (Jacksonville) *Florida Times-Union*. Another possibility is that your stock didn't trade on a particular day. Some stocks that have been listed for trading on a particular exchange or on the Nasdaq don't trade every day. If a stock or bond doesn't trade, the stock will not be included in the listings for that particular day.

What about the possibility the stock I own isn't included in any of these three listings?

Being unable to locate a particular stock price on the New York Stock Exchange, the American Stock Exchange, or the Nasdaq may mean the stock is traded over the counter but doesn't qualify for inclusion in the Nasdaq listings. The stocks of small companies and stocks that trade infrequently in the over-the-counter market are often excluded from newspaper listings because they are lightly traded stocks in the OTC. If you are unable to locate a stock after searching for several days, consider phoning a brokerage firm and asking where to look for the stock price. One thing to keep in mind is that most listings abbreviate firm names, so you may be overlooking the stock by mistakenly thinking the abbreviated name is actually a different company. Listings are generally arranged in alphabetical order as if the firm's full name is completely spelled out.

Is a security price in the same location each day? For example, if a stock is listed on the American Stock Exchange in today's paper, will it be listed on the same exchange tomorrow or next week?

Firms sometimes choose to have their stock listing moved from the over-the-counter market to a national exchange or from one national exchange to another. For example, a company might change the listing for its stock from the American Stock Exchange to the New York Stock Exchange. However, changing a stock listing is an infrequent occurrence for any company. Thus, each day you can expect to find the listing for a given stock at the same location.

Once I locate the stock, how do I interpret the information?

Various publications include different kinds of information for the same security. Some publications include listings that are very complete, while other publications include only the bare essentials. At the very [...] closing price from the previous day's trading. The closing price represents the last pric[e ...] with the security traded on the pre-vious afternoon. For [...] from Monday afternoon. Stock [...] will include closing pr[ices ...] prices, by convention [...] teenths of a dollar. [...] $36.625 per share. A [...] [...]875 per share [...] Thus, 100 shares of a [...] of $3218.75. To cons[...] most financial quotati[...]

$1/16 = 0.0625$ $3/4 = 0.75$
$1/8 = 0.125$ $13/16 = 0.8125$
$3/16 = 0.1875$ $7/8 = 0.875$
$1/4 = 0.25$ $15/16 = 0.9375$
$5/16 = 0.3125$ $8/8 = 1$
$3/8 = 0.375$
$7/16 = 0.4375$
$1/2 = 0.5$
$9/16 = 0.5625$
$5/8 = 0.625$
$11/16 = 0.6875$

What about the numb[er in the] closing price?

Net change represent[s ...] in the net change col[umn ...] and the closing price on the previous day the security traded. Suppose Wednesday's paper shows Exxon's closing price as 45½ and the net change as +1¼. The quotation indicates Tuesday's last trade in Exxon stock was at a price of $45.50 per share, which was $1.25 per share higher than the closing price of $44.25 on Monday. If you own 100 shares of Exxon, you are $125 richer on Tuesday night than you were on Monday night. The net change column is either blank or filled with a series of horizontal dots when the stock closes at the same price as the previous day's closing price. Figure 9-2 provides additional information on interpreting stock quotations.

FIGURE 9-2

Interpreting stock quotations.

52 weeks											
Hi	Lo	Stock	Sym	Div	Yld	PE	Vol 100s	Hi	Lo	Close	Net Chg
28½	17	GenCorp	GY	.60	3.1	9	256	20	19¼	19½	−½

52-weeks hi and lo   The highest price and lowest price attained by this stock during the preceding 52 weeks. Stocks are traded in eighths and thirty-seconds of a dollar. An eighth is 12½ cents and a thirty-second is 6¼ cents. GenCorp reached a high price of $28.50 per share and a low price of $17.00 per share during the preceding 52 weeks.

Stock   The abbreviated name of the company whose stock is listed. Names are sometimes abbreviated to the point that it is difficult to determine the company represented by the abbreviation.

Sym   The ticker symbol for the stock. This series of letters appears in boardrooms and computer screens when a trade in the stock occurs. It is also the coding used to obtain the stock's price on a quotation machine.

Div   The current annual dividend per share. GenCorp is paying an annual cash dividend of $0.60 per share. The owner of 100 shares of this stock will receive a check for $15 every three months. Unusual dividends, such as those paid in stock, are generally indicated with a letter directly beside the dividend amount.

Yld   The percentage dividend yield calculated by dividing the indicated dividend by the closing price of the stock. GenCorp's dividend yield is $0.60/$19.00, or 3.1 percent. Thus, buying the stock at the closing price will result in earning a current yield of 3.1 percent from the annual dividend.

PE   The price-earnings ratio (PE or P/E) is calculated by dividing the closing stock price by the most recent earnings per share

Continued

FIGURE 9-2

Concluded

(not shown). The PE ratio indicates the number of dollars investors are paying for each dollar the firm is currently earning. The PE ratio is a useful investment statistic but can be severely impacted by temporary aberrations in reported earnings.

Vol   The amount of round lot trading in the stock during the day's activity. Total round lot volume is 100 times the number listed in the volume column. Thus, 25,600 shares of GenCorp common stock traded during the day.

Hi   The highest price at which GenCorp stock traded during the session.

Lo   The lowest price at which GenCorp stock traded during the session.

Close   The last price at which GenCorp stock traded during the session. During this session, GenCorp closed at $19.50 per share, $0.25 per share higher than the lowest price of the day.

Net Chg   The difference between GenCorp's closing price this session and GenCorp's closing price during the session in which the stock last traded. The net change of $1/4$ ($0.25 per share) indicates that the $19.50 closing price is $0.25 per share less than the previous day's closing price of $19.75. Thus, the stock closed down $1/4$, or $0.25 per share.

My morning paper also includes a column for volume. What does this mean?

Volume is the number of shares traded during that particular day. Volume is nearly always presented in units of 100 shares, so if a stock's volume column lists 860, the volume of trading for the day was 860 times 100, or 86,000 shares. A volume listing of 11547 is translated as 1,154,700 shares that were traded during the day. Weekly listings found in weekend papers list volume for the week rather than for the day. Most financial analysts consider a stock's trading volume as an important piece of information, especially when the volume is much heavier than normal. Unusually heavy volume indicates substantial investor interest that may well represent new information is forthcoming.

Why is volume usually listed in 100-share units?

Stocks normally trade in units of 100 shares, or *round lots*. If the volume column didn't abbreviate the amount of daily trading, large volume numbers would crowd into the other data because some active stocks trade millions of shares a day. Trading volume in many stocks became so heavy in the 1990s that some publications now list volume in 1000s of shares instead of 100s of shares. Be certain to look at the top of the volume column; it should indicate how volume is being reported. In most instances, the column heading shows *vol. in 100s,* which indicates that numbers in the volume column must be multiplied by 100.

What other information is provided?

Newspapers that devote substantial space to financial listings often include each stock's high price and low price for the day and, less frequently, the high price and low price for the last 52 weeks. The daily price range is of particular interest if you have entered a limit order to purchase or sell a stock at a particular price. Comparing the current price with the price range for the previous 52 weeks indicates if a security is in an uptrend or a downtrend. A stock with a closing price of 75 and a 52-week range of $45\frac{1}{2}$ (the 52-week low) and $76\frac{1}{4}$ (the 52-week high) is near the top of its trading range for the past year.

Why is this important?

Some investors believe that stock prices, like sports teams, can develop a momentum. These investors claim that the way to make money in the market is to jump on the stock and ride its price momentum. A stock with a price near its yearly high has an upward price momentum that is likely to continue, i.e., the stock price is in an uptrend. A stock that is priced near the low end of its yearly price range has a downward momentum, which means the stock should not be purchased. Although not everyone believes in this momentum theory of selecting stocks, being able to compare a stock's current price with the range of prices during the past year adds to the amount of information you have available to use.

What is the PE ratio that is sometimes listed?

Some stock listings (but not bond listings) include a column for each stock's PE ratio. The PE ratio, an abbreviation for price-earnings ratio, is calculated by dividing a stock's closing price by the firm's most recent earnings per share (eps). The price-earnings ratio indicates the number of dollars investors are currently willing to pay for each dollar the firm earns. A PE of 20 shows that a stock is being valued at 20 times the firm's earnings. If a firm with 10 million shares of stock outstanding earned $20 million last year, its earnings for each share is $20 million/10 million shares, or $2 per share. If this firm's stock is trading at a price of $40 per share, the PE ratio would be $40/$2, or 20.

What does this mean?

A high stock price compared to a company's earnings per share, e.g., a stock with a high PE ratio, indicates that investors anticipate the firm's earnings will be growing. The stocks of firms with a potential for substantial earnings growth might enjoy price-earnings ratios of 20, 30, or even higher, while stocks of firms with limited growth prospects might be priced at 8 to 12 times earnings per share. The negative aspect of investing in a stock with a high PE is that actual earnings growth may turn out to be lower than expected, in which case the price of the stock is likely to fall. Thus, even if the earnings per share number grows, if the growth is slower than anticipated, the stock price is likely to decline.

Do the listings provide information about a firm's earnings per share?

Earnings per share is not separately listed, but the statistic can be calculated if the PE ratio is available. Earnings per share equals the closing stock price divided by the PE ratio. For example, if the financial page shows Union Pacific's closing price at $50 and the PE ratio is listed at 25, earnings per share must be $50/25, or $2.00. *Barron's,* a weekly newspaper published each Monday by Dow Jones & Company, includes information on recent earnings as well as the price-earnings ratio.

Does the dividend information relate to last year's dividend?

Unless a symbol is beside the dividend amount, the dividend entry designates a stock's current annual dividend. For example, an entry of 1.60 in the dividend column (remember, dollar signs are not normally used in the financial listings) indicates an owner of the stock is currently receiving an annual dividend of $1.60 for each share owned. Dividends are normally paid quarterly, so the stock is paying $0.40 per share every three months. Some papers also include a separate column to indicate a stock's current dividend yield. This is calculated by dividing the annual dividend by the closing stock price. For example, a stock with a closing price of $50 and an annual dividend of $2 will show a dividend yield of $2/$50, or 4 percent (usually listed as 4.0). A separate yield column really isn't necessary because yield can be easily calculated if the annual dividend and closing price are available.

Do the financial pages indicate the date when the next dividend is scheduled to be paid?

Most publications do not provide dividend dates. These dates can be obtained in *Barron's,* which lists the dividend amount, record date, and payment date for most actively traded stocks. More specialized publications such as the *Value Line Investment Survey, Standard & Poor's Stock Reports,* and *Moody's Stock Handbook* also provide information on dividend dates. One or more of these publications can be located in nearly any public or college library.

What do the letters mean that I sometimes see in stock listings?

Publishers of financial data often use letters or symbols to call readers' attention to a particular piece of information that needs further explanation. An explanation of these symbols is nearly always included somewhere nearby. For example, many publications place the letter *s* beside a stock that has recently experienced a split. Likewise, the letter *n* is often placed beside stocks that have been newly listed. Other symbols are used to indicate special types of dividends and companies that may be in bankruptcy. You can only determine what these symbols mean by looking in the explanation column.

Why are the most active stocks generally included on the financial page?

Very actively traded stocks are owned, traded, and followed by a large number of investors, so price information about these stocks is of interest to most readers. Many investors believe that substantial trading volume indicates something important may be occurring with respect to the company or the stock, especially if more modest volume is the norm. A sudden jump onto the most active list by a stock alerts investors that major investors have suddenly become interested in the stock. Perhaps the company has become the target of a buyout offer from another firm. Maybe the company is getting ready to announce a big increase in earnings. Unusual trading volume may indicate something important before the news becomes public. At least, that is what some investors believe.

Why is it necessary for financial publications to include several market indexes?

Indexes are used for comparison purposes. For example, the consumer price index provides a comparison of the current level of consumer prices with the level on some past date. Stock market indexes compare stock prices relative to their level on some other date. A newscaster may announce the market is up 80 points to 8300. This means an index selected by the newscaster has increased during the trading session by 80 points, from 8220 to 8300, or approximately 1 percent. A stock index is calculated using the prices of selected stocks that, taken as a group, provide an indication of movements for the entire market or for a particular segment of the market.

An index is a proxy for the market?

A stock index is a proxy (substitute) for the market or for a particular segment of the market, depending on the index being used. Some indexes attempt to measure changes in the overall market, while others are better at measuring a narrower segment of the market, such as utility stocks or transportation stocks. Some indexes provide a measure of overall price changes on the New York Stock Exchange, while other indexes are constructed to measure stock price changes in the over-the-counter market. These two sets of indexes do not always move proportionately (the OTC market is generally more volatile) or even in the same direction. You must understand what a particular index is designed to measure to fully appreciate the information it conveys.

Are the stocks that comprise an index ever changed?

Changes in the composition of a stock index are occasionally required for several reasons. A stock included in an index may no longer be traded. Perhaps the firm has gone bankrupt or been purchased by another firm. Likewise, one company may purchase another company and become an entirely different type of firm. Managers of a company may sell a substantial amount of assets, causing the character of the firm's business to change. In each of these cases, the people who construct and maintain a particular stock index may find it necessary to drop one stock from the index and replace it with a different stock.

What are some of the popular indexes?

The Dow Jones Industrial Average (DJIA), often referred to as *the Dow,* is the most frequently quoted stock average. Newspaper headlines that exclaim "Market Down 120!" or "Dow Skyrockets to New High" are both referring to the Dow Jones Industrial Average. The DJIA is calculated using the prices of 30 high-quality stocks listed on the New York Stock Exchange (see Table 9-1). The Dow is not adjusted for the size of a firm or for the number of shares of stock a firm has outstanding. In other words, the stock of a very large company has equal weight with the stock of a medium-size company. The only thing that counts in calculating the Dow is the price of each of the 30 stocks included in the average. Because of the limited number and similar nature of the stocks used in calculating this average, the Dow is considered a better measure of the price activity of the blue-chip segment of the stock market than of the overall market. Dow Jones & Company also calculates and publishes

TABLE 9-1

Stocks used in calculating the Dow Jones industrial average.

Allied Signal	Hewlett-Packard
Aluminum Company of America	International Business Machines
American Express	International Paper
AT&T	Johnson & Johnson
Boeing	McDonalds
Caterpillar	Merck
Chevron	Minnesota Mining & Manufacturing
Coca-Cola	Morgan JP
Disney	Philip Morris
DuPont	Procter & Gamble
Eastman Kodak	Sears
Exxon	Travelers
General Electric	Union Carbide
General Motors	United Technology
Goodyear	Wal-Mart

separate averages for utility stocks, financial stocks, transportation stocks, and the market as a whole.

Is another average a more accurate measure of how the market is performing?

Many financial analysts prefer the S&P 500 index as a proxy for the market. The S&P 500 is heavily weighted with blue chip stocks, but the greater diversity of companies and larger number of issues (500 in the S&P as compared to 30 in the Dow) cause this index to provide a better picture of how the overall market is performing. Unlike the Dow, which considers only the prices of its component stocks, the S&P 500 takes into account both the stock price and the number of shares outstanding for each stock that is included in the index. Every index has its weaknesses, however, and this broad-based measure of blue chip stock prices is no exception. The S&P 500 does not adequately represent certain segments of the market, such as small capitalization stocks, foreign stocks, and high-tech issues. Like the Dow, the S&P 500 is published in nearly all daily newspapers.

Are other indexes and averages better market measures?

Indexes are published for small-cap stocks, utility stocks, transportation stocks, and virtually every other segment of the market. Figure 9-3 lists many of the measures of stock market performance. You may or may not be interested in following these more narrow-based indexes, depending on the types of stocks being held in your portfolio. The S&P 500 is a good representation of the market if you primarily invest in blue chip stocks. The S&P 500 is less indicative of what is going on if you are heavily invested in the stocks of small companies involved in high technology.

What indexes and averages apply to these other groups of stocks?

Nasdaq calculates an average comprised of nearly 5000 over-the-counter stocks. It also publishes indexes for OTC industrials, banks, insurance, finance, transportation, and telecommunications. Many investors watch the Russell Indexes to determine how the stocks of smaller companies are performing. Russell calculates an index for 3000 stocks, a separate index for the largest 1000 of these 3000 stocks, and another index for the smallest 2000 of the 3000 stocks.

FIGURE 9-3

Measures of stock market performance.

Although most investors are thinking of the Dow Jones Industrial Average (the "Dow") when they inquire about how the stock market is performing, numerous measures of stock market performance are utilized.

Dow Jones Industrial Average   A price-weighted average of the stocks of 30 large industrial companies. The sum of the prices of the 30 stocks is divided by a factor that is continually adjusted to take account of stock splits and changes in the composition of the average. Higher-priced stocks tend to have a greater influence on this average because these stocks tend to have greater absolute price movements. Some market watchers consider the Dow to be too narrow and too biased toward blue-chip stocks. Dow Jones also publishes averages for transportation, utilities, and the overall market. It also calculates averages for numerous industry groups.

Standard & Poor's 500 Composite Index   A popular market measure based on the market values (share price times shares outstanding) of 500 stocks: 400 industrials, 40 utilities, 20 transportation, and 40 financial firms. The S&P 500 includes some over-the-counter stocks and is calculated using a base of 10 in the years 1941–43. Standard & Poor's also publishes indexes for specialized stock series.

New York Stock Exchange Composite Index   An index that includes all stocks listed on the New York Stock Exchange. Each stock is weighted according to market value, so stocks of large corporations have a strong influence on index movements. The NYSE also provides other specialized indexes.

American Stock Exchange Composite Index   A market value-weighted index that includes stocks, American depositary receipts, closed-end fund shares, limited partnership units, and warrants listed on the American Stock Exchange.

Continued

FIGURE 9-3

Concluded

Nasdaq Composite Index   An index that includes all the common stocks of domestic companies that are included in the National Association of Securities Dealers Automated Quotation system. Nasdaq also calculates specialty indexes for industrials, insurance, transportation, banking, computer, and telecommunications. The Nasdaq series reflects stock price changes in the over-the-counter market.

Wilshire 5000 Index   A broad-based index of over 7000 stocks traded on the New York Stock Exchange, the American Stock Exchange, and the over-the-counter market. The large number of stocks included in this value-weighted index makes it a good indicator of the overall market.

Russell 2000 Index   An index of 2000 small-capitalization (small-cap) stocks. This index is designed to indicate price movements in the stocks of relatively small firms. Components of the index are selected by eliminating the 1000 largest capitalization firms included in the more broad-based Russell 3000 Index.

Value Line Average   An index of the prices of approximately 1700 stocks reviewed by Value Line. Each stock included in the average is equally weighted (neither price nor market value makes one stock more important than any other stock, as is the case when stocks are weighted according to price or market value), and the index is calculated with a base of 100 in 1961.

Should I examine any other market measures?

Many investors regularly check the number of stock issues advancing in price compared to the number of stock issues declining in price. If the number of advancing issues substantially exceeds the number of declining issues, the market may be exhibiting an upward momentum that is not as evident in the major stock price indexes. On the other hand, if the number of declining issues exceeds the number of advancing issues, market watchers would consider the market to be weak, even when a stock price index such as the S&P 500 staged an advance.

Where do I locate information for advancing and declining stock issues?

Advances and declines are generally contained in a small section of most financial sections termed *Market Diary* or *Market Activity*. The same section will also often provide information on the number of issues traded, the number of issues making new 52-week highs, and the number of issues making new 52-week lows. Each of these statistics provides an indication of the market's underlying momentum. Information about advances and declines is also generally provided for securities traded in the over-the-counter market and on the American Stock Exchange.

What about the lists of percentage gainers and percentage losers?

Many newspapers publish lists of stocks that experienced the biggest percentage price gains and biggest percentage price losses for the day (or week). Most publications include separate lists for the New York Stock Exchange, the Nasdaq, and the American Stock Exchange. Although lists of percentage gainers and losers can be interesting to browse, they typically shed little light on market activity. Most of the entries are low-priced stocks of small firms that the majority of investors have never heard of. Relatively small price changes for low-priced stocks can qualify securities for inclusion in these listings.

How do I interpret bond quotations?

Bond prices are quoted as a percentage of par value. A bond quotation of $95\frac{3}{8}$ indicates the price is 95.375 percent of $1000 (corporate bonds are denominated in units of $1000), or $953.75. A closing price of 103¼ indicates that a bond's last trade occurred at a price of $1032.50. An entry of +¼ in the net change column shows the bond closed up by a quarter of one percent of $1000, or $2.50, compared to the previous closing price. A net change entry of –½ indicates a daily price decline of $15.00 per $1000 bond. As with stock listings, dollar signs are usually omitted in order to conserve space.

What is the meaning of the numbers located directly to the right of the company that issued a bond?

Bond quotations generally include information on the coupon rate and maturity date. Thus, the Bethlehem Steel listing of BethSt 8.45s05 is a bond with an 8.45-percent coupon (i.e., the bond pays annual interest equal to $84.50, or 8.45 percent of the $1000 par value) and a maturity date of 2005. The month and day of maturity can be found in a more comprehensive publication such as *Moody's Bond Record*.

Does the entry for current yield indicate the yield I would earn on the bond?

Some, but not all publications include information for each bond's current yield. Current yield is calculated by dividing the dollar amount of annual interest by the bond's closing price. For example, a bond with an 8-percent coupon and a closing price of 94 offers a current yield of $80/$940, or 8.5 percent. Current yield is an incomplete measure of the return you are likely to earn if you purchase the bond because this narrow measure of yield does not take into account any expected increase or decrease in price of the bond during your period of ownership. The Bethlehem bond just noted will increase $60 in value by maturity, a source of income that is not considered in the calculation of current yield. Unfortunately, more comprehensive measures of yield are generally not included in most of these listings. An entry of *cv* in the current yield column indicates the bond is convertible into shares of common stock. For more details on interpreting bond quotations, refer to Figure 9-4.

Should the entry for volume be multiplied by 100?

Bond volume is listed in full. That is, if the volume column indicates 45, then 45 bonds were traded during that particular day. A bond's daily volume is important if you believe you may want to sell the bond prior to maturity. Actively traded securities, including bonds, are easier to sell without having to give a concession on price. Many financial listings do not include bond volume, and most do not include the daily high and low prices.

Why do bonds often receive an abbreviated listing?

Among individual investors, bonds are not as popular an investment as stocks, which means editors will devote more of their limited space to information about stocks and mutual funds. Browse through the volume column of bond listings and you will notice that bonds are relatively inactive compared to stocks. While a couple of hundred bonds from a particular issue may trade during a given day, the same company's stock might trade hundreds of thousands of shares. In addition, most bond investors have a relatively long investment horizon and little interest in a bond's daily price range. Individual investors often purchase bonds that they expect to hold to maturity.

Why are so many more stocks than bonds listed in the financial pages?

Bond listings are usually confined to debt securities listed on the New York Stock Exchange, and sometimes the American Stock Exchange. In addition, some financial pages include listings for

FIGURE 9-4

Interpreting bond quotations.

Bond	Cur Yld	Vol	Close	Net Chg
Amoco 6¾s05	6.2	247	108¾	−1¼

Bond   The issuer of the bond and the bond's coupon and year of maturity. The Amoco bond has a 6.75-percent coupon rate (the bond pays annual interest equal to 6.75 percent of the $1000 face value). The bond is scheduled to mature sometime in the year 2005 (the exact date is available in other publications), although the possibility exists that the bond is callable and may be redeemed prior to 2005.

Current yield   The bond's yield from interest payments only. Current yield is calculated by dividing the bond's annual interest income ($67.50) by the closing price of $1087.50. Potential changes in the value of the bond are not included in the calculation of current yield.

Vol   The number of bonds that traded during the session. Unlike stocks, for which volume is quoted in hundreds of shares, bond volume is quoted in full. In this instance, a total of 247 Amoco bonds were traded.

Close   The last price at which the bond traded during the session. Bonds are quoted in percent of par value. The Amoco bond closed at 108.75 percent of par value, or $1087.50.

Net change   The amount by which the bond's closing price at the end of this trading session is different from the bond's closing price at the end of the previous trading session. Again, net change is quoted in percent of par value, so a negative change of 1¼ indicates the bond declined in price by 1.25 percent of $1000, or $12.50. Many bond issues trade only infrequently, so the previous trade may have occurred many days or weeks in the past.

U.S. Treasury and U.S. government agency bonds. Although the number of bonds listed on the two exchanges is quite large, many bonds trade infrequently and are not included on a daily basis in the price listings. A big share of bond trading is in the over-the-counter market, which is omitted from most financial publications.

How can I determine the value of bonds traded over the counter?

Price quotations for U.S. Treasury bonds and agency bonds are included in major daily newspapers and financial publications such as *The Wall Street Journal, Investor's Daily,* and *Barron's.* Dealers in the over-the-counter market trade these two types of bonds. Up-to-date price quotations for corporate bonds traded in the over-the-counter market must generally be obtained from a broker, because most newspapers omit data for these securities. Prices for a large number of corporate bond issues can be found in *Moody's Bond Record,* a monthly publication that can be found in many libraries. Unfortunately, the bond prices included in this publication tend to be at least several weeks old, which means that current bond prices are likely to be different than published bond prices.

Does anyone publish a bond index similar to the stock indexes discussed earlier?

Several firms calculate and publish bond indexes. Separate indexes are available for investment-grade bonds, high-yield (i.e., speculative) bonds, global bonds, and convertible bonds. In fact, several indexes are published for the first three categories of bonds. Most newspapers publish at least one bond index. An increase in a bond index means that bond values have increased and interest rates have declined. Prices for investment-grade bonds and high-yield bonds do not always move together.

How do I interpret mutual fund listings?

Mutual fund listings often include only each fund's net asset value (NAV), which is calculated as the market value of securities owned by the fund divided by the number of outstanding shares of the fund. A mutual fund that holds $15 million in bonds and has 1 million shares of its own stock outstanding has a net present value of $15 million/1 million, or $15 per share. The net asset value is the price you will receive if you decide to sell your shares. It is also the price you will pay to buy shares in a fund that does not levy a sales fee.

Sometimes more than net asset value is included? What does this other information represent?

Mutual fund listings sometimes include a column for net change in net asset value. Net change represents the change in the value of one mutual fund share since the close of the previous day's trading. For example, if the net change for a mutual fund is shown as +.23, the net asset value of the fund increased by 23 cents during that day's trading. More extensive mutual fund listings may include information about the rate of return that a fund's shareholders have earned since the beginning of the year or during the last 12 months. Some publications also provide information about sales fees and management fees. Publications such as *The Wall Street Journal, Investor's Business Daily,* and *Barron's* devote substantial space to mutual fund information.

Are any publications devoted solely to mutual fund information?

Mutual funds are very popular investments, and several publications provide extensive information at a fairly reasonable price. Morningstar and Value Line offer similar mutual fund advisory services. Each publication includes information on fees, past performance, management longevity, and risk. Many public libraries will subscribe to one of these services.

How do I interpret option listings?

Option listings represent the previous day's closing option prices as categorized by expiration date and strike price. You may remember from Chapter 7 that an option's strike price represents the price at which the option owner can buy stock (if the option is a call) or sell stock (if the option is a put). The expiration date represents the last day the option may be used. Suppose you are interested in determining the price (also called the *premium*) for Coca-Cola call options with a strike price of $60 per share and an August expiration. Once you locate Coca-Cola options (options are generally arranged in alphabetical order), scan down (or across) the strike price column (or row) to the $60 listing, and then search for an August expiration. A quotation of $4\frac{1}{2}$, for example, indicates that at yesterday's close of trading, the price of the option was $450 (the quotation is the price per share for a 100-share option). This means that for $450, you could have purchased the right to buy 100 shares of Coca-Cola at a price of $60 per share until August. Option prices tend to be very volatile, as you can observe by watching the same listing for several days.

If these investments are so popular, why don't more financial publications include option listings?

Most daily newspapers are unwilling to devote the considerable amount of space required for option listings, especially since these investments appeal to a relatively small proportion of their readers. Most newspapers prefer to devote space to mutual funds rather than to stock options. Even publications devoted solely to providing financial information generally include only an abbreviated listing of option quotations. *The Wall Street Journal, Investor's Business Daily,* and *Barron's* provide good coverage for options.

CHAPTER

How Are Securities Valued?

Chapter summary

Financial analysts believe that stock prices are influenced by numerous identifiable factors, including earnings, dividends, interest rates, inflation, management quality, and so forth. Likewise, several variables, including market interest rates, maturity length, and credit quality, impact the market values of bonds. The concept of discounted cash flows is fundamental in the process of valuation. This chapter discusses some theories concerning security valuation.

How are securities valued?

Most academics and many professionals in the field of finance believe that all investments are valued on the basis of the discounted cash flows that owners of the investments can expect to receive. Cash flows include interest payments, dividends, rent, repayment of principal, proceeds from a sale, and so forth. Although the valuation process is fairly clear-cut in theory, putting it into practice can be quite difficult, especially for investments that have uncertain cash flows, such as common stocks. While the theory tells us that the value of a share of stock is equal to the present value of all future dividends, developing an accurate estimate of a particular stock's future dividend payments is no easy matter. On the other hand, estimating a bond's cash flows is a snap because this security pays a series of fixed interest payments and then returns a known principal amount on a specific date.

How are the cash flow estimates discounted?

Cash flows should be discounted at the rate of return you expect to earn on a particular investment. For example, if you expect to earn a 10-percent annual return from an investment, then you should discount each of the investment's estimated cash flows by 10 percent. A $1000 payment to be received in one year discounted at 10 percent has a value of $1000/1.10, or $909.09. Conversely, investing $909.09 at 10 percent for one year would produce an investment valued at $1000. If the $1000 is not to be received for two years, the current value is less than with a one-year wait because you expect to earn a 10-percent return for each of two years. With a two-year wait, the value of the $1000 payment to be received is calculated as $1000/(1.10)^2$. The process is the same no matter what the investment.

What rates of discount are used for stocks and bonds?

The interest payments and principal repayment from a bond should be discounted at the current market interest rate on bonds of similar risk and maturity. In other words, if newly issued 10-year bonds are yielding 8 percent, then outstanding bonds with 10 years remaining to maturity should also be yielding 8 percent, and that's the rate at which you should discount cash flows from these bonds. This assumes the new bond and the bond you are valuing are of similar risk. Bonds from less creditworthy issuers are discounted at higher rates because investors rightly expect a higher return when they are less certain of receiving the promised interest and principal payments.

What discount rate should be used to value stocks?

Dividends from a stock are discounted at a higher rate than a bond's interest payments because dividends are more risky (less certain) than interest payments. Although you can determine when a company is likely to pay dividends, you can never be certain exactly how much the dividends will be. Thus, accurately forecasting dividends is much more difficult than correctly forecasting interest payments that are guaranteed and fixed in amount. The greater the likelihood of incorrectly estimating the cash flows, the higher the rate of discount that should be used. In general, investors demand a higher return from stocks than from bonds because stocks are more risky to own. At a time when investors are earning a 6- or 7-percent return on bonds, they are likely to be expecting annual returns of 15 to 20 percent on stocks.

If the valuation process is so "scientific," why do analysts disagree on security values?

In truth, security valuation is as much an art as a science. Disagreements regarding a security's value stem from uncertainty regarding the size of the cash flows to be received (What dividend will Exxon be paying five years down the road?), and also regarding the appropriate rate at which to discount the cash flows. Few uncertainties exist with bonds, where cash flows are specified and discount rates are fairly easy to determine. Stocks, real estate, gold, and stock options are much more difficult to value, primarily because great uncertainty surrounds the size of the future cash flows. A company that operates in an emerging technical field is subject to substantial hazards, so a wide range of estimates will exist for the firm's cash flows. This uncertainty of cash flows means it is difficult to determine the true value of the firm's stock.

Why are bonds easier to value than stocks?

Securities and other investments are valued on the basis of all expected future cash payments. Bonds make fixed payments that are easily determined (annual interest equals the coupon rate times the bond's face value), unless the issuer is in a shaky financial condition. Purchase a bond and you know exactly how much cash you will receive and when you will receive it. You can easily determine the rate of return you can earn on comparable bonds by looking in a financial publication such as *The Wall Street Journal.* This return available on comparable bonds is then used as the appropriate rate to discount the interest payments and principal for the bond you are valuing. Bond values are quite precise, at least compared to stock values.

How about preferred stock?

Preferred is much easier to value than common stock because preferred stock dividends remain the same. Although shares of preferred stock are considered units of ownership, the holder of preferred stock is generally guaranteed a fixed stream of income regardless of how profitable the issuing company eventually becomes. While the dividend payments to common stockholders are often adjusted depending on the economic fortunes of the issuing company, dividends to holders of preferred stock do not change. Thus, preferred stock has similar investment characteristics to bonds with very long maturity dates.

What discount rate should be used for preferred stock?

The discount rate for preferred stock is higher than the discount rate for bonds of the same firm. The discount rate is higher because preferred stock is a riskier investment than bonds issued by the same firm. Preferred stockholders have preference to common stockholders but not to the firm's creditors. In other words, creditors of a firm have a claim to interest and repayment of principal that has priority over any claims of preferred stockholders. Thus, creditors are in a more secure position than preferred stockholders in the event a company gets into financial difficulty. As with common stocks and bonds, the discount rate for preferred stock fluctuates depending on market rates of interest and the outlook for the issuer.

If bonds are so easy to value, why do some experts tell investors to sell bonds at the same time other experts are advising investors to buy bonds?

Bond recommendations are generally based on expectations regarding the future direction of interest rates. Bond values move inversely with market rates of interest, so rising interest rates cause a decline in bond prices. Conversely, falling interest rates cause a rise in the value of outstanding bonds. Experts who recommend that you buy bonds are forecasting a decline in interest rates and a resulting rise in bond prices. Experts expecting rising interest rates will recommend selling bonds, or at least not purchasing additional bonds. Although a bond's cash payments are easy to determine, future interest rate changes and the resulting change in bond values are very difficult to accurately project.

If cash payments from a bond are fixed, how do interest rate changes influence the bond's value?

Changes in market rates of interest cause a change in the rate at which a bond's cash flows are discounted. As interest rates rise, the rate at which a bond's fixed cash flows are discounted increases, thereby causing a decline in the present value of the bond's cash flows. Because the discounted cash flows equal the bond's value, a higher discount rate will cause the market price of a bond to decline. When market rates of interest decline, a bond's cash flows are discounted at a lower rate and the value of the bond will increase. Think of it this way: If you own a bond with a $1000 face value and a 7-percent coupon, the bond will have a greater value when comparable bonds yield 5 percent than when comparable bonds yield 10 percent.

How do financial analysts value stock?

As mentioned earlier, stock is valued on the basis of the discounted value of all future dividends. Financial analysts investigate a firm's financial statements (i.e., income statement, balance sheet, and so forth) and the accounting procedures that were used to construct the statements. Analysts are particularly interested in the method used by the firm's accountants to arrive at the dollar amount of income listed in the income statement. Analysts may also visit the firm's facilities and interview the managers. Analysts are always looking for assets that have the potential to produce substantial amounts of additional income but for one reason or another are not being fully utilized. These analysts hope to uncover information that provides a reason to believe future profits and dividends will be different from current estimates.

What do you mean by current estimates?

Stock is valued on the basis of future cash flows (dividend payments) currently expected by the investment community. Financial analysts are constantly searching for information that will help identify companies that will enjoy higher earnings and pay higher dividends than the investment community expects.

The stocks of these firms are likely to be undervalued and offer good investment opportunities.

You mentioned that the value of stock equals the discounted present value of future dividends. What if I eventually plan to sell the stock?

At the time a sale takes place, the value of the stock should equal the discounted cash flow at that time. So even though you plan to eventually sell the stock, the price you receive will be determined by how investors judge cash flows from that point forward. The same reasoning applies to the price to be received when these investors eventually sell the shares purchased from you. That is, these investors will receive a price that is consistent with how other investors view the firm's future.

A company will sometimes announce increased earnings compared to the same period in the previous year and yet the stock price declines. What gives?

Remember, a stock is valued on the basis of investor expectations. If the investment community anticipates a very large earnings increase and a firm announces earnings that are only slightly higher than in the earlier period but substantially smaller than expected, the firm's stock price is likely to decline. Although results improved, they didn't improve as much as expected. It's like weighing yourself after having been on a strict diet. Losing a couple of pounds is good news, but it may still be disappointing if you anticipated a loss of five or six pounds.

Does the same reasoning apply to earnings declines?

It certainly does. A company's stock price is likely to increase if the firm reports a decline in earnings and the decline is less than investors anticipated. Reduced profit is not particularly good news, but investors had been expecting even worse news. Because stocks are priced on expectations, results that are bad, but better than anticipated, often result in rising stock prices.

You're saying investors' estimates of future cash flows have changed?

That's right. When earnings decline less than expected, investors are likely to revise upward their estimates of future cash flows because the firm is in better shape than anticipated. Put another way, it's not in as bad a shape as anticipated. If a company reports an increase in earnings that is less than expected, investors are likely to revise downward their estimates of future cash flows. The downward revision will probably cause the stock price to decline even though increased earnings have been reported. Stock prices are a function of investor expectations regarding the future, and anything that occurs to change these expectations will influence stock prices.

Why will a firm's directors sometimes leave dividends unchanged or even increase dividends when earnings have declined?

Most companies share a portion of their earnings with the owners by distributing dividends to shareholders. The payment of a dividend represents more than a cash distribution, however. Directors often use the dividend announcement to convey information to stockholders and the rest of the investment community. For example, a firm's directors may announce a dividend increase at the same time that reduced earnings are reported in order to reassure investors that the lower earnings are only temporary. The announcement of a dividend increase is a way of telling investors that things are much better than indicated by the current earnings report.

Are these dividend signals generally accurate?

Dividend signals are not always what they may seem, or, at least, they are not always accurately interpreted by investors. The directors of a firm may have several motives for attempting to send investors a signal in order to try and keep the stock price from declining. For example, the directors may be planning to issue additional shares of common stock, which makes it important to maintain a high stock price. Another possibility is that management may be concerned about a takeover attempt by another firm. Maintaining a high stock price makes a takeover more expensive and less likely to occur. Perhaps the directors have simply misjudged the firm's future and don't realize that the company is actually in a very weakened financial position.

How can I judge the value of a security if I don't have the expertise to forecast a stock's future dividend payments?

You can follow the lead of the majority of investors and place your trust in the judgment of professionals who possess more expertise and have the time to evaluate security values. These experts may include your broker, the research department of the firm for which your broker works, or one or more of the hundreds of advisory services that recommend investments. Brokers and financial analysts earn their living from evaluating whether particular securities are undervalued or overvalued. Just as you might trust an attorney to advise you on legal matters or an accountant to advise you on tax matters, a finance professional may be your best source of advice for decisions on securities to buy and sell.

Why do stocks sometimes decline in price when a company makes an offer to purchase another firm?

Investors may believe the acquiring company (the company making the offer) is paying too high a price for the stock of the firm it intends to purchase. Buying another firm is likely to require the acquiring company to borrow a substantial amount of money or issue a large number of new shares of its own common stock. Additional debt may cause investors to worry about the firm's ability to make the required interest payments. If the acquisition is financed with additional shares of common stock, current shareholders will experience a dilution in their proportional ownership of the firm because more shares of stock will be outstanding after the acquisition is completed.

But if one firm purchases another firm, cash flows of the acquiring company should increase. Why would the stock price decline?

If borrowing is used to finance the purchase, interest expense may become so large that future cash flows are severely penalized. At the same time, the increased debt could cause the acquiring firm to be much more risky because of the obligation to make higher interest payments. If new shares of stock are used to pay for the acquisition, the additional shares may more than offset the increase in cash flows on a per-share basis. Also consider that the combination of two firms does not always work out as expected. The possibility of an incompatible union increases the riskiness of the surviving firm, at least until investors are convinced they will benefit from the combination. Union Pacific's purchase of the Southern Pacific is a glaring example of how mergers between firms don't always work as expected, at least in the short run.

If dividends are such an important factor in stock valuation, why are some stocks so valuable even though they don't pay dividends?

The directors of a company must decide whether to pay dividends to the firm's stockholders and, if so, how much. Earnings that are not paid out in dividends are reinvested in the business, hopefully to produce additional sales and earnings in future years. In other words, reinvestment of earnings permits a company to earn increased profits and establishes a base on which to pay higher dividends in future years. Dividends may not be paid next year or even over the next several years. At some point, however, a portion of a firm's cash flows will almost certainly be returned to stockholders in the form of dividends. The bottom line is that lower dividends now generally mean more dividends in the future.

Do stock prices follow trends in economic activity?

Stock prices are definitely influenced by economic activity. After all, sales and cash flows that produce value for investors are a function of the economic environment in which a business operates. However, most analysts believe changes in stock prices lead changes in economic activity. That is, stock values increase prior to economic upturns and decline prior to the beginning of recessions. Remember, financial analysts are continually attempting to estimate *future* cash flows. If analysts anticipate a recession and a resulting reduction in corporate cash flows, stock prices are likely to decline prior to the actual economic recession.

Is it too late to sell my stock if the government declares an economic recession?

It is impossible to determine the exact time when you should sell (or buy) stock. If investors correctly anticipate a recession, stock prices will adjust downward to the expected lower level of economic activity prior to the time the economy actually enters the recession. Thus, by the time the recession becomes official, stock may have suffered a major decline so that it is too late to sell. Of course, the recession may turn out to be much more severe than most investors anticipated, which means additional downward adjustments in stock prices could occur.

Should I select stocks to buy and sell on the basis of news announcements?

Evidence suggests that investors have difficulty profiting from public information because by the time the information is made public, stock prices have adjusted in anticipation of the news. For example, by the time a firm's directors announce a dividend increase, investors have already priced the stock in anticipation of the announcement. Even if news is a major surprise, investors must act immediately in order to have a chance of taking advantage of the news. For the vast majority of individual investors, this kind of reaction is impossible. The bottom line is that individual investors have little chance of profiting from the use of public information. It is probably too late to put the information to profitable use by the time you gain access to the news. Think of all the wealthy and informed investors who are likely to have gained access to news before it comes to your attention.

Is a company's stock valued at least partly on the basis of the assets the company owns?

A company's assets are an important component of valuing the company's stock. However, it is the market value, not the accounting value of the firm's assets, that is important. Assets are valued according to the cash and income the assets produce, not the price the company paid to buy them. A firm's balance sheet values assets according to historical cost adjusted for wear and tear. In other words, balance sheet valuations are based on how much an asset cost, not how much income it produces. Thus, assets are certainly important in valuing a company's stock, but you cannot always determine the relationship by examining the firm's balance sheet entries.

Aren't stock prices sometimes influenced as much by emotion as by fundamentals?

Emotions can play a major part in changing stock valuations, especially near market tops and bottoms. For example, emotions sometimes seem to overpower fundamentals after a long bull market. New players in the market may feel they have discovered innovative methods for selecting stocks so that earnings, sales, and management quality no longer count. Prices of certain categories of stocks sometimes get bid up to lofty levels. At one time, it was manufacturers of color televisions, then nursing homes. At another, it was Internet-related stocks. Likewise, the depths of a bear market might bring so much despair that many individual investors don't feel like buying stocks, regardless of the fundamentals.

A friend uses stock price charts to choose which securities to buy and sell. How does this work?

Charting security prices is a type of technical analysis that attempts to identify variables that accurately forecast security price movements. Some investors try to interpret the data contained in graphs of historical stock prices, while other analysts rely on other technical indicators, such as trading volume, upward price changes compared to declining price changes, the investment quality of actively traded stocks, and so forth. The list of technical indicators is virtually endless.

What is the theory behind technical analysis?

Technical analysis attempts to analyze the supply and demand for stocks and then utilize the analysis to make decisions on securities to buy and sell. In particular, people who practice technical analysis are interested in uncovering the investment activities of major investors such as mutual funds and pension funds. The theory is that major investors have the resources and knowledge to make informed investment decisions. Individuals who are able to determine what institutional investors are doing can follow their lead and take advantage of the investigative work the institutions have already done. Investors who use technical analysis believe certain stock market variables, if correctly interpreted, can provide guidance as to what informed, big-money investors are up to.

What about stock price charts? How can these help?

Stock price charts illustrate a stock's price history, that is, multiple periods of daily, weekly, or monthly stock price movements. Technical analysts believe that viewing past price movements of a particular stock will allow them to discover the buying and selling decisions of large investors. The idea is to interpret stock price movements and determine whether a stock is being accumulated (purchased) or distributed (sold) by institutional investors. If institutional investors are thought to be accumulating the stock, technical analysts hope to profit by purchasing shares of the stock. If institutional investors are believed to be distributing the stock, they must believe it is overpriced, and technical analysts attempt to profit by selling shares of the stock. Technical analysis is a game of following the leader when the leader knows the score. At least this is the theory.

Can charts be utilized to forecast not only the direction but also the extent of a stock price movement?

Some investors who utilize charts feel that certain chart formations are useful in projecting target price levels as well as the direction of future price movements. The size of a projected price movement is sometimes judged on the basis of the extent to which institutional investors have been accumulating (for an upward price movement) or distributing (for a downward price movement) a particular stock. The longer the period of accumulation, the greater the expected price move of the stock.

What type of information is required to maintain stock charts?

Most chartists record price information on a daily basis, although some analysts maintain charts with weekly or monthly prices. A daily price chart requires daily information for stock's high price, low price, closing price, and trading volume. Each of these items is published in *The Wall Street Journal, Investor's Business Daily,* and most large daily newspapers. To keep from beginning a set of charts from ground zero and being required to wait for months to obtain enough data for the charts to be useful, you might want to visit the library and record daily data for the last month or two. Obtaining past price data allows you to get a running start.

How do I use this information once it is obtained?

Security price charts are constructed with stock prices labeled on the vertical axis (up and down) and days, weeks, or months labeled on the horizontal axis (across the bottom). The price of the stock being charted determines the range of prices used on the vertical axis. The dollar amount of difference between the price at the top of the chart and the price at the bottom of the chart needs to be sufficiently wide that the stock can be charted over a relatively long period without having its price move off the chart. Each trading day (or week or month), the high and low prices are connected with a straight vertical line. A short horizontal line is notched to indicate the stock's closing price. The process continues each day, and hopefully, price formations will develop to assist you with making investment decisions. To view a price chart for the Dow Jones Industrial Average, take a look at the third page of the Money & Investing Section of *The*

Wall Street Journal. Better yet check Figure 2-1 in Chapter 2 of this book.

This sounds like too much work. Are ready-made charts available?

Several commercial services sell completed stock price charts. Some firms provide price data via telephone so that you can download data to a computer. Firms selling ready-made stock charts advertise in financial publications such as *Barron's*. Several websites on the Internet have stock price charts that can be viewed without charge. Regardless of how the price information is obtained, it is up to you to interpret the data that is presented.

How do I determine which price formations are useful for forecasting stock prices?

A number of books and investment advisory services are devoted to technical analysis. Most books on technical analysis contain numerous price formations widely used by technical analysts. If you develop an interest in learning more about charting, visit your local library or bookstore and browse through the section on investments. Some brokerage firms also publish technical information from the firms' analysts.

You earlier mentioned technical indicators other than price formations. Can you elaborate a little?

Technical analysts pay close attention to a stock's trading volume. The theory is that something of importance has happened or is happening when trading in a stock becomes unusually heavy. This is true even when no news concerning the firm seems to be available. Technical analysts generally view it as a buying opportunity when a stock increases in price on very heavy trading volume. Conversely, these same investors would be concerned if a stock declines in price on unusually heavy volume. Determining how much trading volume is required to qualify as "unusually heavy" requires that you examine a security's normal trading activity. For stocks that normally exhibit little trading activity, unusual volume might amount to 100,000 to 200,000 shares. For stocks that often trade 500,000 shares a day, trading of 2- or 3-million shares may be required to qualify as unusually heavy.

Are there any other technical tools I should know?

Other technical tools include advancing versus declining stock issues for a given trading day. A significant edge to advancing issues is considered bullish. Large cash holdings by mutual funds is thought to be a bullish indicator because of the substantial buying power these institutions have available. A large number of bearish stock analysts is considered a bullish sign because the consensus is usually wrong. Conversely, a large number of bullish stock analysts is considered a bearish signal. The list of technical tools is virtually endless, although individual technical analysts tend to have their favorites.

Is it better to select stocks using technical analysis or fundamental analysis?

Some professional stock analysts swear by technical analysis, while other analysts choose to use fundamental analysis. Some analysts actually utilize both methods for selecting stocks to buy and sell. For example, some analysts feel that fundamental analysis is a good method for selecting which stocks to buy and sell and that technical analysis should be used to determine when to buy and sell. Technical analysis is much more concerned with timing than is fundamental analysis.

How are mutual funds valued?

The value of a mutual fund is equal to the value of the securities that are owned by the fund. The value of each mutual fund share is equal to the value of the portfolio the fund owns divided by the number of shares of the fund that are outstanding. This is called the *net asset value* of the fund. Mutual funds issue new shares and redeem outstanding shares at the net asset value. The net asset value of a mutual fund will increase if the values of the securities it owns increase in value. Likewise, the net asset value of a mutual fund will decline if the securities owned by the fund decline in value.

How about options?

Options are examples of derivatives, which means they derive their value from another investment. Stock options derive their value from the underlying value of the stock. In addition to the underlying assets, option values depend on the length of time before they expire, the price volatility of the underlying asset, and the price at which they can be used to buy or sell the underlying asset. Other factors such as market rates of interest also influence the value of options. Options tend to be leveraged investments, therefore relatively modest changes in the value of the underlying asset can have a major impact on the value of the option.

11
CHAPTER

Should I Invest in a Mutual Fund?

Chapter summary

Mutual funds are companies that funnel the money of individual investors into professionally selected portfolios of securities. Mutual funds are often a wise investment choice, especially when relatively small amounts of money are available. Investing in a mutual fund allows you to acquire a diversified portfolio of securities with only a modest amount of money. Mutual funds often levy several types of fees, but these can vary significantly in size among the thousands of available funds.

What is a mutual fund?

A mutual fund is a company that pools the money of many individuals and invests the proceeds in financial assets. Rather than owning buildings, equipment, and products held for resale, mutual funds own stocks, bonds, and money market instruments. A mutual fund earns income from the dividends and/or interest it receives and from gains realized from the securities it sells. Basically, a mutual fund is a company that funnels its stockholders' money into financial assets. The proliferation of mutual funds from 1978–1998 can be seen in Figure 11-1.

How can I make money by investing in a mutual fund?

Because of certain federal regulations, mutual funds are required to pass along to their shareholders virtually all of the dividends and interest income received. Thus, as a mutual fund shareholder, you will receive distributions from the fund just as owners of bonds receive interest payments and the owners of stocks receive dividend payments. Mutual funds are also required to pass along any capital gains they realize. In other words, a mutual fund that sells a security it owns for more than it paid must pass along the gain to its shareholders.

Am I able to reinvest the distributions in additional shares of a mutual fund?

You can elect to have distributions automatically reinvested in additional shares of the mutual fund. The election regarding how to handle distributions is made at the time of your initial purchase but can be changed at any time. In other words, it is no problem to initially have distributions reinvested and later change your mind and have the distributions sent to you. Choose the reinvestment alternative and you will receive periodic account statements indicating the amount of money reinvested, the price paid for shares purchased, number of shares purchased, and the number of shares being held in your account. The distributions must be reported as income on your tax return, even though no direct payment is received from the distribution.

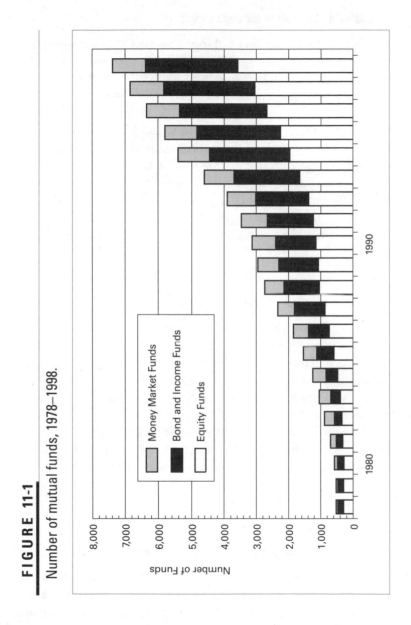

FIGURE 11-1

Number of mutual funds, 1978–1998.

Do mutual fund shares change in value?

The shares of most mutual funds are subject to price changes, some of which can be quite large. The market value of each share of a mutual fund's stock is a function of the value of the fund's portfolio and the number of shares of the fund that are outstanding. A mutual fund that holds $1,500,000 in securities and has 75,000 shares outstanding is worth $1,500,000/75,000 shares, or $20 per share. If the market value of the portfolio subsequently increases to $2,250,000 while the number of shares outstanding remains constant, the value of the fund's shares will rise to $30 each. Assuming an unchanging number of shares outstanding, the price of a mutual fund's shares will vary in relation to changes in the value of the securities held in the fund's portfolio.

What if the number of shares changes?

Mutual funds have an unusual corporate structure that permits them to continuously issue new shares and redeem existing shares. As will be discussed shortly, issuing additional shares or redeeming existing shares affects the overall size of a mutual fund, but it does not cause a change in the value of the mutual fund's shares. A mutual fund's shares will increase in value only if the value of assets owned by the fund increases proportionately more than the number of shares outstanding. Conversely, a mutual fund's shares will decrease in value only when the fund's portfolio decreases in value proportionately more than a decline in the number of shares outstanding.

How does a mutual fund decide which securities to buy?

Mutual funds employ professional investment managers who determine which securities should be purchased and sold. The theory is that professional managers with extensive investment experience and knowledge of the securities markets should be able to make superior investment decisions. Mutual fund portfolio managers have access to sophisticated and expensive investment research that is unavailable to individual investors.

Does a mutual fund buy securities to hold or do the managers of the fund actively buy and sell securities?

Most mutual fund managers engage in active trading of securities, although the amount of trading varies considerably from one fund to the next. Fund managers are constantly attempting to identify and replace overvalued securities (as judged by the managers) with undervalued securities. Mutual funds pay brokerage commissions to buy and sell securities, but the trades are typically very large and the fees on a per-share basis are quite low compared to the commission rates an individual investor such as yourself would be required to pay. Still, turnover of a portfolio does have its disadvantages, including added expense and realized gains that must be distributed to shareholders.

Why are realized gains considered a disadvantage?

Realized gains result in taxable income for a mutual fund's shareholders. Some individual investors prefer mutual funds with stable portfolios so as to minimize their tax liability. Taxes are discussed in more detail in the following chapter.

Do all mutual funds hold similar portfolios of securities?

Mutual funds are categorized according to their investment objectives and the types of securities they own. Mutual funds within each of these categories own similar types of securities. For example, some mutual funds invest only in stocks, whereas other mutual funds limit their investments to bonds. Other mutual funds buy both stocks and bonds. These broad categories are further divided and many mutual funds specialize in particular types of stocks or bonds. For example, some mutual funds limit their holdings to the common stocks of companies from a particular country or from a particular region of the world. Other mutual funds concentrate on owning the stocks of companies that the fund managers consider as having great growth potential. Many mutual funds specialize in owning municipal bonds that pay tax-exempt interest. Some funds even specialize in owning municipal bonds issued in a particular state.

Are money market funds a type of mutual fund?

Money market funds are a specialized type of mutual fund with investments in short-term debt securities that pay interest and exhibit little price change. Thus, rather than invest in stocks and bonds in hopes of profiting from changes in asset values, money market funds invest in U.S. Treasury bills, commercial paper, certificates of deposit, and other high-quality, short-term debt that pays interest income but offers very limited potential for changes in market value. Some money market funds further specialize by owning only tax-exempt debt securities, which allows the funds to collect and then pass through tax-exempt interest to their own shareholders. Because the investments held by a money market fund have stable market values, the share price of a money market fund is also stable. In fact, sponsors attempt to maintain money market shares at a constant price of $1.

What type of return can I expect from a money market mutual fund?

Money market funds offer returns that are competitive with short-term interest rates. Buy shares in a money market fund and you can plan on earning about the same rate as that being paid on U.S. Treasury bills. Sometimes the return may be a little less and sometimes it may be a little more. Money market funds invest in short-term debt instruments, collect interest paid by these securities, and distribute the income to shareholders in the form of more shares of stock. Thus, you earn what the fund earns except for a relatively small fee that is deducted to cover the fund's operating expenses. The return from owning shares of a money market fund constantly changes as maturing debt securities are replaced with new debt securities. If market rates of interest have risen and replacement securities yield more than maturing securities, your own return will increase. If interest rates on short-term debt instruments fall, the return earned by shareholders of a money market mutual fund will also decline.

Do some mutual funds also specialize in bonds?

Many mutual funds specialize in bond investments. Bond funds often have subspecialties, but to a lesser extent than mutual funds that concentrate on stock ownership. Most mutual funds that specialize in bonds choose to invest in a particular category of bonds. For example, bond funds that invest in municipal bonds are able to pay their shareholders tax-exempt income. Some of these municipal bond funds restrict their portfolios to municipal bonds issued in a particular state so that shareholders can receive dividends that may be free of both federal and state taxation. Mutual funds that specialize in bonds often choose to hold debt securities within a particular range of maturities. For example, a fund might choose to limit its portfolio to bonds that have maturities of five years or less, while a different fund might specialize in owning bonds with very long maturities. These two types of bond funds produce very different results for their shareholders, depending on the level and direction of interest rates.

Why all this specialization?

Mutual funds with specialized portfolios attract investors who wish to acquire a professionally managed portfolio within a particular segment of the stock market or the bond market. For example, investing in a mutual fund that specializes in municipal bonds allows you to earn tax-exempt income from a diversified portfolio of municipal bonds. Even though you may not have enough money to purchase a $5000 municipal bond, you are likely to be able to afford shares of a mutual fund that owns a large portfolio of municipal bonds. Likewise, you can acquire part interest in a diversified portfolio of growth stocks by investing in a mutual fund that specializes in these securities. Mutual funds even permit you to acquire a stake in a portfolio of common stocks issued by companies from a particular foreign country. Specialized mutual fund portfolios are offered to individuals who want to invest in a particular industry, a particular country, or a particular region of the world. Specialized bond funds allow you to choose whether to own a part interest in a portfolio of long-term bonds, intermediate-term bonds, or short-term bonds. The graph in Figure 11-2 provides a look at overall mutual fund sales and redemptions from 1975 to 1997.

Do any mutual funds own both stocks and bonds?

Some mutual funds, called *balanced funds,* own both stocks and bonds. Balanced funds are considered "middle-of-the-road" funds that offer growth potential, i.e., an increase in share value, at the same time they provide current income to their shareholders by paying dividends from the interest and dividends that are received. Owning a balanced fund produces the same effect as investing in both a mutual fund that specializes in stocks and a second mutual fund that specializes in bonds. View a balanced fund as a place for one-stop shopping. The bonds held by balanced funds offer stability of value and high current income, and the stocks that are owned offer the potential for gains in value. The result is a compromise investment.

FIGURE 11-2

Mutual fund sales and redemptions, 1975–1997.

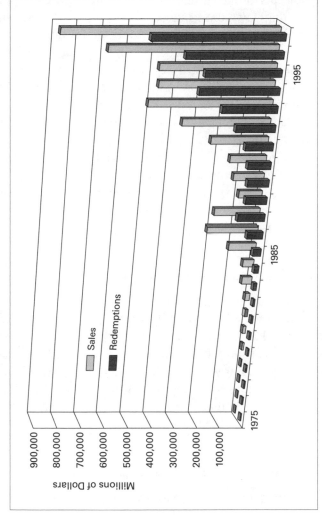

What are the index funds that I hear so much about?

Index funds are a special type of mutual fund that attempts to track the performance of a particular stock index or average such as the Dow Jones Industrial Average or the Standard & Poor's 500 Index (S&P 500). Changes in the value of an index fund's shares will parallel changes in the value of the index. If the underlying index declines, the price of an index fund's shares will decline by approximately the same proportion. The portfolio manager of an index fund designs the portfolio around the stocks that comprise the index. These funds offer a way to actually "own the market" rather than owning a particular stock or a sector of the market. In general, index funds incur low expenses because no research and little buying and selling of securities are necessary. Low portfolio turnover also results in relatively small capital gains distributions and a reduced tax liability for shareholders.

How can I purchase shares of a mutual fund?

Some mutual funds are sold directly by their sponsors, while other funds are sold through a variety of financial institutions, such as brokerage firms, insurance companies, and financial planners. You must phone or write the sponsor to purchase shares directly. For your trouble, you are likely to save paying a sales fee that goes to compensate a salesperson. Buying direct cuts out the middleman. A selected listing of large mutual fund distributors can be seen in Table 11-1.

Am I required to invest a minimum amount of money?

Each mutual fund establishes its own minimum investment. Some funds require a minimum initial investment of $2500 or more, while other funds allow you to open an account with as little as $100. Minimum purchases of additional shares once an

TABLE 11-1

Selected list of large mutual fund distributors.

Colonial Investment Services One Financial Center Boston, MA 02111-2621 800-225-2365	Putnam Financial Services P.O. Box 41203 Providence, RI 02940-1203 800-225-1581
Dreyfus Service Corporation 144 Glenn Curtiss Boulevard Uniondale, NY 11556 800-782-6620	Scudder Fund Distributors P.O. Box 2291 Boston, MA 02107-9913 800-225-2470
Fidelity Distributors Corporation 82 Devonshire Street Boston, MA 02109 800-544-6666	USAA Investment Management 9800 Fredricksburg Road San Antonio, TX 78288 800-531-8181
IDS Financial Services IDS Town 10 Minneapolis, MN 55440 800-328-8300	Value Line Securities 331 West Ninth Street, Fourth Floor Kansas City, MO 64105 800-223-0818
Kemper Financial Services 222 South Riverside Plaza Chicago, IL 60603 800-621-1048	Vanguard Group of Investment Companies P.O. Box 2600 MS 136 Valley Forge, PA 19482 800-662-7447
Massachusetts Financial Services P.O. Box 2281 Boston, MA 02107-9906 800-225-2606	
T Rowe Price Associates P.O. Box 89000 Baltimore, MD 21289-0250 800-638-5660	

account has been opened are nearly always smaller than the initial investment requirement. For example, a fund that imposes an opening minimum of $2500 may allow subsequent investments of as little as $50. Both the initial minimum amount of money to open an account and the minimum requirement for subsequent investments vary by firm. Depending on your financial resources, the minimum amount required to open an account will be an important consideration in selecting a fund.

What determines the value of a mutual fund?

The value of a mutual fund's shares is determined by the value of the securities owned by the fund and the number of the fund's outstanding shares. Suppose a mutual fund holds stocks and bonds with a current market value of $200 million. If the fund has 10 million shares of its own stock in investors' hands, each share has a value of $200 million/10 million shares, or $20. This is called the mutual fund's *net asset value* (NAV). The net asset value of a mutual fund is very important because it determines the price you will pay when shares of the fund are purchased and the price you will receive when shares of the fund are sold. Everything about a mutual fund revolves around the net asset value.

Should I be able to buy and sell shares of a mutual fund at the net asset value?

Shares of a mutual fund are sold and repurchased at the net asset value only if the fund has no sales charge or redemption fee. If a sales fee is charged, you will be required to pay the net asset value plus the sales fee. If a redemption fee is charged when shares are sold, you will receive the net asset value less the redemption fee. Invest $2500 in a mutual fund with an NAV of $10 and you will purchase 250 shares if no sales fee is charged. If the mutual fund levies a 4 percent sales fee, $100 will be deducted from the money invested and you will receive credit for only 240 shares.

Will I be able to purchase additional shares of the same fund?

Mutual funds are structured such that new shares of stock are continuously made available for sale except in the rare instances when a fund has been closed to new investments. Current owners of a fund may purchase additional shares and outside investors who desire to become owners can buy shares for the first time. For example, you can purchase 100 shares of the fund today and several months later buy an additional 50 shares of the same fund. Mutual funds do not normally limit the number of shares that may be sold or the number of shares an individual investor can purchase. Thus, a successful mutual fund may grow very large as new investors buy shares in the fund and existing shareholders purchase additional shares.

What price will I pay to purchase additional shares?

The price to purchase additional shares of a mutual fund will depend on the fund's NAV at the time of the purchase. The net asset value of the fund's shares will change with variations in the value of securities owned by the fund. Thus, you may pay more or less than the price you paid for the original shares. If the fund's manager has made good investment choices, the fund's net asset value will have increased and you will pay a higher price than you paid for your original shares. On the other hand, if the mutual fund's investments have done poorly, you will be able to buy additional shares for a lower price than you paid for the original shares, because the fund's NAV will have declined.

So the value of my shares of a mutual fund is directly affected by the value of the securities owned by the fund?

The investment decisions of the fund's portfolio manager are the driving force behind the value of your shares in the fund. If securities owned by the fund increase in value, then the net asset value (i.e., the price) of the fund's shares will also increase. Likewise, if a falling market or poor investment decisions by the manager cause the fund's portfolio to decline in value, the fund's own shares will decline in price. The strength of the market combined with the investment decisions of the fund manager are the determining factors in the performance of your investment in the fund.

Does the price of a mutual fund's shares move up and down very much?

The volatility of a mutual fund's shares depends entirely on the price volatility and diversification of the securities being held in the fund's portfolio. If a mutual fund owns securities with volatile prices, then the price of the fund's own shares will be subject to large changes. For example, a mutual fund that is heavily invested in volatile high-tech stocks will experience great volatility in the value of its portfolio and in the price of its own stock. A relatively stable share price will prevail for a mutual fund that invests in securities with stable market values. The ultimate in share price stability is enjoyed by money market mutual funds, which invest in short-term debt securities. These securities register only minor changes in value, thus causing shares of money market funds to have a very stable price.

Will mutual fund shares experience less price volatility than individual stocks?

The price of a mutual fund's shares tends to be less volatile than the prices of most of the individual stocks owned by the fund because price movements of some stocks will tend to cancel out price movements of other stocks. In other words, the prices of all the securities owned by a mutual fund will not always move together. The more specialized a fund's holdings, the more stocks owned by the fund will move together. Therefore, specialized funds tend to experience greater price volatility than funds that hold broadly diversified portfolios.

Is price volatility of a mutual fund's shares important?

The importance of the price volatility of a mutual fund's shares depends on your investment goals. Price volatility is likely to be an important consideration in selecting a fund if you anticipate the possibility of needing to sell shares on short notice. On the other hand, if you are a long-term investor who intends to ride out short- and intermediate-term price changes, then price volatility is likely to be much less important.

You mentioned that expert management is one of the main benefits of investing in mutual funds. Are there any other benefits?

A major benefit of investing in mutual funds is the instant diversification (i.e., owning many different securities) that can be achieved with a limited investment. Diversification means that the value of your investment is not so dependent on a few different securities. The diversification of a mutual fund is virtually impossible to match unless you have available a very large amount of money that would allow you to invest in a substantial number of different securities.

Are some mutual funds more diversified than other funds?

Many mutual funds formed in the 1980s and 1990s offer specialized portfolios. For example, a mutual fund might specialize in owning stocks of high-technology companies. Other mutual funds specialize in the stocks of companies in a certain foreign country or in a certain geographic region. Mutual funds with specialized portfolios offer limited diversification compared to mutual funds that invest in a wide range of industries.

Why should I worry about investing in a specialized fund?

Specialized mutual funds are more risky than well-diversified mutual funds because the performance of a specialized fund is tied to a single type of investment. The stock prices of similar companies tend to move in tandem. That is, if the price of Exxon stock declines, the stock prices of BP Amoco and Royal Dutch Petroleum are also likely to decline. Owning all four stocks or holding shares in a mutual fund that limits its investments to petroleum stocks provides little diversification. Thus, the net asset value of a specialized mutual fund is likely to be more volatile than the net asset value of a well-diversified mutual fund, especially if the diversified fund invests in both stocks and bonds.

What kinds of fees will I pay for investing in a mutual fund?

Several types of fees can be applicable for individuals who invest in mutual funds. Fee structures differ among the thousands of mutual funds that are available for purchase, and not all funds charge every fee. All mutual funds do levy a fee that goes to pay the portfolio managers and cover the fund's operating costs. This annual fee generally ranges between one-half of one percent and slightly over one percent of a fund's assets. A mutual fund with $800 million in assets that levies a fee of one percent will take in $8 million to cover its expenses. This particular fee comes out of the fund's earnings and reduces the return that is earned by the mutual fund's shareholders. A higher fee means a greater hit against the fund's earnings. The dollar amount (but not the percentage) of the fee will increase as a fund grows in size. The percentage size of this fee sometimes declines as a fund grows larger and a greater amount of assets are subject to the fee.

How can I determine the size of a mutual fund's management fee?

The type and size of each fee charged by a mutual fund is spelled out in the prospectus that is available from the fund or from the fund's salesperson. Fee information is also included in mutual fund advisory services published by firms such as Morningstar and Value Line. It is worthwhile to examine a mutual fund's prospectus before investing in the fund.

What other types of fees are charged by mutual funds?

Mutual funds sold by brokers and other salespeople nearly always entail a transaction fee, generally at the time shares are purchased. Some mutual funds require a redemption fee that is charged when shares are redeemed rather than when shares are purchased. A transaction or sales fee that is paid when shares are purchased, referred to as a *load,* generally rewards the person who sells the shares. Loads typically range from 3 percent to 6 percent of the money invested, although fees can climb to 8 percent for the purchase of some funds. Keep in mind that paying a sales fee reduces the amount of your investment that goes to buying shares of the fund. Also, don't expect to attain better portfolio management when a fee is charged to reward the salesperson instead of the portfolio manager.

How are redemption fees applied?

Some mutual funds levy a redemption charge, also called an *exit fee* or *back-end load,* when shares are redeemed. Often, redemption charges are a percentage fee that is reduced each year the shares have been held. For example, a fund might charge an exit fee of 6 percent of the sales price if shares have been held less than a year, 5 percent if shares have been held between one and two years, 3 percent if held between two and three years, and so forth. Under this type of fee schedule, no redemption fee would be charged if shares have been held for a specified number of years. Both the sales fee and redemption fee will be described in the mutual fund's prospectus.

Can you provide an example?

Suppose three years ago you invested $4500 in a mutual fund whose shares sold at a price of $15. Without a sales fee, you would have purchased $4500/$15 per share, or 300 shares. If the firm levied a sales fee of 4 percent, $180 of your $4500 investment would go to cover the sales fee, meaning that only $4320 was actually invested in shares of the fund. Now suppose the fund didn't charge an initial sales fee but, instead, levied a redemption fee equal to 4 percent of the net asset value at the time of redemption. If you sold all 300 shares for $50 per share, the redemption fee would amount to $600 (4 percent of $15,000). The redemption fee would be deducted from the proceeds of the sale, so that you would receive $14,400 in proceeds from the sale.

Are any other fees involved in buying and owning mutual funds?

Some mutual funds levy what is termed a *12b-1 fee*. This is an annual percentage fee charged against the market value of the fund. Although the 12b-1 fee is similar to the annual management fee discussed earlier, proceeds from this charge are utilized to cover the fund's distribution expenses, which may include compensation for the salesperson, rather than for paying management expenses. Essentially, a 12b-1 fee is a charge paid by current shareholders that reimburses the fund for recruiting new shareholders. A rundown of the costs of investing in ten equity and balanced mutual funds can be seen in Table 11-2.

Can I find mutual funds that don't charge any of these fees?

Some mutual funds do not charge an initial sales fee, a redemption fee, or a 12b-1 fee. These fees are designed to cover distribution and sales expenses, not the costs of operating a fund. All funds levy a management fee designed to cover management

TABLE 11-2

Expenses Involved in investing in the ten largest equity and balanced funds.

Fund	Sales Charge (%)	Redemption Fee (%)	12b-1 Fee (%)	Expense Ratio (%)
Fidelity Magellan	3.00	0.00	0.00	0.61
Vanguard Index Trust 500 Port.	0.00	0.00	0.00	0.19
Washington Mutual Investors	5.75	0.00	0.25	0.62
Investment Company of America	5.75	0.00	0.25	0.56
Fidelity Growth & Income	0.00	0.00	0.00	0.69
Vanguard Windsor II	0.00	0.00	0.00	0.37
American Cent: Twentieth Cen. Ult.	0.00	0.00	0.00	1.00
Vanguard Wellington	0.00	0.00	0.00	0.29
Fidelity Puritan	0.00	0.00	0.00	0.64
Fidelity Adv. Growth Opp.	3.50	0.00	0.65	1.18

and operating expenses. Somebody has to pay the cost of operating the fund, of course, but this charge varies widely among the different funds. This means you should be certain to determine the size of the management fee before putting your money into a fund.

If some funds don't charge sales, redemption, or 12b-1 fees, is there any reason I should consider a fund that does charge one or more of these fees?

Some financial planners advise individuals to limit their choices to mutual funds that levy only a management fee and then to further narrow the selection to a fund with a relatively low management fee. An important consideration is the degree of assistance you may require in selecting a fund. Perhaps you do not feel you have the expertise to make an informed selection from among the more than 7000 funds available for purchase. Should you purchase a stock fund, a bond fund, or a balanced fund? If you decide on a stock fund, should you choose a fund that specializes in growth stocks, income stocks, or the stocks of foreign companies? Many choices are available, and it is important to narrow the selection to funds that have investment goals appropriate to your financial needs.

With thousands of mutual funds available, how do I decide which ones to buy?

You must first determine what it is you want to accomplish with the money you expect to invest. Are you after current income or capital appreciation? Choosing between these two investment goals will significantly narrow the list of appropriate funds. After deciding between income and capital growth, consider the degree of risk you can afford to assume. If you are after current income but are unwilling to accept much risk, the list of funds is narrowed even more. On the other hand, if you are willing to accept considerable risk in the pursuit of current income, a different set of mutual funds can be eliminated from consideration.

After establishing my investment goals, won't I still have hundreds of funds from which to choose?

Numerous funds are included in each category, so you will need to further narrow your choices among funds with a similar goal. First, investigate the intermediate-term and long-term track records of the funds. Both are more important than short-term performance. You should check the fees charged by each of the funds you are considering. Several inexpensive publications, including *Money, Forbes,* and *Business Week,* publish special editions that list the fees and historical investment performance of individual mutual funds. Morningstar and Value Line each publish much more comprehensive information. Both of these publications provide a performance rating of individual funds and an assessment of the relative riskiness of owning each fund.

Are mutual fund shares traded on a stock exchange?

Mutual fund shares are not traded in the secondary market. Thus, mutual funds are not listed on the New York Stock Exchange or the American Stock Exchange and they are not traded over the counter. Mutual fund shares are purchased from and sold to the fund sponsor, although a salesperson will sometimes handle the transaction. Because mutual funds guarantee to redeem their shares at net asset value, there is no need for you to locate another investor when you decide to sell shares you own.

How do I check on the price of a mutual fund's shares?

Mutual fund quotations are published daily in *The Wall Street Journal, Investor's Business Daily,* and many metropolitan newspapers. Other newspapers publish weekly quotations, usually in their Saturday or Sunday editions. During each week, *The Wall Street Journal* publishes data for the net asset value, fees, and investment performance over several time periods. Nearly all funds have toll-free telephone numbers for shareholder use.

Do mutual fund companies offer retirement options such as IRAs?

Mutual funds have been very aggressive in pursuing investors interested in establishing retirement accounts. Most of these

companies offer a variety of retirement accounts, including individual retirement accounts, Keogh plans, and 403(b) plans.
You may or may not be required to pay a fee to open and/or
maintain a retirement account at a mutual fund. Fees are sometimes waived when an account reaches a specified dollar
amount. Some sponsors also levy a fee when a retirement account is moved to another firm. These fees are in addition to any
other fees a mutual fund charges.

I have heard about investments similar to mutual funds. What are these?

Mutual funds are one type of investment company. Another less
popular kind is the closed-end investment company. Closed-
end funds are organized in an identical manner to most corporations. That is, a closed-end investment company issues a specific number of shares to investors when the company is
formed. No further shares are issued except in rare instances.
Unlike mutual funds, which agree to redeem their shares,
closed-end investment companies do not provide for the redemption of their own shares. Thus, while mutual funds expand
and contract in size depending on whether investors are buying
additional shares or redeeming outstanding shares, closed-end
investment companies begin business with a fixed number of
shares that will remain unchanged throughout the life of the
companies (see Table 11-3 for a list of some such companies).

How do I liquidate shares of a closed-end fund?

Shares of closed-end investment companies are traded in the
secondary market in the same manner as the shares of Coca-
Cola, Microsoft, General Motors, and all other publicly traded
corporations. The shares of many closed-end funds are traded
on one or more of the stock exchanges, while other closed-end
investment companies have stock that is traded in the over-the-

TABLE 11-3

Partial listing of closed-end single country funds.

Fund	Exchange
Argentina Fund	New York
Brazilian Equity Fund	New York
Canadian General Investment Fund	Toronto
Chile Fund	New York
China Fund	New York
First Australia Fund	American
First Israel Fund	New York
First Philippine Fund	New York
India Fund	New York
Indonesia Fund	New York
Jakarta Growth Fund	New York
Japan Equity Fund	New York
Korea Fund	New York
Malaysia Fund	New York
Mexico Fund	New York
New South Africa Fund	New York
Pakistan Investment Fund	New York
ROC Taiwan Fund	New York
Singapore Fund	New York
Taiwan Fund	New York
Templeton Vietnam Fund	New York
Thai Fund	New York
Turkish Investment Fund	New York

counter market. In other words, instead of shares being redeemed by the sponsor, as is the case with mutual funds, shares of a closed-end fund must be sold to another investor. This type of transaction in the secondary market is facilitated by a broker, which means that you will pay a commission both to buy shares of a closed-end fund (unless you purchase stock as part of an original issue) and later to sell those same shares.

Will I be able to sell shares of a closed-end fund at net asset value?

It's possible, but unlikely you will receive a price that exactly equals net asset value. It is just as unlikely that you will purchase shares of a closed-end fund at net asset value. Shares of a closed-end investment company are traded among investors rather than redeemed by the sponsor, so at any particular time, the shares may trade at a price that is higher or lower than net asset value. A closed-end fund with an NAV of $10.50 may sell for $9.75, for $12.10, or anywhere in between. Thus, you may purchase shares of a closed-end investment company for less than NAV and later sell the same shares for more than net asset value. This is the best of all worlds because you are buying at a discount and selling at a premium. Of course, it may turn out to be just the opposite: you may buy shares above net asset value and subsequently sell the same shares at a discount to net asset value.

Why do shares of closed-end investment companies sell at discounts and premiums?

No one seems to have a definitive answer to this question. As with stocks, bonds, or tangible investments, the share prices for closed-end investment companies are affected by supply and demand. With no additional shares being issued, investors can only buy the stock of a particular closed-end fund from other investors. The price at which stock is available may be above or below the net asset value. Past investment performance and the perceived quality of a fund's management certainly have an effect on supply and demand, and therefore on the price of a fund's shares.

What are unit investment trusts?

A unit investment trust (UIT), also called an *investment trust,* is a basket of assets packaged by an investment firm such as Merrill Lynch, Salomon Smith Barney, or Prudential Securities. The sponsor of the trust issues a fixed number of ownership units that are sold to cover the cost of acquiring the assets in the trust. While mutual funds and closed-end investment companies hold managed portfolios in the sense that assets are subject to being bought and sold, an investment trust begins life with a portfolio of assets that remains unchanged throughout the life of the trust. Unit investment trusts devoted to holding bonds are particularly popular with investors. Other unit trusts specialize in a fixed assortment of stocks. The unit trusts pass through to their owners all the cash received. In the case of UITs holding bond portfolios, cash received from interest and bond redemptions is passed through to the owners. Unit investment trusts holding stocks pass through dividends and proceeds from the sale of stock.

If these investments have unchanging baskets of assets, why is stock sold?

Some unit trusts specializing in stocks have a maturity date that is established when the trusts are formed. At maturity, all of the stocks in the portfolio are sold and proceeds are distributed to the trust owners. Unit trusts specializing in bonds distribute cash when debt securities mature or are called by the issuers. A bond trust is dissolved when all of its bonds have been redeemed.

What about the money I receive when the trust is dissolved?

A unit trust holding a portfolio of bonds will return a portion of your money each year as bonds are called or mature. After years of payments, most of the bonds originally held by the unit trust will have been redeemed and the value of the remaining portfolio will be relatively small. At this point the sponsor will distribute the remaining assets and dissolve the trust. Your cash needs and investment goals will determine whether the cash you receive can be spent or reinvested. Perhaps you will decide to devote cash distributions to buying another unit investment trust.

Can ownership units of an investment trust be resold?

Ownership units of an investment trust can be resold, but these investments are generally not as liquid as shares of mutual funds or closed-end investment companies. The sponsor of a unit investment trust will generally make a secondary market in ownership units, but selling your ownership back to the sponsor means you are likely to receive a price that is somewhat lower than you might consider fair. The sponsor purchases the units for resale to other investors. Unit trusts specializing in bonds should generally be purchased with the intention of holding the investment until the trust is dissolved.

Do unit investment trusts hold specialized portfolios?

Most unit trusts specialize in the types of assets they hold. Many of the trusts hold portfolios of municipal bonds. These trusts pass through to their owners interest payments that are exempt from federal income taxes. Some unit trusts specialize in bonds with particular maturity lengths. For example, some unit trusts hold bonds with maturity lengths of from seven to ten years. Other trusts specialize in owning bonds with very long maturities. Some unit trusts even specialize in bonds issued within a particular state. One popular unit trust specializes in owning high dividend-paying stocks included in the Dow Jones Industrial Average. Basically, a sponsor will put together any specialized type of unit investment trust that the sponsor believes will appeal to investors.

Is a unit investment trust superior to a mutual fund?

The unmanaged portfolio of a unit trust requires a much lower management fee than is charged by most mutual funds. On the other hand, you are likely to pay a sales fee of about 4 percent of the amount invested to purchase units of ownership in an investment trust. Some but not all mutual funds charge a similar sales fee. If an investment is to be retained many years, the unit investment trust is likely to be the superior investment because of the significant savings that will be achieved from the nominal management fee. On the other hand, little savings will result from a holding period of two or three years. Unit trusts are particularly applicable if you plan to invest a nominal amount of money, are mostly interested in owning bonds, and intend to hold the securities to maturity.

How do I choose between investing in individual issues of stocks and bonds and investing in the ready-made portfolio of a mutual fund, closed-end fund, or unit investment trust?

A mutual fund is likely to be the best choice if you don't have much money to invest at any one time. For example, a mutual fund is an excellent choice if you intend to regularly invest several hundred dollars a month. Buying a few shares of stock at a time is usually an expensive proposition because of brokerage commissions. A mutual fund is also a good choice if you don't have the time to investigate individual stock or bond issues. Mutual funds hire professional portfolio managers who are paid a lot of money to select stocks to buy and sell. Investing in a closed-end fund requires somewhat more work on your part than investing in a mutual fund, in part because you are likely to find less material providing analysis of these funds. Unit investment trusts are a good choice if you are investing in either taxable or nontaxable bonds.

Can you give me some final pointers on investing in mutual funds?

First, choose from among the mutual funds that have investment goals compatible with your own financial goals. Second, investigate the fees you will be required to pay. Take time to look at a fund's past performance. This can be checked in several places, including well-known mutual fund publications from Morningstar and Value Line. Realize that long-term performance, not short-term performance, should be a consideration in your selection. Consider choosing a fund that is part of a family of funds so that you will be able to shift money from one fund to another without incurring substantial sales charges.

Is there anything else?

Once you settle on which funds you wish to buy, invest on a consistent basis rather than trying to time the market. In other words, don't attempt to determine if the market is too high or too low. Even professional investors have difficulty judging the market's direction on a regular basis. Invest $100 or $200 each month, regardless of whether the market is rising or falling. Financial people call this *dollar-cost averaging*. If the market declines, a constant investment will allow you to purchase a larger number of shares. Dollar-cost averaging is particularly effective with mutual funds because of the ability to invest relatively modest sums of money.

CHAPTER

How Are Wall Street Investments Taxed?

Chapter summary

Taxes are an unfortunate fact of life for investors. You must report as income and pay taxes on gains realized from the sale of securities, just as dividends and most interest payments you receive are subject to taxation. Even investment income exempt from federal taxes may be subject to taxation by states and municipalities. Taxation is an important consideration for investment decisions, which should be based on after-tax returns, not before-tax returns. This chapter discusses some of the important tax issues that are likely to be faced when investing in Wall Street.

Will I be able to avoid taxes by investing in Wall Street?

With some exceptions, Wall Street investments produce income that is subject to taxation. Dividends are taxable, most interest is taxable, and realized gains (you must sell an asset to realize a gain) in asset values are taxable. Of course, Wall Street investments sometimes lose value, in which case you may actually save taxes if you use realized losses (i.e., you sell assets for less than you paid) to offset realized gains or other types of income. However, saving taxes by investing in assets that lose value is not a goal of most investors.

Why should I invest in Wall Street if no tax benefits result?

Wall Street investments offer an opportunity to earn relatively high rates of return compared to the returns you are likely to earn on savings accounts, insurance policies, and certificates of deposit. Investments offered by Wall Street firms also offer the opportunity to acquire a diversified group of investment assets that can provide protection from some of the risks discussed in Chapter 13. A reduction of overall risk and the potential for higher returns are two good reasons to consider investing in Wall Street. In addition, certain tax advantages are available from Wall Street investments.

What kinds of taxes will I be required to pay on Wall Street investments?

If you choose to purchase shares of stock in a corporation—either common stock or preferred stock—you will be required to pay income taxes on any dividends you receive. Dividends are taxable at the same rate as your wages or salary. Invest in corporate bonds or U.S. government bonds and you must pay taxes on the interest income you receive. Like dividends, interest income is taxed at the same rate as the income earned from wages or salary. Keep in mind that the tax rate you pay will depend on the amount of taxable income you report. Interest income and dividend income are listed separately on your federal tax return.

How does the Internal Revenue Service know I have received dividends or interest?

Organizations that pay dividends or interest are required to report annually both the amounts and the recipients to the Internal Revenue Service (IRS), state tax authorities, and investors who received the payments. Thus, the IRS doesn't rely only on your word for the amount of interest and dividends you received. The information included on your tax return must agree with the information reported by the payers to the IRS, or you can expect an IRS letter requesting an explanation.

Are dividends and interest subject to withholding?

It is unlikely that dividend and interest income you receive will be subject to withholding, although you must sign a form confirming that withholding is not required. The federal government at one time attempted to initiate withholding on investment income, but a public outcry ensued (sponsored primarily by commercial banks rather than investors) and the proposal was scrapped.

I understand some interest is not taxable. Is this correct?

The federal government does not tax interest income from most bonds issued by state and local governments. Certain exceptions exist, including bonds issued to finance sports stadiums, private businesses, and some types of housing. However, most state and local bonds (often called *municipal bonds,* or *munis*) pay interest that is exempt from federal taxes. Depending on the tax code of the state in which you reside, interest from municipal bonds may also be exempt from state and local income taxes. For example, residents of Georgia are not required to pay either federal or state income taxes on interest received from bonds issued by the state of Georgia or municipalities within the state of Georgia. However, Georgia residents do have to pay state income taxes (but not federal taxes) on interest received from bonds issued by states and municipalities outside Georgia. State tax policy regarding municipal bond interest varies from state to state. To see how such tax-exempt instruments stack up against taxable investments, refer to Figure 12-1.

Why doesn't everyone invest in municipal bonds?

The tax-exempt interest from municipal bonds is so desirable that the issuers of these securities are able to pay relatively low interest rates in order to attract buyers. For example, at a time when big corporations might have to pay an interest rate of 6 percent to borrow money, a city or state with comparable credit quality may be able to issue its own tax-exempt bonds with an interest rate of $4\frac{1}{2}$ percent. Investors with modest income are likely to find that the tax benefit of owning a municipal bond does not offset the reduced interest rate from the bond. If you pay a relatively low tax rate on income, more after-tax income will be earned by investing in taxable bonds and paying the taxes than by investing in tax-exempt municipal bonds. Municipal bonds are primarily of interest to investors who pay a relatively high tax rate on income.

How do I determine if I should invest in municipal bonds?

First, municipal bonds are a wise investment choice only if you desire a fixed stream of income. Tax-exempt bonds are alternatives to taxable bonds, annuities, and certificates of deposit, but they are not necessarily good substitutes for tangible assets or common stocks. If you are interested in investing for fixed income, the decision as to whether municipal bonds are a superior choice hinges on two factors: the combined federal, state, and local income tax rate you pay and the spread between taxable and tax-exempt interest rates. Tax-exempt bonds are more

FIGURE 12-1

Comparing taxable and tax-free yields.

Comparing the returns from owning tax-exempt municipal bonds with taxable certificates of deposit or corporate bonds requires that you evaluate the yields on a comparable basis. For example, the return from investing in a high-grade municipal bond with 20 years to maturity should be compared to the *after-tax* return available on a high-grade corporate bond or a U.S. Treasury bond of similar maturity.

CALCULATING THE AFTER-TAX RETURN OF A TAXABLE INVESTMENT

The after-tax yield from a taxable investment is calculated by multiplying the investment's taxable return by one minus your effective federal tax rate. Suppose you pay federal taxes on the highest dollar amount of your income at a rate of 28 percent. This rate is termed your *marginal tax rate* because it applies only to the extra, or marginal, dollars of income you earn. Subtract the marginal rate of 28 percent from one and multiply the difference of 0.72 by the return that can be earned on the taxable investment being evaluated and you have the after-tax yield. For example, a taxable return of 10 percent translates into an after-tax return of 10 percent times 0.72, or 7.2 percent. In formula form, the calculation is shown as:

After-tax return = taxable return × (1 − marginal tax rate)

The resulting after-tax return from the taxable investment is then compared with the tax-exempt return available on the municipal bond. In the above example, a municipal bond offering a tax-exempt return of 6 percent would not be acceptable if you had the choice of a taxable bond offering 10 percent.

CALCULATING THE EQUIVALENT TAXABLE RETURN OF A TAX-EXEMPT INVESTMENT

The equivalent taxable return from a tax-exempt investment allows you to determine the return you would require on a taxable

Continued

FIGURE 12-1

Concluded

investment that would equal the return provided by the tax-exempt investment. Equivalent taxable return is calculated by dividing the tax-exempt return by one minus your marginal tax rate. Suppose a tax-exempt money market fund offers an annual return of 5 percent. The equivalent taxable return is calculated as 5 percent divided by 1 minus 0.28, or 6.94 percent. In formula form, the calculation is shown as:

Equivalent taxable return =
after-tax return/(1 – marginal tax rate)

Thus, you should choose a taxable investment whenever the yield is higher than the equivalent taxable return of a tax-exempt investment. In the above example, you should choose a taxable money market fund that yields more than the 6.94 equivalent taxable yield of the tax-exempt money market fund.

Treasury securities and some municipal securities are also exempt from state and local taxes, which can tip the balance to favor these securities when the comparison of yields is close. Notice that a higher personal tax rate makes it more likely that tax-exempt securities are the superior choice.

likely to be a desirable investment choice if you pay a high tax rate and if the spread between interest rates on taxable and nontaxable bonds is relatively small. Municipal bonds should be considered only when they produce a higher after-tax return compared to the return available on taxable bonds. Stated another way: the taxable equivalent yield of a municipal bond should be compared to the taxable yields of corporate bonds. Taxable equivalent yield is the taxable return that would have to be earned to produce a given tax-exempt return. Your broker can help determine if municipal bonds are a good choice in your particular situation. See Table 12-1.

TABLE 12-1

Taxable equivalent yields.*

Tax-Free Yields	Marginal Tax Rate				
	15%	28%	31%	36%	39.6%
3.00%	3.53%	4.17%	4.35%	4.69%	4.97%
3.50	4.12	4.86	5.07	5.47	5.79
4.00	4.71	5.56	5.80	6.25	6.62
4.50	5.29	6.25	6.52	7.03	7.45
5.00	5.88	6.94	7.25	7.81	8.28
5.50	4.68	7.64	7.97	8.59	9.11
6.00	7.06	8.33	8.70	9.38	9.93

* This table does not include any effect from a state income tax on the taxable equivalent yield.

Is interest from a U.S. government obligation taxable?

Interest received from U.S. Treasury securities is taxed by the federal government but not by state and local governments. Ownership of Treasury obligations can produce significant tax savings if you pay a high state and city tax on personal income. Although the savings is considerably smaller than if the interest was exempt from federal taxation, investors in high-tax states such as New York and California can still reap substantial benefits from government securities. Keep in mind that U.S. Treasury securities carry slightly lower interest rates than high-grade corporate bonds of equivalent maturity. The lower yield stems from investor demand for greater safety and for state and local tax exemption.

What other taxes apply to Wall Street investments?

Gains and losses that are realized when securities are sold will impact the income you report and the taxes you are required to pay. Securities that are sold for more than they cost result in gains that are considered taxable income. Securities that are sold for less than they cost result in losses that reduce taxable income and cause a reduction in your tax liability. You must maintain a record of the cost of securities that are purchased so you will be able to calculate the gains and losses that are realized when the securities are sold.

Will I have to pay taxes if I continue to hold securities that increase in value?

Appreciation in the value of an asset must be realized through a sale before a gain is considered taxable income. No gain is realized and no tax is due as long as you continue to hold a security that has appreciated in value. The same rule holds true for a loss in value. It cannot be used to reduce taxes until a sale occurs. Controlling the timing of when gains become taxable and when losses are used to reduce taxable income offers important benefits in financial planning.

What if I never sell a security that has appreciated in value?

If you hold a security until your death, then you will never have to realize a gain and pay a tax. Your estate and the people who inherit the security will also not have to pay a tax on the appreciation that occurred during your lifetime. Your heirs will inherit the security at its market value as of your death. Suppose you bought a stock for $10 per share that had gone up in value to $90 per share by the time you died. Whoever inherits the stock will have a cost basis of $90, not $10. Now that's a deal.

Can you provide an example of how a gain is calculated?

Suppose you pay your broker a $100 commission to purchase 100 shares of Union Pacific common stock at a price of $54 per share. The cost basis equals the principal amount of the trade (100 x $54, or $5400), plus the $100 commission for a total of $5500. If you later pay a commission of $125 to sell the stock at a price of $65 per share, net proceeds from the sale equal the principal amount from the transaction (100 x $65, or $6500), less $125 for the brokerage commission, or $6375. Taxable income from the sale is the difference between the proceeds ($6375) and the cost basis ($5400), or $975. You will be required to report $975 as income on your income tax return.

Will the entire gain of $975 be taxable?

The entire amount of the gain is considered taxable income, although the applicable tax rate is likely to be less than the tax rate you are required to pay on income from wages, interest, and dividends. At one time, only a portion of a capital gain was taxable, but the entire gain is subject to taxation under current law.

Why is the tax rate on gains from security sales lower than the tax rate I pay on other types of income?

The theory is that a lower tax rate on capital gains will encourage individuals to invest more of their income, which, in turn, will make more capital available for corporate investment in research, equipment, and new factories. Increased corporate spending should stimulate employment and cause the economy to grow. In other words, a lower tax rate for investors will stimulate saving and investing, thereby making the American economy more productive and competitive. At least, that's the theory.

How will the Internal Revenue Service learn about gains I realize from the sale of stocks and bonds?

The brokerage firm that sells your bonds or stock will report the dollar amount of the sale to the Internal Revenue Service. This means the IRS has knowledge of the transaction, including the amount of money you received. The proceeds reported on your tax return must conform with the proceeds reported to the IRS by the brokerage firm. The IRS does not know the amount of the gain you realized because it doesn't have a record of the price that you paid to purchase the securities that were sold. However, in the event of an audit, you must be able to prove how much you paid for the securities in order to show that the gain or loss is what you reported.

What if I own a bond that is redeemed by the issuer?

The brokerage firm will report the redemption if the bond is held in a brokerage account. The company redeeming the security will report the proceeds (no commission will be charged) if you hold the bond in your possession and send it in for redemption. Thus, you must report gains and losses from securities sales regardless of whether the securities are being held by you or are in a brokerage account.

What tax rate will I pay on a gain realized from a stock sale?

The maximum federal tax rate on gains from assets held longer than 12 months is 20 percent. For the $975 capital gain in the above example, you would pay a federal tax of 20 percent of $975, or $195. Remember that the tax is on the gain, not the proceeds from a sale. The 20-percent maximum rate applies no matter how high a tax rate you pay on the other income you earn. The tax rate on capital gains is only 10 percent if the tax on your regular income is at the lowest federal tax rate of 15 percent. Depending on your residence, a state tax is likely to be added to your federal liability. Not all states afford capital gains a special tax rate.

How does the tax rate for capital gains compare with the tax rate applied to regular income?

The federal government currently taxes regular income at five different rates, depending on the amount of taxable income reported. The rates begin at 15 percent and top out at 36.9 percent (see Table 12-2). Legislators often talk about reducing the highest rates and/or moving to a single-rate tax (called a *flat tax*), but

TABLE 12-2

Federal income tax rate schedules, 1998.*

Single	
Taxable Income	**Tax**
$ 0 to $ 25,350	15 percent of taxable income
25,350 to 61,400	$ 3,802.50 plus 28 percent over $25,350
61,400 to 128,100	13,896.50 plus 31 percent over $61,400
128,100 to 278,450	34,573.50 plus 36 percent over $128,100
More than $278,450	88,699.50 plus 39.6 percent over $278,450
Married Filing Jointly	
Taxable Income	**Tax**
$ 0 to $ 42,350	15 percent of taxable income
42,350 to 102,300	$ 6,352.50 plus 28 percent over $42,350
102,300 to 155,950	23,138.50 plus 31 percent over $102,300
155,950 to 278,450	39,770.00 plus 36 percent over $155,950
More than $278,450	83,870.00 plus 39.6 percent over $278,450

* Separate schedules apply to heads of households and married filing separately.

don't hold your breath. There has also been talk that the income tax will be replaced with some type of national sales tax. Again, don't count on it anytime soon. It is pretty obvious that high-income individuals benefit most from the favorable tax treatment accorded to capital gains. These investors pay taxes on long-term capital gains at a rate of 20 percent, compared to a rate on regular income (including dividends and interest) of 36 to 39.6 percent.

What if I sell shares of stock that I bought only a few months earlier?

Short-term capital gains are taxed at the same rate as regular income. If you earn sufficient salary, interest, and dividends so that the top part of your income is taxed at a 31-percent rate, then short-term capital gains will be added to this other income and also be taxed at a 31-percent rate. In fact, if short-term gains add a substantial amount of income to your return, a portion of your overall taxable income may shift into the next higher tax bracket. Thus, a part of a short-term gain may be taxed at 36 percent if you already earn sufficient income to be taxed at 31 percent. Investors with substantial income generally try to ensure that securities are not sold at a gain until the holding period qualifies as long-term.

Does a maximum capital gains rate of 20 percent apply no matter how much in gains I realize in a year?

With the tax rates currently in effect, the maximum federal tax rate you will pay on capital gains is 20 percent, as long as the securities have been held over 12 months. Of course, tax rates are subject to change, so no guarantee exists that the maximum rate on capital gains will remain at 20 percent. Also, there is no guarantee the holding period to qualify for the 20-percent rate will continue to be 12 months plus a day.

If I purchase stock now, will I lock in the 20-percent rate on gains, even though I sell the stock when rates may have changed?

Capital gains tax rates are not grandfathered. That is, you will likely have to pay whatever rate is applicable at the time a sale takes place. The tax rate on the sale date, not the purchase date, determines the tax you will pay. Not knowing the rate of taxation that will be applicable to the sale of an investment introduces a degree of uncertainty into investing. You may invest in stock tomorrow at a maximum capital gains tax rate of 20 percent and find when you sell the stock 20 years later, the tax rate on capital gains is 30 percent. On the other hand, you may find that it is 10 percent.

What if I sell several different securities during the same year?

Gains and losses realized during the same year offset one another. Suppose that during one year you sell three securities, one for a loss of $3000, and two for gains of $2000 and $5000, respectively. The loss offsets $3000 of the combined gains of $7000, leaving a net capital gain of $4000. You will be required to pay taxes on $4000 of net gains.

What if in one year my total realized losses exceed total realized gains?

The same rule of consolidating gains and losses applies. If the consolidation results in a net loss (i.e., losses exceed gains), the net loss can be used to reduce other taxable income up to a maximum of $3000 per year. Net losses above $3000 must be carried over to future years, when they can be used to offset regular income up to the $3000 annual maximum or to offset capital gains.

Does any cap apply to the net gains I must report in a given year?

Although the amount of net capital losses you may use to offset regular income is capped at $3000, the entire amount of net capital gains in a given year must be reported. This may seem unfair, but the government figures you have the ability to manipulate the gains and losses that are realized in a given year by timing security sales. The degree of flexibility is reduced somewhat by limiting the amount of net capital losses you can utilize in a given year.

Am I required to pay taxes on realized gains from municipal bonds I sell?

Although most municipal bonds pay interest that is exempt from federal income taxes, taxes must be paid on any gains you realize from the sale or redemption of these bonds. In short, capital gains on municipal bonds are taxed in the same manner as capital gains from selling shares of stock or corporate bonds. Surprisingly, capital losses realized from municipal bonds bought at a premium (a price above par) are not allowed to offset gains or other income. If you purchase a municipal bond in the secondary market for $1150 and the bond is later redeemed at its par value of $1000, you may not use the $150 loss to reduce taxable income.

Is there some way to keep from paying a tax on capital gains?

As mentioned previously, taxation of gains can be avoided, or at least deferred, by not selling a security that has appreciated in value. The problem with this is you can't get your money out of the security unless it is sold or you take out a loan using the security as collateral. Another possibility is to sell securities that have declined in value in order to realize losses that will offset the gains that have been realized from selling securities that have appreciated in value. Investors find it particularly rewarding to offset short-term gains that do not receive favorable long-term capital gains tax treatment.

What are the tax consequences of making a gift of a security that has appreciated in value?

Give away a security and you will not realize a gain nor will you be taxed on any appreciation. Many investors give appreciated securities to charities in order to claim a tax deduction at the same time that they escape taxation on increases in value. Suppose stock currently worth $5000 was purchased several years ago for $2000. Give the security to a qualifying charity and you are able to claim a $5000 charitable contribution at the same time you escape being taxed on the $3000 gain. You cannot realize a gain on a security you no longer own. The charity is a tax-exempt organization and will not be required to pay a tax if, as is likely, it subsequently sells the stock. Make a charitable donation of a security that has appreciated in value and you will not only escape tax on the gain, you will also be able to claim a tax deduction on the full value of the gift. Not a bad deal.

What about a security that has declined in value?

It doesn't make sense to make a charitable contribution of a security that has declined in value since it was acquired. You still get the tax deduction for the market value of the gift, of course, but there will be no gain in value to avoid realizing. You would be better off to sell the security, realize the loss for tax purposes, and then give cash to the charity.

What if I give an appreciated security to another person rather than to a charity?

Give the security to your son, daughter, mother, niece, or anyone other than a charity and you won't have to pay a tax on any increase in value that has occurred. Of course, you won't receive a tax deduction, even if your son doesn't have a job and appears to be a charity case. The recipient of the stock will assume your cost basis or the value of the security at the time of the gift, whichever is lower. In other words, any unrealized capital gain is transferred to the recipient. This may still prove advantageous, however, especially if the recipient pays a lower tax rate than you.

If I purchase a zero-coupon bond at a discount from face value, will I be able to defer capital gains taxes until maturity or until the bond is sold?

Zero-coupon bonds purchased at substantial discounts from face value result in an annual tax obligation even though you will not receive semiannual interest payments. The bond issuer will send both you and the Internal Revenue Service a form indicating the dollar amount the bond should have increased in value during the year, based on the bond's issue price, face value, and maturity date. As an owner of the bond, you must report this appreciation, or *accretion,* as income for tax purposes. Zero-coupon bonds create a cash flow problem because taxes must be paid on "paper" income. The taxability of appreciation and assured return makes these bonds popular for tax-deferred accounts such as IRAs.

What if a state or local government issues the zero-coupon bond?

Tax-exempt bonds issued at a discount from face value create a different situation. The accretion in value of a zero-coupon bond is considered tax-exempt interest income and is not taxable, just as interest payments on regular municipal bonds are not taxable as income. Tax-exempt municipal bonds do not create the cash flow problem of corporate zero-coupon bonds.

What method is used to tax income I receive from mutual funds?

Income from mutual funds is taxed in the same manner as income from any other security. Mutual funds own stocks and bonds and pass through to their own shareholders the interest and dividend payments they receive. As a mutual fund shareholder, you must report these payments as income on your tax return. Likewise, mutual funds that sell securities for more than they have paid distribute the gains to their shareholders, who must report and pay taxes on the gains. A mutual fund does not pay taxes on the interest or dividends it receives or on the gains it realizes from the sale of securities.

What about mutual funds that invest in tax-exempt municipal bonds?

Mutual funds, closed-end investment companies, and unit investment trusts that invest in municipal bonds pass through tax-exempt interest to their own shareholders, who are not required to report the payments as taxable income. These investments are particularly popular with high-income individuals who wish to earn investment income that is exempt from taxes. Money market mutual funds that invest in tax-exempt securities also pay dividends that are exempt from taxation.

Are changes in the value of mutual funds shares taxable?

Changes in the value of mutual funds shares are treated in the same manner as changes in the value of other securities. That is, any gain realized from the sale of mutual fund shares must be reported as a capital gain and included as income on your tax return. Likewise, realized losses from the sale of mutual fund shares have the effect of reducing taxable income. Realized gains and losses are calculated by subtracting the cost basis from net proceeds received from a sale. Changes in the market value of mutual fund shares have no effect on taxable income until shares are sold and gains and losses are realized.

How do I determine the gain or loss if shares of the same fund are purchased at different prices over a period of time?

Determining the tax is not particularly complicated if you sell all of your shares. Calculate the gains or losses by subtracting the cost basis of each purchase from the proceeds that were received. Paperwork confirmations from mutual fund share purchases should be retained in order to provide the cost data necessary for the calculation. A partial sale of the shares you own will be more of a headache because you will need to determine which of your shares have been sold. The Internal Revenue Service assumes that shares are sold in the order in which they were purchased. That is, the first shares purchased are the first shares sold. This method is commonly called *first in, first out*. If the shares you own have gone up in value, this method will produce the largest gain and the largest tax liability.

What other methods are available for calculating gains and losses?

You are permitted to determine gains and losses by calculating the average price you paid for all the shares you own. The average price then becomes your cost basis for the shares that are sold. This cost is then subtracted from the proceeds received in order to determine the gain or loss. The average-cost method lumps together the cost of all your shares and may result in larger gains and a bigger tax liability than the other methods. This is the method used by most mutual fund shareholders. Another more complicated method is to specifically identify the shares that have been sold. In this method, you are able to sell your highest-cost shares, which will result in the smallest gains and the lowest tax liability. Keep in mind that you must hold mutual fund shares over a year in order to qualify for long-term capital gains treatment. The last method is to calculate the average cost of all the shares that have been held over a year and a separate average for all the shares that have been held a year or less.

How can I reduce the taxes of being a mutual fund shareholder?

Remember that no capital gains tax is due (other than distributions you receive from the fund) until you sell your shares and realize a gain. Thus, continue to hold your shares and no tax from an increase in the value of your shares will be due. Investors who frequently buy and sell mutual fund shares pay more in taxes than investors who adopt a buy-and-hold strategy. This doesn't mean you have to keep your shares forever, of course, but you should consider the tax consequences of trading shares in one mutual fund for shares in another mutual fund. You can also reduce taxes by selecting a mutual fund with a management that does not engage in rapid portfolio turnover. The more securities are bought and sold by a mutual fund portfolio manager, the more taxable distributions you will receive.

What types of mutual funds have stable portfolios?

Index funds typically have low portfolio turnover. These funds attempt to track a particular stock index such as the Standard & Poor's 500, which means there is little need to buy and sell stocks. The index underlying the composition of the fund's portfolio occasionally changes, but not often. Other mutual funds peg their portfolios to different indexes. Regardless, index funds typically trade very little compared to most common stock funds. In fact, several funds have been established to minimize shareholder taxes. If taxes are a concern, consider a fund's portfolio turnover when you are selecting a mutual fund to buy.

If I borrow money to finance my investments, will I be permitted to use the interest I pay as a deduction on my tax return?

Interest expense that is incurred in order to produce investment is deductible. Thus, if you borrow money to buy shares of stock, you may use the interest you pay on the borrowed money to offset dividend income you earn from the stock. An exception is that interest paid on a loan to finance the purchase of municipal bonds is not deductible.

Can I deduct interest I pay on a loan used to buy U.S. Treasury securities?

Yes, you may deduct interest from loans used to buy Treasury securities. Interest income you receive from U.S. Treasury securities is considered taxable income in calculating your federal tax liability, and interest expense used to finance the purchase of these securities is a deductible expense.

Can I deduct the interest expense only when I use my broker to borrow money for a security purchase?

It doesn't matter whether you borrow money through your broker or arrange the loan yourself through a financial institution, as long as proceeds from the loan are used to finance income-producing assets.

Can I deduct other expenses involved in earning investment income? For example, can I deduct the cost of this book?

Most investment-related expenses, including the cost of financial publications, may be used to reduce taxable income, but only when you itemize deductions rather than use the standard deduction in calculating your tax liability. Investment expenses fall into a category of expenses called *miscellaneous deductions*. These expenses are permitted as itemized deductions only to the extent that total miscellaneous deductions exceed 2 percent of your adjusted gross income. Many taxpayers use the standard deduction and are unable to deduct investment-related expenses.

Should I take advantage of investment plans that defer taxes until retirement?

Individual retirement accounts (IRAs), Keogh plans (for the self-employed), 401 plans, and other tax-deferred investment plans should be viewed as tax-protected shells in which investments can earn income and be bought and sold without tax consequences. Realized gains are not taxable and realized losses have no gains to offset. Tax-deferred retirement plans provide several advantages. First, your contributions are made with before-tax, not after-tax income. Contributing with before-tax income results in contributions that are less painful because of the resulting tax reduction in the year of the contribution. This process eventually reverses itself when funds are withdrawn from the account and taxes must be paid. In addition, deferral of taxes on income earned in the account allows you to accumulate a larger retirement nest egg because your investment returns compound without being depleted by taxes. Not having to pay taxes on dividends, interest, and realized capital gains means that all of the funds in the account continue to earn income. These two tax benefits allow you to end up with a substantially

larger fund at retirement compared to when you save using after-tax income.

Are there any negative aspects to these plans?

Be aware that all of the dollars you eventually withdraw from
one of these plans will be fully taxable at whatever rate is effective at the time of the withdrawals. No portion of the withdrawals will benefit from capital gains treatment, as would occur for
investments outside a retirement plan. Most individuals are
likely to face a lower tax rate during retirement than during the
years of contributions, but a lower rate is not a certainty because
there is no way to predict future tax rates. Who knows what
Congress may do next year or, if you are in your twenties or thirties, several decades in the future?

What if I need to withdraw money prior to retirement?

Although rules are somewhat different for different types of retirement plans, in general, funds withdrawn prior to age $59\frac{1}{2}$ are
subject to a 10-percent penalty. The penalty is waived if withdrawn funds are used for a limited number of specified reasons.
In addition to the penalty, withdrawn funds are subject to taxation at whatever your effective tax rate happens to be at the time
the withdrawals occur. Funds contributed to a retirement account should be intended for retirement.

CHAPTER

What Are the Risks of Investing in Wall Street?

Chapter summary

Investing money in products offered by Wall Street firms is often accompanied by substantial risks. Products with high potential returns tend to entail substantial risks. Several types of risks are encountered in most investments. Understanding the various types of risks associated with specific investments should play an important role in determining the investments you choose. In general, it is best to avoid investment products you don't fully understand.

Is investing in Wall Street more risky than putting my money in certificates of deposit?

Probably, but investments peddled by Wall Street are so diverse that the particular investment being compared with a certificate of deposit must be specified. In fact, brokerage firms actually sell insured certificates of deposit issued by financial institutions. It is important to understand that several types of risk are inherent in owning nearly any investment, and even certificates of deposit are not completely free of risk.

Does risk refer to the possibility of losing the money I invest?

The possibility of losing the money you invest is certainly a risk of investing, but the concept of risk is actually more comprehensive than this. Risk is generally considered as the uncertainty of the return you will earn, where return includes both current income and changes in the value of your investment. The greater the uncertainty of the return, the greater the risk of owning the investment. An investment such as common stock, which may provide a return in a given year of from minus 30 percent to plus 30 percent, is a riskier investment than a bond, which may provide a return that ranges between minus 5 percent and plus 15 percent. Each return is calculated using both current income (dividends or interest) plus changes in the value of the investment. The bond produces a narrower range of outcomes and would generally be considered the less risky of the two investment alternatives.

What is the risk of putting my money in a certificate of deposit?

You actually face a couple of risks from having money invested in a CD. First, the purchasing power of the interest income and principal may be eaten away by unexpected inflation, especially if you choose a certificate with a relatively long maturity. Imagine investing in a 10-year CD with a 6-percent annual interest rate, only to find that within a couple of years the inflation rate increases to 8 percent annually. An inflation rate higher than the rate of return means you will earn a negative "real" rate of return. In other words, your purchasing power declines, even after accounting for the interest you receive. On the other hand, suppose you choose a CD with a short maturity with the intention of rolling over the principal into a new CD at maturity. When the certificate comes due and you are ready to reinvest in a new certificate, you may discover that interest rates have declined and your annual interest income will be much smaller than anticipated. Ask someone who retired in the early 1980s and invested in certificates of deposit what happened to their interest income in the 1990s. Also take a look at Figure 13-1, which will give you an idea of how inflation becomes a factor in investing.

So the risk of an asset is the uncertainty of the return I will earn?

Well, sort of. Actually, it's a little more complicated than that. A comprehensive view of risk is the effect a particular asset has on the risk of your entire portfolio. In other words, an investment's risk should be viewed from the perspective of how ownership of the asset affects the uncertainty of the returns of your overall portfolio. It is misleading to consider the risk and return expected from a particular asset without considering how that asset will affect the risk and return of your total portfolio of investments.

This is confusing. Can you provide an example?

Most experts believe that ownership of real estate entails substantial risk compared to investing in insured certificates of deposit. Real estate is often subject to wide variations in value and is likely to be difficult to resell on short notice. Despite the risks of owning real estate, the risk of your overall investment portfolio may be reduced by adding real estate investments to the assets you already own, especially if your current investments are mostly financial assets such as bonds and stocks.

FIGURE 13-1

Annual inflation, 1975–1998.

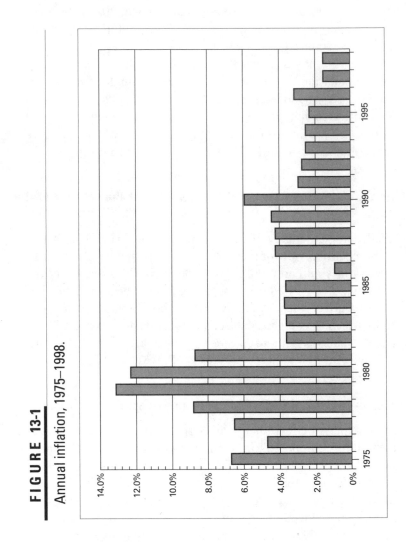

I still don't understand how adding a risky asset to a low-risk portfolio reduces risk?

The possibility of losing purchasing power to unexpected inflation is one of the important risks faced by any investor. Inflation can devastate the real value of a portfolio of financial assets that most investors would consider to be low risk. For example, the real values of the fixed interest income and principal of a long-term Treasury bond are subject to being seriously eroded by rising consumer prices. Interest income from the bond will remain the same each year, but this fixed dollar amount buys less and less as consumer prices rise. Thus, the real return earned from a portfolio heavily weighted with Treasury securities or any other investment that pays a fixed return is subject to substantial uncertainty because of the possibility of unexpected inflation. The addition of tangible assets—precious metals, investment-grade coins, stamps, diamonds, or real estate—can help protect this type of portfolio from losing value to unexpected inflation.

How do tangible assets help protect a portfolio from the risk of unexpected inflation?

Tangible assets often perform best in an inflationary environment as investors move their money from financial assets to tangible assets. The strong demand for tangible assets causes the prices of these assets to increase. For example, increased buying of collectible baseball cards will cause these assets to increase in value. Thus, during an inflationary period when financial assets such as stocks and bonds are likely to suffer, tangible assets are likely to appreciate in value. Adding tangible assets to a portfolio of financial assets will tend to reduce the overall risk of the portfolio because different types of assets are subject to different risks.

But isn't the possibility of a reduction in the value of my investment the major risk I face?

The potential for a loss of value of an investment is an important risk faced by any investor, but other aspects to risk should also be considered. A major risk faced by conservative investors who devote a heavy proportion of their portfolio to a money market fund is a potential reduction in interest income caused by a decline in market rates of interest. The possibility of lower interest rates is a very real risk, especially for individuals who utilize interest income to meet current consumption needs. A money market fund has a stable market value, so there is little possibility of a loss in value, yet an overreliance on this particular investment could place you at substantial risk by reducing your income.

I recently heard a financial commentator refer to beta as a measure of risk. What is beta?

Beta is a relative measure of the volatility of returns provided by a particular asset or a particular portfolio of assets as compared to the overall market. The mathematical calculation of beta uses historical data and is complicated, but the application is fairly simple. The overall market is assigned a beta of one. Stocks or portfolios of stocks that have betas greater than the market benchmark of one are considered to be more risky than the market. Conversely, stocks or portfolios of stocks with betas of less than one are considered to be less risky than the market. The higher the beta, the riskier the investment.

Where can I locate stock betas?

Betas are calculated and published by several organizations. The most readily available source is likely to be the *Value Line Investment Survey,* which is carried by most public and college libraries.

Value Line research includes the beta of each stock it includes in its weekly service. Firms calculate betas somewhat differently (e.g., the beta of IBM stock as calculated and published by Value Line may be different from the beta of the same stock as calculated by Merrill Lynch), so you are likely to find somewhat different betas from two different firms for the same stock.

Anything else I should know about beta?

A stock's beta may change over time, especially if the company significantly alters its financing mix or undergoes a major change in the business it conducts. For example, a company may make a major acquisition that causes it to do much of its business in an entirely different industry. The beta of the company's stock is bound to change. The less stable a beta, the less useful beta becomes for measuring an investment's risk. In fact, some researchers believe that beta is unstable enough to make it a poor measure of risk.

What other risks will I face by investing in Wall Street?

Chapter 3 discussed the importance of market rates of interest to owners of long-term bonds. Invest in a long-term bond and a subsequent increase in market rates of interest will cause a decline in the market value of your bond. The bigger the change in interest rates and the longer the maturity length of your bond, the greater the change that will occur in the value of the bond you own. (See Figure 13-2.) Increases in market rates of interest are a major risk faced by most investors, including those who own preferred and common stocks.

Why would a stockholder be negatively affected by rising interest rates?

Rising interest rates exert downward pressure on the prices of nearly all assets, including stocks. Stocks must compete for in-

FIGURE 13-2

U.S. Treasury yields, late 1998.

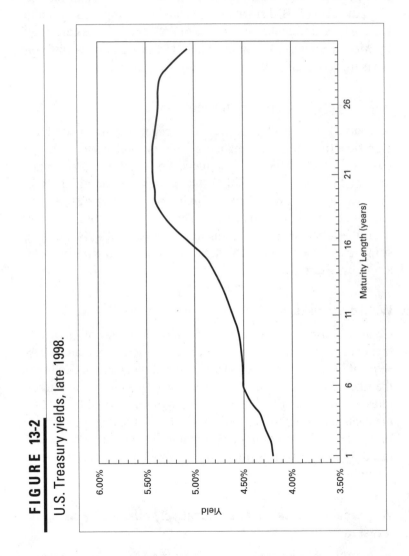

vestment dollars with other assets, bonds, certificates of deposit, money market accounts, and so forth. If these investment alternatives begin offering higher returns (e.g., higher interest rates), then investors will begin demanding greater returns from stocks. Without a corresponding increase in expected earnings and dividend streams, stocks can only offer higher returns if they can be purchased at a lower price. Thus, rising interest rates cause a decline in stock and bond prices so that new investors are able to purchase these securities at a reduced price. At the same time, the existing owners of these securities suffer losses as the prices of the securities decline.

Do falling interest rates benefit owners of bonds and stocks?

Falling interest rates tend to boost the market values of both stocks and bonds. The decline of interest rates during the 1980s and 1990s was a major factor in the bull markets of stocks and bonds. Remember, however, that falling interest rates result in reduced interest income for investors who are just investing their funds or reinvesting money received from the sale or redemption of another investment. Having a large portion of your portfolio in a money market account or short-term certificates of deposit means you will have to accept lower current income from subsequent investments. As interest rates fall, your investments will produce less and less income.

If rising interest rates are bad for stocks and bonds, why doesn't the government have a policy to keep interest rates low?

Pushing interest rates too low for too long is likely to require ever bigger increases in credit expansion that may result in inflationary pressures. Rising inflationary expectations will then make it even more difficult for the Federal Reserve to successfully pursue a policy promoting lower interest rates because creditors expecting higher inflation will charge borrowers a higher interest rate. This is a vicious circle that causes the Federal Reserve to walk a fine line on money creation, credit expansion, and interest rates.

What other risks do I face as an investor?

Another risk is the potential difficulty you may have in selling your investment. Some investments lack an active secondary market, which can result in a lower-than-expected price when you are ready to sell. Tangible assets like baseball cards, gold, and real estate often suffer a price reduction when they must be sold in a short period of time. These relatively illiquid tangible assets compare with U.S. Treasury bills and actively traded stocks, which are easily sold without incurring a price penalty.

Are tangible assets the only investments that may be difficult to sell?

Inactive stocks and bonds often suffer from a large spread between the bid price and the ask price. With inactive trading and few buyers, securities must sometimes be sold below what might be considered a fair price. However, a lack of liquidity may not be particularly important when you have a long investment horizon. If you intend to hold stocks for many years or plan to hold bonds to maturity, then the lack of active trading in the secondary market is not a major consideration in selecting securities to purchase. If you may be required to liquidate a security on short notice, it becomes a more important consideration.

What about variations in the market value of an investment?

Many assets are subject to substantial variations in market value, an important factor to consider if you may be required to sell an investment on short notice. For example, it is very risky to invest in a stock that has exhibited a very volatile price when you may be required to sell the stock within a year. This type stock can also be risky to own if you are of a temperament to find steep price declines so unnerving that you might sell at an inopportune time. Like a lack of liquidity, variations in value are less of a problem if you invest for the long term and have the temperament and financial ability to ride out temporary (hopefully) declines in value.

What types of investments are subject to major price variations?

Tangible assets and some financial assets, including many common stocks, are subject to large fluctuations in value, although the extent of the fluctuations varies. For example, some stocks have much more volatile prices than other stocks. Preferred stocks and long-term bonds also vary in value, but not to the extent of most common stocks. Investments subject to little variation in value include Treasury bills and other short-term debt securities. Money market funds, money market deposit accounts, savings accounts, and short-term certificates of deposit exhibit virtually no changes in market value. In fact, stability of value is the major positive attribute of these types of investments, and they generally offer a low return as a consequence.

Should I favor investments with stable values?

Your investment portfolio should include at least some assets that have relatively stable values and excellent liquidity. These assets have a place in any portfolio because nearly everyone faces a possibility of unexpected expenses that will necessitate liquidating some investments. Unfortunately, investments with stable values tend to produce relatively meager rates of return, meaning that obtaining some liquidity and safety is likely to cost you some income. Look at holding these assets as a form of insurance that will protect you from suffering a substantial loss, i.e., being forced to sell assets at a low price, in the event you need to come up with some cash.

What about the possibility of a company or government entity going out of business or halting dividend or interest payments?

The possibility of a reduced income stream is a risk unless you stick to the very safest investments, such as insured CDs or U.S. government securities. The risk is especially great if you own common stocks. Businesses prefer not to reduce the dividends they pay to their stockholders, but a decline in a firm's earnings may cause the directors to reduce or omit dividends. A reduction in payments to bondholders is less likely because interest payments and principal repayment are legal obligations of the issuer. However, investing in bonds issued by businesses or government entities with shaky finances can result in the substantial risk of not receiving all of the promised payments.

So I'm better off as a bondholder than a stockholder in the event a company goes out of business?

If a company goes out of business, you are almost certainly better off being a bondholder than a stockholder because claims by bondholders are paid prior to claims by stockholders. In other words, as a bondholder, you should be paid what you are owed before the firm's stockholders recover any money. In practice, bondholders do not always recover their full claim because a firm may have insufficient assets to pay all of the outstanding claims. Be aware that many companies have several classes of outstanding bonds, each with a different claim. Thus, one class of bondholders may have a superior claim that allows the recovery of what they are owed before the other bondholders are paid. Investors who are holding subordinated debentures have a very low claim and may recover little in the event the issuer encounters financial difficulties and goes out of business.

How can I determine the likelihood a company will default on its debt obligations?

Individual investors are generally forced to judge the credit quality of a bond by relying on credit ratings provided by commercial rating firms such as Standard & Poor's or Moody's. Ratings range from AAA for the highest quality bonds, on which issuers will almost certainly meet their commitments, to ratings of C and D for bonds with an uncertain outlook. Individual bond ratings can be obtained from your broker or from publications in most public and college libraries.

If a reduction in bond interest is less likely than a reduction in stock dividends, why should I invest in stocks?

Although bond interest payments are rarely decreased or omitted, they are never increased. This means that the promised payments are the most you can expect, and you might actually receive less. On the other hand, stock dividends are sometimes reduced or eliminated, but they are also subject to being increased if the company that issued the stock prospers. A company that currently pays a dividend of $2.00 per share is likely to have once paid a dividend of 10 cents per share. In fact, at one time it probably didn't pay any dividend. Stock ownership offers the potential for increased dividend payments.

Are fixed interest payments the reason bonds provide little protection against inflation?

The coupon rate on a bond takes account of the inflation expected by investors at the time the bond is issued. An expected inflation rate of 3 percent may result in a borrower paying 6 percent on a new 20-year bond issue. A higher expected inflation rate is likely to result in a bond being issued with a higher coupon rate. Expected inflation is built into the interest rate established on the issue date. It is *unexpected* inflation that causes pain for bondholders, who can only watch as the purchasing power of fixed interest payments declines more rapidly than anticipated. Buy a 7-percent coupon bond when inflation is anticipated at 4 percent and you are expecting an inflation-adjusted return of 3 percent. If inflation subsequently increases to 8 percent annually, you will continue to earn the 7-percent return on your original investment, but 7 percent will be 1 percent less than the inflation rate. A return lower than the inflation rate results in earning a negative return. This is the same type of risk mentioned earlier in this chapter in the discussion of certificates of deposit and U.S. Treasury securities.

How will an increase in interest rates affect all my investments?

An increase in interest rates will cause a decline in most investment values. The inverse relationship between interest rates and investment values is easiest to understand with bonds but it also applies to most investments. Suppose you buy a bond with a 6-percent coupon and interest rates subsequently begin to increase so that new bonds have 8-percent coupons. It is fairly obvious that your 6-percent coupon bond will be worth less than what you paid for it when investors can now buy newly issued bonds that have a much higher coupon rate. Higher interest rates also impact the prices of common stocks, preferred stocks, and most other investments. The longer the maturity length of the bond, the greater the price volatility of the bond in response to changing interest rates. Short-term bonds change very little in price when market rates of interest change. On the other hand, bonds with long maturities are subject to very large swings in market price.

So I should stay away from bonds with long maturities?

Not necessarily. Bonds with longer maturities generally offer higher yields than bonds with short maturities. Even though bonds with long maturities are subject to greater price fluctuations in response to changes in interest rates, the fluctuations in price may be unimportant if you plan to hold a bond to its maturity. On the other hand, buying a long-term bond that you may be required to sell can present a real risk that you will receive less than you paid for the bond.

How do takeovers and buyouts affect the risk investors face?

Takeovers and buyouts often create additional risk for investors, especially when debt is used to finance the transaction. Bondholders are especially vulnerable to the change in risk because their claims may be undermined by the substantial amounts of additional debt that is issued in the takeover. Stockholders can also encounter additional risk when a company takes on additional debt in order to make an acquisition. Of course, if you are lucky enough to be a stockholder of a company being purchased for cash, you will not take on any additional risk when your shares of stock are swapped for cash.

Are stock options risky to own?

Stock options are generally very risky investments to own, although the degree of risk depends on how they are used. Buying a call is a speculation on an increase in the value of the underlying stock. Buying a put is a speculation on a decrease in the value of the underlying stock. It would not be at all unusual to lose all of the money you invest in either buying a put or a call. On the other hand, it would also not be unusual to double your money in a relatively short period of time. Option prices are very, very volatile. On the other hand, using options to offset other investment positions, a technique called *hedging,* can actually reduce overall risk. Hedging with options is a fairly sophisticated investment procedure that most individual investors should avoid. In fact, most individual investors should probably avoid options altogether.

How about futures contracts?

Futures contracts are also very risky and should be avoided by most investors. Futures contracts generally involve substantial leverage, so a relatively modest change in the price of the underlying asset can produce a very large change in the value of the contract. Unlike options, where you cannot lose an amount greater than your investment, futures contracts can produce financial losses that far exceed the initial amount of money you put up.

Is any risk involved when investing in a money market fund?

First, the ever-changing income stream from a money market fund can be a very important risk if you require the interest income to meet regular living expenses. This risk of facing a declining income stream was discussed earlier in this chapter. With regard to other risks, it is necessary to differentiate money market funds offered by Wall Street firms from money market deposit accounts that are offered by commercial banks and savings and loan associations. Deposit accounts at banks and savings and loans qualify for Federal Deposit Insurance Corporation coverage and are free of credit risk as long as your account doesn't exceed the established insurance limit. Money market funds offered by Wall Street firms are specialized mutual funds that invest in high-grade short-term debt securities. Money market funds are generally very safe, but the money you place in these investments is not insured. Most of these funds invest a portion of their shareholders' money in corporate securities, so there is always the possibility of a loss of income because of a corporate default. Unless the fund's sponsor is willing to absorb the loss by reimbursing the fund for the defaulted debt, the money market shares may decline in value.

What about money market funds that invest in Treasury securities?

Money market funds that limit their investments to U.S. Treasury securities do not subject investors to loss of value because of credit risk. This specialized segment of money market funds is considered ultrasafe because of the safety of U.S. Treasury securities. The downside is that Treasury securities generally offer a lower yield than corporate securities, which means a money market fund that limits its investments to Treasuries will pay a lower return to its own shareholders. The upside is that interest payments from Treasury securities are exempt from state and local income taxes, so the income passed by the money market fund to its shareholders is also exempt from these taxes. The state and local tax exemption is important if you live in a high-tax state like New York or California.

Why would the manager of a money market mutual fund choose to invest in securities in which a possibility of default exists?

The managers of the fund apparently believe that the higher yields available on the securities they purchase are worth the increased risk. The managers also know that individual investors are attracted to money market funds that provide the highest yields. Investors often seem to paint all money market funds with the same brush by assuming all of the funds are of equal risk. This isn't true, of course, but those who believe it to be true simply search for the fund that offers the highest yield.

Is this also true of mutual funds that invest in bonds?

A much greater gap in risk exists among bond funds than among money market funds. Some bond funds even specialize in high-risk, high-yield debt. These "junk bond" funds tend to be quite risky compared to the average bond fund. Other funds restrict their investments to U.S. Treasury securities, which means that they offer a portfolio of bonds with a substantially higher credit quality than the average bond fund.

How can I guard against risk when I invest in Wall Street?

Several points should be kept in mind when you are investing. First, never invest in an asset you do not fully understand. Putting money in a complex asset is a recipe for disaster because you are less likely to perceive the risks involved. Investments that are sold primarily on their tax advantages are often both complicated and risky.

So I need to understand the investments I put my money into. Anything else?

Choose assets that fit your particular investment needs. Accomplishing this bit of investing wizardry requires two things: First, gain an understanding of the characteristics of stocks, bonds, convertible bonds, and each of the other Wall Street investments you will be considering; second, understand your investment needs by establishing realistic financial goals. Knowing your investment goals and understanding how various investments can accomplish those goals will go a long way in allowing you to reduce unnecessary risks. It is a mistake to acquire long-term investments to meet short-term goals, just as you should not acquire short-term investments to meet long-term goals.

Can too much of my money be invested in a single asset?

Regardless of how strongly you feel about the advantages of investing in a particular security or a particular type of asset (i.e., common stock, municipal bonds, real estate, and so forth), do not surrender to the temptation to put all your eggs in one basket. Even "sure things" occasionally turn sour, and a downturn can come when you are least expecting it. Diversification—putting your money in a number of assets with a variety of investment characteristics—is a key to reducing risk. Never invest only in stocks, only in bonds, or only in real estate. Concentrating all your money in a single stock or one type of asset offers the potential for earning a very high return. You also stand to lose a substantial part of your investment in the event you make a mistake. It is also unwise to sock away all of your funds in very safe investments such as a money market account or Treasury securities. These investments have high liquidity and little credit risk, but they provide a low return.

Is it worthwhile to try and determine the right time to invest?

Many financial consultants suggest that you are best served by a diet of steady investing. That is, be consistent in your investing, regardless of whether the market is going up or down. Individuals often become frightened when the market suffers a major decline and, as a result, stop investing and begin selling their investments. This is likely to turn out to be exactly the wrong action, since security prices are relatively low. Individuals also often start investing more heavily when the market has gone through a sustained advance. One way to overcome this tendency is to use *dollar-cost averaging,* in which you invest equal amounts at periodic intervals. Thus, you may invest $500 per month regardless of what the market is doing. See Table 13-1 for an illustration of how dollar-cost averaging works.

TABLE 13-1

Example of dollar-cost averaging.

Suppose you commit to a program of dollar-cost averaging by investing $1000 in the shares of a particular mutual fund every three months. Regardless of the price of the fund, you continue to plow $1000 into the shares. The results after a period of three years are illustrated below.

	Amount Invested	Price Paid	Shares Purchased	Shares Owned	Average Cost per Share
Year 1					
Quarter					
1	$1000	$30.00	33.33	33.33	$30.00
2	$1000	$28.50	35.09	68.42	$29.23
3	$1000	$25.00	40.00	108.42	$27.67
4	$1000	$26.25	38.10	146.52	$27.30
Year 2					
Quarter					
1	$1000	$29.50	33.90	180.42	$27.72
2	$1000	$32.00	31.25	211.67	$28.35
3	$1000	$33.75	29.63	241.30	$29.00
4	$1000	$35.25	28.37	269.67	$29.67
Year 3					
Quarter					
1	$1000	$35.50	28.17	297.84	$30.22
2	$1000	$33.50	29.85	327.69	$30.52
3	$1000	$37.25	26.85	354.54	$31.03
4	$1000	$36.00	27.78	382.32	$31.38

I have read that most investors should place part of their money in foreign bonds or foreign stocks. Does this make sense for me?

Improved diversification results from including securities of foreign companies in your portfolio. Some experts believe that investors should devote 10 to 15 percent of their portfolios to foreign investments. The diversification can be achieved by purchasing the stocks or bonds of foreign companies or by investing in mutual funds or closed-end investment companies that invest in foreign securities. Stocks of some foreign companies are acquired by purchasing American depositary receipts, which trade on organized exchanges or in the over-the-counter market.

Any other ideas on how I can reduce my losses?

Don't become greedy. We all hear stories about a particular investment that is a sure thing. Maybe your brother-in-law told you about a stock that is certain to double in the next six months. A broker might tell you the same thing in an unsolicited telephone call. Plunging into a "sure thing" you would ordinarily avoid is nearly always a mistake born of greed. Trying to make as much money as possible in the shortest possible time is a risky course of action.

Does this mean I should not invest all my money in Wall Street?

Don't be embarrassed to keep insured certificates of deposit or a bank money market account as a part of your investment portfolio. These investments provide a relatively low return, but they also let you sleep at night. You may want to adjust the composition of your portfolio devoted to these assets, depending on the comparative returns available from these and alternative investments. Fine-tune your investments so that you are not penalized too heavily for maintaining balances in risk-free assets.

Does asset allocation affect investment risk?

Asset allocation refers to the proportion of your portfolio devoted to different classes of assets. For example, you may decide the proper allocation is 50-percent common stock, 30-percent bonds, and 20-percent real estate. Each person's desired allocation is different, depending on his or her age, income, investment goals, and so forth. The allocation you choose when you are in your thirties is unlikely to be the same as the allocation you choose in your fifties. Thus, it is important to review both your investment goals and your portfolio to make certain your portfolio represents your current investment goals, not your past investment goals. You may find it necessary to reallocate funds from stocks to bonds or bonds to stocks, depending on how the two classes of assets have been performing. For example, if stocks have experienced large gains while bond values have been stable, you may want to sell some stock and use the proceeds to purchase additional bonds. Moving money from stocks to bonds will allow you to adjust your overall allocation to the desired proportions.

I have read that I should only invest in Wall Street with money I can afford to lose. Is this good advice?

Not really. Invest in a high-grade corporate bond or a Treasury bond and you have an assured stream of cash income in addition to the return of the principal that you invested. Each of these investments is offered by nearly every Wall Street firm and involves little risk of nonpayment. Each is a good substitute for a long-term certificate of deposit and is likely to offer a slightly higher rate of return. Blue-chip stocks exhibit more price volatility, with the added possibility of dividend reductions, but these securities offer an opportunity to receive a stream of income that increases over time. Common stocks also offer the opportunity to own assets that increase in value over time.

How about only investing money I can afford to lose?

Limit your investments to blue-chip stocks, investment-grade bonds, or other low-risk assets when investing money you cannot afford to lose. Do not invest your grocery money in warrants, options, junk bonds, and the multitude of limited partnerships offered by Wall Street. This same advice also applies to your retirement money, especially if retirement is relatively near.

Any last bit of advice?

Take much of what you read or hear about investing with a grain of salt.

Does this apply to the information in this book?

You will have to be the judge of that, but don't call collect.

GLOSSARY

Account statement   A statement of investment activity and investment position that is periodically sent by brokerage firms to their customers.

Accrued interest   Interest that is owed but not yet paid. Most bonds trade with accrued interest, which means the buyer must pay some interest to the seller.

Active   Describing a security in which there is substantial trading.

After-hours trading   Trading in securities following the close of an organized exchange.

Agency security   See *Federal agency security.*

Aggressive investing   Investing in risky assets in an attempt to earn relatively high returns.

Alternative minimum tax (AMT)   A federal tax on taxable income as adjusted for certain specified deductions and income items.

American depositary receipt (ADR)   A receipt for a foreign security that is being held in trust.

American Stock Exchange (AMEX)   An organized securities exchange located in New York City that trades securities that have national interest.

Arbitrage   Simultaneously purchasing and selling different assets that are substantially the same in order to take advantage of price differences that exist between the assets.

Ask   The quoted price at which a security will be sold.

Asset   Something of value that is owned by an individual or by an organization.

Asset allocation   Separating investment dollars into particular categories of assets, such as bonds, stocks, and real estate.

Averaging down   An investment strategy of reducing the average cost of a stock holding by purchasing additional shares as the price declines.

Basis   The cost of an asset for the purpose of calculating gains and losses.

Basis point   One-hundredth of one percent.

Bear   Someone who believes a particular stock or the entire stock market is headed for a decline.

Bear market   An extended period of declining investment prices.

Bid   The price being offered by a potential buyer.

Big Board   See *New York Stock Exchange.*

Blue chip   A high-quality company or security.

Bond   A long-term promissory note.

Bond rating   A grading of the likelihood that a bond's interest and principal will be paid in a timely manner.

Book value   The accounting value of an asset or a company. The book value of a company is calculated by subtracting the outstanding debts from the accounting value of assets. The book value of an asset is calculated by subtracting accumulated depreciation from the price that was paid to acquire the asset.

Bottom   The lowest value to which a particular stock or the stock market will fall.

Broker   An individual or firm that serves as an intermediary between a buyer and a seller.

Bull   An individual who expects the price of a particular stock or the general stock market to increase in value.

Bull market   An extended period of rising security prices.

Buy-and-hold   Pertaining to an investment strategy of holding securities for long periods in order to reduce transaction costs.

Buyback   A firm's repurchase of its own securities.

Call   1. An option that permits the owner of the call to purchase a certain asset at a specified price until a certain date. 2. The redemption of preferred stock or of a bond prior to the scheduled maturity.

Capital gain   The amount by which the proceeds from the sale of an asset exceed the cost basis of the asset.

Capital gains tax   The tax on realized gains from the sale of capital assets such as stocks and bonds.

Cash account   A brokerage account that requires payment in full for security purchases.

Certificate   Evidence of ownership of shares of stock or of a bond.

Churning   Excessive trading in a customer account by a broker who wishes to generate additional commissions.

Close   The last price at which a security trades or the last valuation of a stock price average or index during a trading session.

Common stock   A class of stock that has no preference with regard to dividends or to assets in the event the business is liquidated.

Composite tape   A security price reporting system that includes trading from all of the organized exchanges and from the over-the-counter market.

Confirmation   Written acknowledgment that a security order has been executed.

Conversion price   The price at which shares of common stock will be exchanged for a convertible security.

Convertible security   A security that the owner can convert into another security or securities. Many bonds can be converted into shares of common stock of the issuer.

Coupon   The annual percentage rate of interest paid by a debt security as calculated on the basis of the security's face value.

Creditor   The person or organization to which a debt is owed.

Current yield   The rate of return earned from an investment based upon the investment's expected annual cash payment compared to the investment's current market price.

Cyclical   The stock of a business with revenues and profits that are subject to substantial swings throughout a business cycle.

Day order   An order to buy or sell a security that will be automatically cancelled at the end of trading on the day the order is entered.

Dealer   An individual or organization that purchases assets for and sells assets from its own portfolio.

Debenture   A corporate debt security that has no specific assets pledge as collateral.

Declaration date   The date when a firm's directors announce the amount and date of the firm's next dividend payment to stockholders.

Defensive stock   A stock that tends to resist declines in the stock market.

Delivery   Transfer of a security to the seller's broker.

Derivative   A security that derives its value from some other asset. Call options, put options, and convertible bonds are examples of derivatives.

Discount bond   A long-term debt security that sells at a price below its face value. See also *Premium bond.*

Discount brokerage firm   A brokerage firm that executes security trades for commissions that are less than those charged by most full-service firms.

Diversify   To acquire several different assets with returns that are not directly related.

Dividend   A payment from profits that is distributed to stockholders.

Dividend reinvestment plan   A corporate plan in which stockholders may elect to have the firm utilize dividend payments to purchase additional shares of stock.

Dollar-cost averaging   An investment plan in which an individual makes equal dollar investments each period.

Dow Jones Industrial Average (DJIA)   One of the oldest and most widely quoted measures of stock market price movements. The DJIA is calculated using the market prices of 30 blue-chip common stocks. Also called *The Dow.*

Downtrend   A series of declines in value for a specific security or for the overall market.

Earnings per share (eps)   A corporation's net income after taxes and preferred dividends divided by the number of shares of the firm's common stock outstanding.

Equity   1. Stock, either common or preferred. 2. The market value of assets being held in a brokerage account, less the amount borrowed in the account. 3. Funds in a business that have been contributed by the owners.

Ex-dividend   Pertaining to a stock that no longer carries the right to the next dividend payment.

Ex-dividend date   The first date a buyer of stock will not receive the next dividend. The ex-dividend date is generally three days prior to the stockholder of record date.

Federal agency security   A security of a federal agency such as the Government National Mortgage Association. Also called *agency security.*

Fixed-income security   A security that makes fixed periodic payments.

Flat   Pertaining to a bond that is traded without accrued interest.

Full-service brokerage firm   A brokerage company that provides customers with a wide range of financial products and services, including advice concerning what assets to buy and sell.

Going public   See *Initial public offering.*

Good-till-canceled order   An order to buy or sell that remains in effect until executed or until canceled by the investor who placed the order.

Growth fund   An investment company with an investment objective of long-term capital growth.

Growth stock   A common stock of a company that is expected to have above-average growth in revenues and profits.

Hedge   Limiting potential losses on an investment position by taking another investment position in a similar asset.

Hedge fund   An investment partnership of wealthy, sophisticated individuals and institutions. Hedge funds are generally unregulated, and ownership can involve substantial risks for its partners.

High-yield bond   See *Junk bond.*

Inactive   Pertaining to a security that seldom trades or that trades in small amounts.

Index fund   A mutual fund that maintains a portfolio of stocks designed to match the performance of a particular stock index.

Initial public offering (IPO)   A corporation's first public offering of common stock.

Institutional investor   An organization such as a bank trust department or pension fund that invests substantial amounts of money.

Investment banker   A firm that provides assistance to organizations that are in need of raising capital.

Investment company   A firm that pools and then reinvests funds. Mutual funds are the most popular type of investment company.

Issue   1. A particular class of an organization's securities. 2. To sell securities in the primary market.

Joint ownership   Ownership of an asset by two or more parties.

Junk bond   A bond in which there is considerable doubt that the terms of the bond will be satisfied. Also called *high-yield bond.*

Limit order   An investor order to buy a security at a specified price or lower or to sell a security at a specified price or higher.

Liquidity   The degree to which an asset can be readily converted to cash.

Listed security   A security that has been admitted to trading on a particular exchange or in a particular market.

Load   The fee that investors are charged when they acquire shares of a mutual fund.

Low-load fund   A mutual fund with a relatively low sales fee that ranges from 1 percent to 3 percent of the amount invested.

Maintenance fee   The annual fee charged by some brokerage firms to maintain a brokerage account.

Major turn   A reversal in the intermediate- or long-term direction of the stock market's movement.

Management fee   The annual fee charged to investors who own shares of an investment company.

Margin   The amount of unencumbered value that must be deposited in order to purchase or maintain a security position.

Margin account   A brokerage account that permits an investor to purchase securities on credit or to borrow against securities that are being held in the account.

Market order   An investor's order to immediately execute a security trade at the best possible price.

Market price   The price at which a security currently trades in the secondary market.

Maturity   The date on which a financial obligation is to be paid.

Money market   The market for short-term debt securities such as negotiable certificates of deposit, commercial paper, and U.S. Treasury bills.

Money market fund   A special type of mutual fund that purchases short-term, high-quality debt securities and passes through to its shareholders the interest received on these securities.

Multiple   See *Price-earnings ratio.*

Municipal bond   A debt security issued by a state, city, county, or some other political subdivision. Most municipal bonds pay interest that is exempt from taxation by the federal government.

Mutual fund   An investment company that continually stands ready to redeem existing shares of its own stock.

National Association of Securities Dealers (NASD)   A self-regulatory association of over-the-counter brokers and dealers that establishes legal and ethical standards of conduct for its members.

National Market System   A Nasdaq system for reporting transactions of active over-the-counter securities.

Net change   The amount by which a security's closing price is different from the closing price in the previous trading period.

Net proceeds   The amount of funds that are received from the sale of an asset. Net proceeds are calculated after any commissions are paid.

Net worth   The value of all assets less the amount of money that is owed.

New issue   A security that is being offered to the public for the first time.

New York Stock Exchange (NYSE)   The oldest and largest organized securities exchange in the United States. Also called the *Big Board.*

No-load fund   A mutual fund that is sold without a sales charge.

Odd lot   A quantity of securities that is less than the standard trading unit. Fewer than 100 shares of most common stocks is considered an odd lot.

On the sidelines   Describing an investor who has decided to wait before committing funds for investment.

Opening   The beginning of a trading session.

Option   A contract that allows the owner to either purchase or sell (depending on the type of option) an asset at a specified price until a certain date. See also *Call, Put.*

Overbought   Pertaining to a market that has recently experienced a significant rise and is likely to experience declines in the near future.

Oversold   Pertaining to a market that has recently experienced a significant decline and is likely to experience increases in the near future.

Over-the-counter market (OTC)   The linking of dealers that make markets in securities.

Par value   A security's stated value as printed on the certificate. Most corporate bonds have a $1000 par value.

Payment date   The date on which interest or a dividend will be paid to a security's owner.

Payout ratio   The proportion of net income that a firm pays out in cash dividends.

PE   See *Price-earnings ratio.*

Penny stock   A low-priced stock whose ownership generally entails substantial risk.

Point   A measure of change in the value of a security or of a market average.

Portfolio   A group of investments.

Post   The location on the floor of an organized securities exchange at which a particular stock or group of stocks is traded.

Preemptive right   The right of a stockholder to maintain proportional ownership of a firm by acquiring a portion of new shares that are being sold to the public.

Preferred stock   Shares of business ownership that give the owner of the stock priority over common stockholders with respect to dividends and assets in the event of a liquidation.

Premium bond   A long-term debt security that sells at a price above its face value. See also *Discount bond.*

Price-earnings (PE or P/E) ratio   The current market value of a stock divided by the firm's earnings per share of common stock. Also called *multiple.*

Principal   A bond's face amount.

Profit taking   Widespread selling of a stock or of securities in general following an extended rise in value.

Prospectus   A formal document containing relevant facts concerning an issue of securities.

Proxy   Written authorization to act for a stockholder.

Publicly traded company   A business with shares of ownership that are traded on an organized exchange or in the over-the-counter market and that are available for purchase.

Put   An option that gives the owner the right to sell a particular asset at a specified price until a given date.

Quotation   A listing or statement of the value of a security. Also called *quote*.

Range   The high price and the low price a security or a market average has attained during a given period.

Rating   See *Bond rating*.

Rating agencies   Companies that grade the credit quality of debt obligations.

Record date   The date on which an organization determines who holds securities for the purpose of paying dividends, sending financial statements, and so forth.

Redemption   The retirement of a security by the security's issuer.

Regional exchange   An organized securities exchange that specializes in the securities of companies located in the region of the exchange.

Registered representative   A brokerage firm employee who is registered with the Securities and Exchange Commission to handle investor accounts.

Registration statement   A formal document filed with the Securities and Exchange Commission by an organization planning a public securities issue.

Rights offering   The distribution to existing stockholders of rights to purchase shares that are part of a new common stock issue.

Round lot   The standard unit of trading for a particular type of security.

Secondary market   The market in which outstanding securities are traded.

Sector fund   An investment company that concentrates on investing in securities having a commonality. For example, a sector fund may buy only the stocks of companies in a particular industry.

Securities and Exchange Commission (SEC)   The federal government agency that regulates most activities connected with issuing and trading securities.

Securities Investor Protection Corporation (SIPC) A government-sponsored organization that insures cash and securities held in brokerage accounts. Limits apply to insurance coverage for each account.

Short sale The sale of a security that is not owned and must be borrowed. Short-sellers generally anticipate a decline in the market value of the security that is shorted.

Size The number of bonds or shares of stock that are being offered for sale or bid for at the quoted price.

Specialist A member of an organized securities exchange who makes a market in one or more securities.

Speculation Taking large risks in order to earn above-average returns. Speculation generally involves holding securities for a relatively short period of time.

Split An increase in the number of shares of stock outstanding without an accompanying increase in assets. A two-for-one split involves sending out one additional share for each share already held.

Standard & Poor's 500 Stock Index A comprehensive measure of stock price movements that is calculated using the market values of the common stocks of 500 large companies.

Stock Shares of ownership in a corporation.

Stock dividend A dividend of additional shares of stock (rather than cash) that is paid to stockholders.

Street name Registration of an investor's security in the name of the brokerage firm that is holding the security.

SuperDOT A New York Stock Exchange system that automatically routes customer orders to the appropriate specialist.

Tax-loss selling Selling securities in order to realize a loss in value for tax purposes. Tax-loss selling often occurs at the end of a calendar year in which securities prices have experienced substantial losses.

Technical decline A short-term decline in the stock market that is an interruption of a longer-term increase.

Technical rally A short-term rise in the stock market that is an interruption of a longer-term decline.

Tender offer An offer to purchase stock from investors.

Top The highest value to which the stock market or a particular stock will rise.

Total return   A security's yield to investors which includes both current income and changes in market value.

Trader   A person who buys and sells securities in an attempt to profit from short-term changes in value.

Treasury bill   A short-term (one year or less) debt security issued and guaranteed by the U.S. Treasury.

Unlisted   Describing a security that trades in the over-the-counter market and has not been approved for trading on an organized securities exchange.

Uptrend   A series of increases in value for a specific security or for the overall market.

Value investing   The purchase of securities based upon the market value of assets that are owned by the firms that have issued the securities.

Volume   Units of trading in a security or in the overall market for a specified period.

Voting stock   Stock that gives the owner of the stock the right to vote for the firm's directors.

Warrant   A security that allows an investor to purchase a specific number of shares of stock at a predetermined price.

When-issued   Pertaining to a security that has not yet been issued.

Yield   The rate of return to be earned on an investment. See also *Current yield.*

Yield to maturity   The annual rate of return to be earned by buying a debt security at the current market price when the security will be held until the scheduled maturity.

Zero-coupon bond   A bond that is issued at a large discount from face value and that makes no periodic interest payments.

Index

INDEX

Active stocks, 178-179
ADR (*see* American depositary receipt)
American depositary receipt (ADR), 21, 93, 281
American Stock Exchange, 8, 94, 131, 168, 171, 231
American Stock Exchange Composite Index, 183
Annuities, 124
Ask, 76
Asset allocation, 282
Asset management accounts, 161-163
Atlanta, 80
AT&T, 68, 82
Average (*see* Stock index)

Back-end load, 227
Balanced funds, 218
Bankers acceptance, 41
Barnett Banks, 94
Barron's, 147, 168, 177, 178, 189, 190, 192, 208
Beta, 266-267
Bid, 76
Big Board (*see* New York Stock Exchange)
Birmingham, 80
Bonds:
  book entry, 159
  call feature, 47-49

Bonds *(Cont.):*
  comparison to stock, 42-43
  convertible, 124, 134-138
  coupon rate, 40, 43-44
  definition, 4, 38-39
  denominations, 43-44
  interest payments, 49-52
  liquidity, 47, 69-70
  maturity, 40
  quotations, 185-189
  ratings, 57-59, 273
  and unit investment trusts, 235-237
  valuation, 53-56, 267-269, 271, 274-275
  with put option, 47
  yields, 52-53, 56, 58
Book entry (*see* Bonds, book entry)
Boston Stock Exchange, 92
BP Amoco, 226
Brokerage commissions (*see* Commissions)
Brokerage firms:
  commissions, 144-146
  locating, 144
  insurance, 163-164
Brokers:
  providing price quotations, 76
Broker call money, 41
Broker-dealers, 74

ABOUT THE AUTHOR

David L. Scott is Professor of Accounting and Finance in the College of Business Administration at Valdosta State University, Valdosta, Georgia. Born in Rushville, Indiana, he earned a B.S. at Purdue University, his M.S. at Florida State University, and a Ph.D. in economics at the University of Arkansas in Fayetteville.

The second edition of *How Wall Street Works* is the twenty-sixth book authored by Dr. Scott. He has published numerous articles and presented seminars and workshops on various aspects of investing and personal finance. He has been a guest on radio and television shows, including CNBC and NBC's *Today*. Previous books include *The Guide to Personal Budgeting, The Guide to Investing in Common Stocks,* and *The Guide to Investing in Mutual Funds.* He is also the author of the best-selling reference guide *Wall Street Words,* published by Houghton Mifflin. Along with his wife, Kay, Professor Scott has authored three popular guidebooks to America's national parks.

Other books on finance and investments by David L. Scott

Dictionary of Accounting

Fundamentals of the Time Value of Money

The Guide to Buying Insurance

The Guide to Investing in Bonds

The Guide to Investing in Common Stocks

The Guide to Investing for Current Income

The Guide to Investing in Mutual Funds

The Guide to Managing Credit

The Guide to Personal Budgeting

The Guide to Saving Money

The Guide to Tax-Saving Investing

Investing in Tax-Saving Municipal Bonds

The Investor's Guide to Discount Brokers

Municipal Bonds: The Basics and Beyond

Understanding and Managing Investment Risk & Return

Wall Street Words